DATE DUE

Port Moody PL		
due. 12 July 11		

GENDER IN HISTORY

Series editors:
Pam Sharpe, Patricia Skinner and Penny Summerfield

The expansion of research into the history of women and gender since the 1970s has changed the face of history. Using the insights of feminist theory and of historians of women, gender historians have explored the configuration in the past of gender identities and relations between the sexes. They have also investigated the history of sexuality and family relations, and analysed ideas and ideals of masculinity and femininity. Yet gender history has not abandoned the original, inspirational project of women's history: to recover and reveal the lived experience of women in the past and the present.

The series Gender in History provides a forum for these developments. Its historical coverage extends from the medieval to the modern periods, and its geographical scope encompasses not only Europe and North America but all corners of the globe. The series aims to investigate the social and cultural constructions of gender in historical sources, as well as the gendering of historical discourse itself. It embraces both detailed case studies of specific regions or periods, and broader treatments of major themes. Gender in History titles are designed to meet the needs of both scholars and students working in this dynamic area of historical research.

Myth and materiality in a woman's world

Manchester University Press

MYTH AND MATERIALITY
IN A WOMAN'S WORLD
SHETLAND 1800–2000

⊷ Lynn Abrams ⊶

Manchester University Press
Manchester and New York

distributed exclusively in the USA by Palgrave

The right of Lynn Abrams to be identified as the author of this work has been
asserted by her in accordance with the Copyright, Designs and Patents Act 1988.

Published by Manchester University Press
Oxford Road, Manchester M13 9NR, UK
and Room 400, 175 Fifth Avenue, New York, NY 10010, USA
www.manchesteruniversitypress.co.uk

Distributed exclusively in the USA by Palgrave
175 Fifth Avenue, New York, NY 10010, USA

Distributed exclusively in Canada by UBC Press
University of British Columbia, 2029 West Mall,
Vancouver, BC, Canada V6T 1Z2

British Library Cataloguing-in-Publication Data
A catalogue record for this book is available from the British Library

Library of Congress Cataloging-in-Publication Data applied for

ISBN 0 7190 6592 5 *hardback*
EAN   978 0 7190 6592 7

First published 2005

14 13 12 11 10 09 08 07 06 05   10 9 8 7 6 5 4 3 2 1

Typeset in Minion with Scala Sans display
by Graphicraft Limited, Hong Kong
Printed in Great Britain
by Biddles, King's Lynn

Contents

CONTENTS

List of figures, table and plates

Figures

Table

Plates

All plates reproduced courtesy of Shetland Museum

Preface and acknowledgements

This book is about the relationship between myth-making and historical materiality. It is about the ways in which the people of the most northern archipelago of the British Isles – Shetland – imagine their past and, at the same time, it is an attempt to reconstruct this woman's world from fragments of cultural experience captured in written and oral sources. It is a book in which I recreate and explore Shetland women's worlds, then and now, based upon their material experience and personal testimony. It is an interrogation of imaginations.

Shetland has a history unique in Europe – of women dominating the family, the economy and the cultural imagination. Women ran households and crofts without men. They maintained families and communities because men were absent. And they constructed in their minds a 'liberated', autonomous identity of themselves long before organised feminism was invented. And yet, in the popular imagination, Shetland is a place made by 'hard men' – Picts, Scots and above all Vikings. It is an archipelago whose contemporary identity still draws on the heroic exploits and sagas of medieval Norsemen. Against this history how did the most isolated community of the British Isles come to be a woman's island?

This book is a singular case study of the position and experience of women in a 'peripheral' society distanced – geographically, economically and culturally – from the British mainland. The history of Shetland is at present dominated by the symbols of male power and masculinity: fishing, farming, oil and the winter festival of Up-helly-aa, reinforcing a view that the islands were characterised by a rigid division of labour and male dominance. Yet for the whole of the nineteenth century Shetland was a community where women were demographically dominant to an exceptional degree. Nowhere else in the United Kingdom was the sex imbalance so pronounced, and women's role in maintaining the continuous life on the islands is undisputed. Shetland was a woman's place. Here, women were numerically preponderant and economically vital. These material circumstances determined women's experience and have shaped the past and present representation of Shetland women – as pre-modern survivors of a lost world on the one hand and as heroines on the other, well into the twentieth century.

The historiography of European women in the nineteenth and twentieth centuries is shaped by a western European perspective with a focus on the industrialised economies of Britain, France and Germany. The key explanatory frameworks derived from this focus are the ideology of separate spheres and of domesticity, the centrality of marriage and motherhood, the gendered division of labour and the rise of organised feminism. In Shetland though, and in other economically marginal communities in Europe such as Iceland, northern

Norway, parts of Ireland and the Basque country, as well as in much of rural eastern and southern Europe, these conceptual models seem inappropriate. In these places the story of women's lives has to be told against a different backdrop. This study of an exotic, different place will not only draw attention to those areas which do not fit the dominant story of women in European history, but will also show how there might be a different story to tell which places women at the centre of economic processes and demographic trends, and which uses women's voices to construct an alternative narrative of women's agency. This book, therefore, inverts the geographical focus of much women's history and subverts the narrative. It shifts attention from the European geo-political centre to Shetland and it subverts the narrative by disturbing the story of 'progress' from peasant oppression to women's liberation via domestic ideology and first- and second-wave feminism, and replacing it with an alternative narrative of a rural society of European women whose vision and experience was of female agency and of power. Adopting a perspective far removed from the metropolitan heart of Europe forces one to think differently about the prime motors of change and the chronology of that change.

This book is about what happened to women in a community in which they were demographically dominant and where they sustained the economy. It examines the opportunities and life experiences of women in a place where more of them worked and fewer got married than anywhere else in the British Isles. What did this do to women? How did this experience impact upon women's sense of agency and power? Through the analysis of woman-centred narratives, I seek to unravel the threads of competing versions of Shetland history by placing women centre stage, by listening to their voices and by reassessing social relations in this unique place. Women's stories take us to another place: a Shetland dominated by women's imaginations, by stories constructed and passed on through women's memory and by women's confidence in their identity as workers. The result is an alternative narrative of a society of women constructed around reciprocity and community, women's knowledge and female power. The story being told sweeps from around 1800 to 2000 as we explore how the intensity of Shetland women's material experience of the nineteenth century gave substance to a distinct women's culture that lingered long through the twentieth century.

My research in Shetland has been sustained and stimulated by many people who have been generous with their time and their thoughts. A visit to Shetland Archive in Lerwick is always a delight, for one is invariably assailed by interested members of the Shetland community whose engagement with the history of their islands offers the novice a rich diet of knowledge and anecdotes. In particular, though, I am indebted to the archivist Brian Smith and the assistant archivist Angus Johnson, whose commitment to preserving and understanding the history of Shetland is a joy to behold. I would have floundered without their indefatigable help and particularly their willingness to aid my research when I returned home. Angus probably now knows more about

Shetland women in the past than he ever imagined. Residents of Shetland have been unfailingly courteous. In particular I would like to thank Mary Blance, Gordon Johnston, Thelma Watt and especially my oral history respondents, Netta Inkster, Agnes Leask and Mary Ellen Odie. Mary Prior and Claire Jack, historians of Shetland women themselves, have also been a constant source of stimulation. I would not have been able to utilise the Shetland census if it were not for the hours of painstaking work undertaken by volunteers at Shetland Archive, transcribing entries from the original microfiche into user-friendly databases. The illustrations are courtesy of Shetland Museum's marvellous photographic archive.

Back on the Scottish mainland my enthusiasm for Shetland has been supported by my friends in Women's History Scotland, who have heard more papers on Shetland women than they probably care to remember. Anne Coombes, Claire Jack, Barbara Mortimer, Brian Smith, Nancy Wachowich and Perry Willson read earlier drafts of some of the chapters and provided valuable insight and trenchant criticism. Nigel Fabb, Nyree Finlay and David Hopkin helped me to look at my material through unfamiliar lenses. I would also like to acknowledge the financial support received from the Arts and Humanities Research Board, the British Academy, the Carnegie Trust, the John Robertson Bequest and the Department of History and Faculty of Arts of the University of Glasgow, all of whom facilitated my expensive flights to and from Shetland and the time to complete the manuscript.

I have loved writing this book. Shetland is magical and its history addictive. My partner Callum Brown discovered this before me and has been unable to kick the habit. Since our first trip to Shetland together Callum has found himself drawn into this woman's world, both practically and intellectually. This book is for him.

Glossary and note on Shetland dialect

Bere	a kind of barley
Bigg	to build
Böd	a fisherman's booth or hut
Delling	digging using traditional Shetland method
Dyke	stone wall
Haaf	deep-sea fishery
Hairst	harvest
Hap	small hand-knitted shawl
Howdie	untrained midwife
Kishie	basket made of straw and carried on the back or on a pony
Plantiecrue	stone enclosure to protect small plants
Peerie	small
Roo	to pluck wool from a Shetland sheep
Runrig	a form of land use whereby land is parcelled out in individual and often discontinuous strips or rigs
Scattald	common pasture attached to a township
Skekkler	a guiser clad in a suit of straw
Skroo	corn stack
Spencer	under-vest
Trow	fairy or 'little folk' with magical properties
Voar	spring

Note on Shetland dialect

Where appropriate, quotations from oral history interviews have been reproduced as they were transcribed from the tapes, in Shetland dialect. Oral history interviews conducted by the author were transcribed by the author into standard English and are reproduced as such.

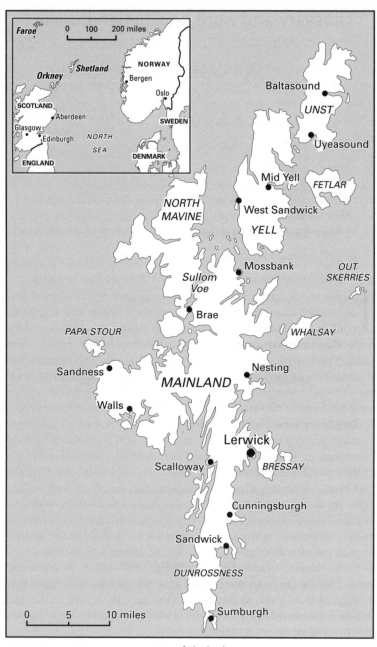

Map of Shetland

1

Pasts, peoples, selves

Here is a story of the sea and of strong men who wrest their living from the sea; of salt sprayed islands where waiting wives knit their souls into woollen masterpieces. (*Chicago Daily News*, October 1927)

Arrivals

ARRIVED IN SHETLAND for the first time on one of the worst days of January 1999, accompanied by gale force winds and horizontal rain. As we entered the warm and comforting surroundings of the airport terminal I was confronted with a departure lounge crowded with men. There were very few women present at all. The weather had grounded the oil workers who were awaiting their flights to the rigs. Since the 1970s oil boom women have been in the minority in these islands, although many of the 'surplus' men are transient workers. Shetland today is often characterised as a masculine society. Its own men are portrayed as burly, bearded individuals who are proud of their genetic links to the Norsemen or Vikings, and who act out their identification with this culture at the annual festival of Up-helly-aa. Yet I knew that Shetland had been a 'woman's island'. Throughout the nineteenth century and right up to the 1960s women outnumbered men in the population. Shetland was a woman's world, not just in numerical terms but also in respect of women's active presence in economic and social life. Indeed, in 1849 one official referred to them as 'the best men in Shetland'.[1]

The Shetland Islands are the northernmost landmass of the British Isles. They lie 120 miles north-east of the Scottish mainland, closer to Norway than to Scotland. For the modern traveller a visit to Shetland entails a fourteen-hour journey by sea from Aberdeen or a shorter, but often heart-stopping, flight. Either way, the first-time visitor will certainly be struck by a sense of difference or otherness. Arriving by ferry one encounters a magical coastal landscape as the ship glides into the relatively calm waters along the east coast of the mainland, passing the gigantic pictish Mousa Broch and the island of Bressay and then into Lerwick harbour. Alighting from the ferry, one is immediately confronted with the hustle and bustle of this compact, cosmopolitan town. It was described in 1897 as 'like no other place except itself', and this phrase remains apposite.[2] Travellers by air encounter another Shetland as the plane swoops in from the open sea, over the cliffs to land at the southernmost tip of the mainland. This is the Shetland of seabirds and ponies, wild landscapes and pre-historic archaeology. This northern archipelago resembles no other part of the British Isles.

Otherness

In 1980, a columnist for a London-based newspaper wrote of the Shetland Islands that they are not only 'much further away than most people suppose. They are much more foreign places, much harder, odder and more distinct.'[3] His comments on the 'otherness' of this place echo the sentiments of nineteenth-century travellers, scientists and missionaries who made the intrepid journey north and reported upon their observations in the style of amateur ethnologists and explorers. In a lecture to the Dumfries Mechanics' Institute in 1861, the Revd Murray remarked that 'the Zetlanders are a century behind the rest of Britain' and proceeded to characterise the islands and their inhabitants as isolated, backward, hospitable, moral and religious.[4] Indeed, such was the ignorance amongst many mainland Scots – not to mention inhabitants elsewhere in the British Isles – of their most northerly neighbours, that the following apocryphal tale may contain an element of truth. An Edinburgh lady invited to tea a young Shetland girl who had arrived to study in the capital. 'I particularly wish you to meet a young friend of mine from the Isle of Skye,' she remarked. 'Perhaps you have met one another already, *living so near*. And, at any rate, as I daresay you are both a little homesick, it will do you good to talk to one another in your own native – *Gaelic*.'[5] This remark is as much a mark of ignorance of the Gàedhealtachd as it is of Shetland. Gaelic has never been the language of these islands.

In the twenty-first century it is still not uncommon for Shetland to be conflated with 'the Highlands', a tendency perhaps exacerbated by the depiction of Shetland on weather maps in a box just off the coast of Aberdeen, which tends to reinforce mainland Scots' ignorance of Shetland's geographical position. The islands' peripheral location is accentuated by the rough seas separating the islands from Orkney and the Scottish mainland and by the weather, which in winter often curtails air and sea links, both to the mainland and to the more distant islands of Skerries, Foula and Fair Isle. The majority of Scots have never visited Shetland on account of the distances and expense incurred.

Shetland's sense of otherness and distance from mainstream and mainland Scotland is accentuated by its Norse heritage. Shetland was settled by the Norse in the ninth century and was administered by the Orkney earls until the twelfth century, when it was ruled directly by Norway. In 1469 Shetland became part of the Scottish Kingdom. Until the eighteenth century Shetlanders spoke a language derived from Norse called Norn.[6] In the words of one native Shetlander who tired of explaining that Shetland was not in the Hebrides, 'The Shetlander is proud of his Viking descent . . . The people of Shetland do not understand Gaelic. There are no "Macs" among them. The bagpipes are an importation . . . Whisky is not a native drink.'[7] The late Victorian winter festival of Up-helly-aa, which still thrives today, is the most visible symbol of Shetland's appropriation and maintenance of its distinct history and culture.[8] However, the discovery and exploitation of oil just off Shetland in the 1970s, and the resulting influx of construction and oil workers, has done more to heighten awareness and knowledge of Shetland beyond the islands without necessarily diluting the sense of 'differentness' within the islands. In the twenty-first century Shetland's 23,000 inhabitants are still, comparatively speaking, geographically isolated from the rest of the United Kingdom, but in terms of internal communications, community infrastructure, employment and housing, to name just a few indicators, the islands appear relatively prosperous. In these terms it is difficult to regard them as a backward outpost of the United Kingdom.

In the nineteenth century, representations of the islands and their inhabitants were in the hands of a few educated travellers who trumpeted their own bravery in choosing to travel to such a place and who commonly saw Shetland through the colonial lens. This was a moment of imperial adventure for Europeans. The visitors' gaze, the lens through which they viewed the islands, and the ways in which they interpreted and related what they saw were informed by discourses on the colonised peoples of British imperial possessions in Africa, India and the Caribbean. Travellers to Shetland utilised a language and a set of ideas, already familiar to readers of missionary magazines, journals and newspapers, which rested on notions of what constituted 'civilisation'. In this way, nineteenth-century Shetland was understood in the terms of already familiar discourses on the 'uncivilised' native of the European colonies. 'Shetland truly appears to be the skeleton of a departed country', commented Samuel Hibbert in 1822.[9] And that country was not Scotland. 'How foreign everything around me', exclaimed Edward Charlton in his aptly titled *Journal of a Visit and Residence in the Shetland Islands* published in 1832. 'Fields without hedges, a fort without soldiers, a town a seaport without wharves or piers, and a country all without a tree, how different, how wild and yet to my eyes how strangely beautiful.'[10] 'The traveller in search of novelty, whether of scenery or of customs, might find here enjoyment', enthused a partisan of Shetland's charms in the 1840s.[11] Shetland's beauty was all in the eye of the beholder. An American journalist was less enamoured, describing it as 'drear country', 'monotonous' and 'desolate'. 'They are lonely and dreary little islands; they are windswept and battered'; and yet even this sceptical writer was eventually won over. 'If you have stood on the wine-red moors at sunset and seen the great swells of the Atlantic pounding in on you, you will never forget them.'[12]

But it was the people who inhabited this desolate place who attracted the most comment. Eighteenth-century visitors were pleasantly surprised to find that well-to-do Shetlanders were relatively sophisticated and knowledgeable about the outside world. As early as 1701 a visiting minister found the people to be 'not so Rustick and Clounish as would be expected in such a place of the world'.[13] Just a few decades later, the Londoner Thomas Preston was astounded to discover a gentry class, including women 'well drest, genteel in Carriage, well-behav'd in Company, and spart and pleasant in Conversation', which was nothing short of miraculous 'considering they live in such a remote island, which has so little correspondence with the rest of the World.'[14] By the nineteenth century, however, amid the colonial craze, and influenced by the popularity amongst intellectuals of theories of race and eugenics, it was the rural labouring Shetlanders who became the focus of attention. Just as the indigenous peoples of the colonies had been analysed in racial terms, so now Shetlanders were identified as a race apart. 'Situated as these islands are, out in the wide ocean . . . their inhabitants form a race by themselves, and differ so remarkably from the people of the mainland of Scotland . . .', remarked a contributor to the newspaper *The Scotsman* in 1885.[15] These differences were largely explained by 'the large infusion of Scandinavian blood'.[16] According to the anthropologist Dr Edward Westermarck, 'The Shetlanders reveal their Scandinavian origin not merely by their racial type and their ancient traditions and sagas, but also by their temperament. The Scottish stiffness is foreign to the Shetlander. He is lively, sprightly and talkative.'[17]

Writing at the end of the nineteenth century Westermarck, an ethnic Swede from Finland who was visiting Foula, the most isolated of the Shetland islands, found the people there to be the last remnants of a pure race of 'the Scandinavian type' and the last speakers of the ancient Norse language. 'My experience is mainly taken from a place where tourists seldom land', he wrote, 'and where the original characteristics of the islanders have been preserved in all their purity'.[18] Westermarck's rather crude observations are not untypical.

Geographical isolation and Norse influences were widely credited with influencing Shetland's 'otherness'. The people spoke with a 'peculiar accent'[19] and were described by the Revd Reith, visiting around 1900, as 'hard-featured and weather beaten, scraggy, lean and bony'.[20] The young women of the island of Papa Stour, who were observed carrying home peats with ponies, were described as 'picturesque' in *Chambers' Journal* of 1889, in contrast with the older women, who looked 'Moorish' with their heads covered with black shawls.[21] Walter Scott, during an excursion to Shetland to locate sites for lighthouses, wrote in his journal that he found the islanders 'a strong, clear complexioned handsome race and the women very pretty'.[22] Almost all aspects of everyday life were intimately noted and commented upon by these visitors, from the islanders' style of dress to their living conditions and their character. Shetlanders were commonly said to be a 'curious' race, hospitable, oppressed, intelligent, ingenious and unsophisticated. In language which imitated that of imperial explorers, the author Arthur Conan Doyle used the image of the noble savage in the shape of a woman to convey his impressions. In 1880, upon going ashore on one of the outer islands:

> [I] wandered among the peat bogs, meeting strange, barbarous, kindly people who knew nothing of the world. I was led back to the ship by a wild, long-haired girl holding a torch, for the peat holes make it dangerous at night – I can see her now, her tangled black hair, her bare legs, madder-stained petticoat, and wild features under the glare of the torch.[23]

Shetland was exotic. Yet, Shetland was not as isolated and as 'other' as educated visitors supposed. They chose to disregard Shetland's long history as a centre of legal and illegal trade, as a fishing and whaling port and as a thoroughfare for Europe's seamen. Many inhabitants possessed a working knowledge of several languages, including Dutch, English and Norse, in order to be able to do business with visiting traders. This cosmopolitan Shetland rarely appeared in nineteenth-century travellers' accounts (or was characterised as a degenerate and uncharacteristic part of Shetland) probably because it did not square with the image they had already constructed for themselves, of a place largely left behind by the modern world, an uncomplicated, rural society where one might find throwbacks to a world that had been lost on the industrialising continent of Europe. Most visitors preferred to focus on Shetland's crofter and fisher families as representing a kind of simple ideal in a world so changed by industrialisation and urbanisation. Descriptions are frequently patronising and sometimes humorous, but almost without exception they seek to amplify the 'otherness' of Shetland life. This applied to references to Shetland ponies, the Shetland dialect, the absence of trees, the physical characteristics of the Shetland people and almost invariably, the condition of women. It was the prominence of women in Shetland life and landscape that surprised visitors to the islands, and it was this particular feature that became the benchmark for highlighting the 'backwardness' of Shetland in comparison with the British mainland.

Belonging

The otherness of Shetland was primarily an outsider's perspective, one of educated visitors whose standpoint was located somewhere else. Few Shetlanders consciously contributed to this characterisation of Shetland as different from the neighbouring Scottish mainland. Amongst native inhabitants there was an everyday familiarity with difference or otherness. During the sixteenth and seventeenth centuries Shetland was a key trading nexus, attracting Dutch fishermen and German merchants from the Baltic and North Sea ports as well as smugglers, so Shetlanders were familiar with seasonal migrants. Also at this time Scots administrators, legal officers and churchmen as well as landowners began to arrive on the islands. In the nineteenth century a new migration of professionals (such as teachers and doctors) and tradesmen (such as English whalers) added to the mix.[24] Difference was something that Shetlanders had always lived with, and by the nineteenth century it was experienced in a variety of ways. It was cultural: Norn as a working language had disappeared as early as 1700, but most Shetlanders spoke a strong local dialect which included a large vocabulary of words of Norse derivation, whereas English was the language of the legal, educational and clerical elite. In Lerwick, moreover, there was the creation of a respectable culture which bore more resemblance to the culture of Scottish bourgeois evangelicalism, encompassing temperance, moral restraint and philanthropy, than to the 'rough' culture of misrule to which Lerwick had become accustomed.[25] And difference was experienced through the legal system.

The letter and the implementation of the law were in the hands of Scottish-trained lawyers and sheriffs, which meant that any Shetlander who participated in a legal case was obliged to see his or her words 'translated' from the Shetland dialect into formal legal prose.

A Norse revival movement amongst intellectuals and socialists at the end of the nineteenth century did seek to inculcate in popular consciousness an appreciation of Shetland's Norse heritage, including the history, culture and language of Norse 'civilisation'. However, although it probably influenced the views of educated visitors it would be wrong to exaggerate the reach of this movement amongst Shetland labouring people at the time.[26] It was not until the late twentieth century, then, that Shetlanders consciously embraced difference as a constituent element of identity. The vast structural, economic and social changes that have impacted on the islands, especially since the discovery of North Sea oil in the 1970s, have prompted a great deal of what I call 'identity work' amongst Shetlanders. In 1979 Shetlanders voted overwhelmingly 'No' in the devolution referendum; almost three-quarters of voters here rejected the proposal compared with just 48 per cent in Scotland as a whole. Coterminous with this was the formation of a new political entity, the Shetland Movement, a party favouring autonomy for Shetland, with a more general aim of exploiting Shetland's new-found oil wealth and preserving Shetland identity.[27] Along with the long-standing Lerwick fire festival of Up-helly-aa (and the revival of the festival in some of the smaller communities such as Scalloway, Brae and Mossbank) these were the outward manifestations of a broader Shetland revivalism, bolstering the perception amongst mainland Scots that Shetland was indeed other. But there have been many other expressions of this identity which have not had such an impact on the 'outside world' but which are, nevertheless, instrumental in bolstering or reinforcing a sense of otherness or distinctiveness amongst Shetlanders themselves.

In the late twentieth century Shetland experienced an economic and demographic resurgence which made it unlike many other parts of Scotland, where economic decline, incorporating the collapse of traditional heavy industries and the crisis of community, was a more common theme. The Scottish east coast has witnessed the gradual decline and more recent collapse of the fishing industry. In the Highlands and the Western Isles population has fallen, and some remoter areas have seen the inexorable movement of people from the land to urban centres. In the south-west problems affecting lowland farming have caused rural uncertainty. All these developments since the 1970s have fuelled attempts to re-imagine and recreate heritage and identity in a variety of forms: the revival of language and dialects, the recording and archiving of memory, the concrete representation of the past in museums and heritage centres and so on.[28] Since the 1970s the United Kingdom has witnessed intense popular interest in and enthusiasm for the preservation of 'heritage'. What the historian Raphael Samuel described as the 'historicist turn in national life' has been manifested in a national, local and individual obsession with the recovery and recreation of the past.[29] This preoccupation with the past – its discovery, preservation and recreation – has perhaps had greatest resonance in communities experiencing crisis, such as former mining villages and fishing communities where it is not simply an occupation but a whole 'way of life' that has been lost. In these places, the value of heritage work is that it bolsters or even creates a sense of identity and distinctiveness in a community now devoid of a common purpose.

In Shetland, though, it was not economic crisis but economic revival that stimulated the heritage culture. The arrival of the oil industry transformed the economic, material and social infrastructure of the islands, but for Shetlanders its impact was at first double-edged. On the one hand the oil industry was perceived by some as a cultural invasion. Large numbers of workers from mainland Scotland and England moved in, some with their families, as temporary construction workers on the new oil terminal at Sullom Voe, or as permanent staff at the terminal and in servicing and technical support. Almost overnight Shetland had a new workforce and a new industry. The influx of 'foreigners' created a renewed interest in what it meant to be Shetland. This was manifested in various ways, such as much greater financial investment by individuals in the festival of Up-helly-aa and an increase in locally produced publications on all aspects of Shetland culture. However, in contrast with nineteenth-century attempts to raise consciousness of Shetland's Norse links, this time the work to bolster identity was conceived as a defensive project, protecting the community and its interests against the incursions of alien modes of living. As the anthropologist Anthony Cohen argues, we become aware of a culture 'when we are brought up against its boundaries', when we are confronted with another culture or set of behaviours which deviates from our own.[30]

Oil wealth facilitated Shetland heritage work or what might be described as excavating the old 'authentic' Shetland (as opposed to the new and inauthentic oil community). From the 1970s Shetland in a big way embarked upon heritage work, which encompassed official and popular representations of the past. In the former category one might include the establishment of Shetland Archive in 1976, and initiatives aimed at increasing awareness and understanding of Shetland culture in schools, for instance through teaching Shetland dialect. Shetland also has an energetic archaeology programme. Throughout the summer, teams of archaeologists dig away at some of the best-preserved early sites in Britain, and their findings are regularly reported in the *Shetland Times* in a regular column called 'Dellin inta da past' which, in turn, uses prevailing Shetland myths to frame the findings. At the interface between the official and the popular there have been numerous projects, including oral history, family history and the establishment of community heritage centres.

However, what distinguishes this heritage work from other initiatives elsewhere in Scotland is its intended audience. Shetland heritage productions are aimed, first and foremost, at Shetlanders themselves and to visitors with a Shetland connection. The occasional 'hamefarins' or homecomings – a designated week of events organised for visiting exiled or emigrant Shetlanders and their offspring – provide a ready-made audience for representations of the 'authentic' past. The narratives which have had most resonance within this community are those embedded in Shetlanders' intimate relationships with the sea and the soil, and it is these stories which are retold and represented in a variety of forms – oral, visual, written – and in a range of locations: museums, galleries, tourist information centres, heritage centres. Perhaps this production of the past for internal consumption creates fewer tensions here, in terms of the message or stories being represented, than in other places where heritage has been conceived as one plank in a survival strategy aimed at economic regeneration and encompassing employment for local inhabitants and attracting tourists.[31] Shetland will never become a heritage theme park. It is too remote and, at present anyway, relatively wealthy.

The past that is being excavated in modern Shetland fits a small number of key stories. The boundaries of this imagined past are mostly internally defined within Shetland so that the landscape of the past is perpetually discovered and rediscovered and then re-circulated in a variety of forms and genres. At the heart of this past are the eighteenth- and nineteenth-century fishing-crofting household and the values or 'way of life' associated with it. In 1979 a study of the impact of development on the south mainland identified three common elements of Shetlanders' collective image of themselves: the crofting and fishing tradition, self-sufficiency and egalitarianism.[32] And it is this conception of the Shetland way of life that has framed most heritage productions, whether they be large-scale, ambitious exhibitions like the Unst Boat

Haven or more grass-roots oral history or publication projects. What I shall be arguing is that these narratives of the past, including personal memory narratives, tend to be constructed within a larger myth system which *excludes* as much as it includes. Narratives and voices which counter the myth tend to be marginalised, while those that conform are incorporated and reproduced and thus serve to reinforce it. The myth is not necessarily untrue, but is just a highly emotive grand story that is embedded in Shetland culture and into which every aspect of Shetland's past and present tends to be forced to fit.

One way of understanding this is to see how for Shetlanders, and increasingly for long-staying 'incomers', these narratives assume the function of 'symbolic boundaries', policing difference, reinforcing otherness, creating identity in a context of change.[33] According to the ethnologist John Gray, identity making is 'a cultural process through which, in creating places . . . and forming attachments to them, people implicate an historicised image of themselves as people of [a particular locality].'[34] In Shetland it is only an historicised image or representation of Shetlanders and their way of life that has any real purchase in expressions of identity. Although most inhabitants have embraced change they still set great store by material referents of local identity that provide a link to the past.[35] Peat is a good example of something which has assumed great symbolic importance even though it is no longer a necessity. Peat is decayed wood and vegetation which, over millennia, has broken down into a main constituent of the hill and moorland of the island, resting a few centimetres beneath the heather and grass. When cut, drained and dried it makes a slow-burning and effective domestic fuel and was the basis of Shetland energy. But in the 1970s many households converted to oil-fired heating and cooking on account of the cheapness, cleanliness and convenience of oil and the difficulty in finding the necessary labour to cut the peats. Some continued to cut peat for their fires on a much smaller scale, albeit using plastic sacks and tractors to transport it down from the hill instead of 'kishies' (baskets) and ponies. These activities recall the old days when the peat cutting and raising was a community activity symbolic of the Shetland way of life. Indeed today, going to the peat banks represents a 'direct link to the past' in terms of the tools used and the evidence of generations of previous workings on the hill.[36] One oral interviewee recalled working the peats for her elderly mother, who 'you couldn't expect to cope with anything else other than a peat fire which she'd always been used to'.[37] Cohen describes this as 'perception of dissonance' – that things are not quite right when peat is replaced by coal or oil.[38] But peat changed in the 1970s from an economic resource to a cultural resource. Similarly, the remnants of former croft houses and fishing booths scattered around the islands not only present a constant reminder of Shetland's past but also provide a concrete link with previous generations of crofters and fishermen. The Weisdale crofter Agnes Leask described to me the various archaeological remains discovered on her croft land, from quern wheels to ash pits. On coming across 'two big brown stripes' through earth that was being dug for foundations, Agnes contacted the Shetland Council archaeologist, who confirmed that the stripes were ancient ash and the ground had previously been a settled site. The history of Shetland was important to Agnes, as she explained: 'One of the main pulling powers of staying here is just being . . . connected [to the past]. You go out on a nice summer evening, you stand outside and you think how many people have stood here, seen the same things, the moon shining on the water etc, what was their life like, how did they live.'[39]

By contrast, the oil industry seems to provide no link to the past. It has not fitted into the myth system of Shetland. Indeed it provides a counter-narrative or anti-narrative to the Shetland way of life. Recollections of the oil industry are rarely incorporated in a positive way into people's accounts of Shetland's past. Moreover, until recently, the impact of oil (together with other external influences such as the Royal Air Force base on Unst and the airport at Sumburgh) has not featured prominently in public representations of the past. The original Shetland Museum, for instance, contained no exhibits on the oil industry. Oil is still regarded as an alien or foreign element, not an authentic one. There is no sense of ownership of the oil industry (despite the fact that oil income has financed massive improvements to transport infrastructure and community facilities), and therefore it cannot perform any work in helping to frame memories. This may be changing in the early twenty-first century, as a new Shetland Museum may incorporate a sizeable oil-industry display.

So Shetland sits on the cusp of a reinterpretation of its past. The old markers of belonging have resonance only as long as some remnants of that particular past still exist, and many of those remnants are fast disappearing.

Understanding

Shetland is interpreted to the outside world today by a host of professional scholars. Historians, anthropologists, ethnologists, archaeologists, geographers and linguists have played their part in the construction of

Shetland identity as 'other' in their conversations with the 'outside world'. This book is part of that tradition. Scholars have chosen Shetland as the focus for their research precisely because of their own perception or preconception of its otherness. Nineteenth-century writers went there, in part, to find the authentic other of the Norse sagas or of an imagined pre-modern, 'backward' society. Some of today's scholars would be unwilling to own up to such essentialist preconceptions. But there are other factors luring the academic to this place which were shared by those travellers who went before us. There is a fascination with a place which is part of the British Isles and yet which is so palpably different from any other part of that geographical, political and cultural entity. So-called peripheral societies have long attracted the anthropologist, the ethnologist and the folklorist keen to record remnants of surviving cultures and to investigate identity and cultural ritual in places seemingly at a distance from the centre.[40] In these localities, situated at the geographical and cultural edge or fringe of industrialised societies, one is afforded the opportunity to observe what happens as the peripheral culture is exposed to that of the metropole. Such an approach is common in Scotland, where Skye and the Western Isles have provided fertile soil for studies of identity and culture, and in Ireland on the Blasket, Aran and Tory islands.[41] In Shetland it is also the Norse heritage that offers the researcher a fascinating insight into a crossover culture. In practical terms the islands are a treasure-trove of rich materials. Archaeologists go there in droves for the opportunity to work on such early undisturbed sites on a large scale. Historians are probably better served in Shetland than anywhere else in Scotland by archives offering rich sources which can be consulted in the context of where they were produced rather than at a distance in Edinburgh, thus offering the historian the benefit of local expertise.[42] But perhaps more than anything else it is the combination of Shetland's geographical proximity and its sense of remoteness that makes it so special for anthropologists, ethnologists and historians, who have the illusion of travelling into the past and yet not travelling any distance at all. Shetland still has the aura of an ethnological rarity which attracts scholars like bees to a honey pot. There can be few places in the world – perhaps with the exception of Papua New Guinea – that have attracted quite so much academic interest so far out of proportion to their size.

But Shetland is no common periphery. It differs markedly from other island places in Europe. It does not conform to the model of the declining and decaying peripheral region incorporating 'an increasingly feminised and aged population . . . a fall in agricultural output and income . . . a deterioration in services and living standards' which characterises other parts of Europe that have turned to tourism as an economic lifeline.[43] In many European regions, such as western Ireland, rural Brittany and parts of the Basque country, as well as parts of western Scotland, young women have fled to urban centres, creating a 'bride-famine' and social dislocation. Shetland, though, has avoided the fate of many of Europe's peripheral regions – that of dependency on the centre – on account of its ability to maintain its position in the fishing industry (until the present crisis) and because of the benefits accrued from oil.[44] The result is a vibrant culture and society which envelops the researcher in an atmosphere of positive interest and engagement. One is researching the history not of a dying culture but of a culture that is very much alive.

For the historian of women, however, Shetland would at first appear an unpromising case study. Once a year, on the last Tuesday in January, images from Lerwick are broadcast across the country. It is the night of Up-helly-aa, the winter festival when hundreds of Lerwick men dress up as Vikings or as guisers, parade around the town with fiery torches and burn a Viking galley. This festival is masculinity on display, and it bolsters a more subliminal image of modern Shetland, the Shetland of oil, probably the most masculine of occupations. These two images – of Vikings and Up-helly-aa, and of the oil industry – framed my introduction to Shetland. I first visited the islands accompanying my partner, who was promoting his book about the festival. During our visit we were convivially hosted by that year's Jarl's Squad – the premier squad of forty-three Viking-clothed male guisers – who were busy preparing the Viking galley for the celebrations. Shetland life and culture seemed an epitome of male strength and female subordination. It seemed, at first glance, a place where oil wealth had deterred rather than promoted second-wave feminism.

Yet it soon became clear to me that these representations of Shetland were superficial and that in fact Shetland had always been a woman's place. It was a place where women were the majority of the population and were active producers in the market, and it was a place where women possessed a degree of confidence in their role and their identity as workers, so much so that it is women's voices that, with clarity and assurance, articulate and convey the past through contemporary sources and through retrospective testimony. Shetland was a woman's place in material terms; it was also such in representational terms. It was this realisation that determined my approach to the research and writing of this book.

My starting point was to use Shetland as a unique case study in order to test certain widely held assumptions amongst historians of women. As I began my primary research in Shetland Archive, I was simultaneously writing a survey-history of women in nineteenth-century Europe. I was engaged in an internal dialogue, constantly using the standard models and interpretations commonly applied to industrialising Europe to think about Shetland women and, conversely, using Shetland women's experiences to rethink or at least challenge some of these models.[45] To simplify and to paraphrase, the story of women in nineteenth-century Europe is dominated by a western European perspective with a focus on the industrialised economies of Britain, France and Germany. Women's historians of Britain and Europe are now accustomed to a post-Enlightenment meta-narrative which goes something like this. The intellectual and scientific revolution of the Enlightenment had a profound and long-term impact on the ways in which gender roles were conceived. The French Revolution and subsequent liberal and national revolutions across Europe entrenched women's place as second-class citizens, and with the industrial revolution the role of both middle- and working-class women – as mothers and wives – was defined within the private sphere. This definition of appropriate femininity was used by middle-class women to create a feminine public sphere and ultimately led to the self-consciousness of organised feminism. For working-class women the ideology of femininity and separate spheres limited their working opportunities and consigned them to low wages and exploitation in the home and the workplace. Ultimately, though, this is a story of 'progress' from peasant oppression to women's liberation via domestic ideology and first- and second-wave feminism.

Despite much regional variation, women's historians have largely used this narrative as the core for understanding the female experience in a male past, for explaining the progression from subordination to liberation across the past two centuries. This story is, of course, a travesty of the complexity that is European women's history in the modern period. National, regional and local studies have gone a long way towards refining and redefining this narrative. However, I came to realise that Shetland reveals an alternative story, not just a regional variation or a minor complication in the European narrative, but a wholly different way of understanding women's history. Instead of a progression from subordination to liberation, the story of European women could have a fundamentally different thread. Adopting a perspective far removed from the metropolitan heart of Europe forces one to think differently about the prime motors of change and the chronology of that change. It dawned on me that Shetland women harboured a story that may well have a wider resonance in European consciousness – a story of female agency and of power.

My aim was to take this place on the European periphery, the continent's second-most isolated island group, and use it to question and subvert the dominant narrative, replacing it with an alternative narrative of a rural society of European women whose vision and experience was characterised by female agency and power. I set out to analyse the extent to which demographic and economic factors influenced women's experience. In a place where the sex imbalance was so pronounced for such a long period of time (there was arguably nowhere else in nineteenth-century Europe where the ratio of women to men was tipped quite so dramatically to the females), and where economic opportunities were severely constrained, I hypothesised that I would find a historical narrative that, at the very least, disturbed our understandings of continuity and change in nineteenth-century Europe. But the materialist story was not all I found. What I had not counted on was the tremendous power of narratives of the past in Shetland which used women and women's position in the economy as the leitmotif for historical change. I found that women have always been at the centre of Shetland's own story of its past.

Interpreting

Existing frameworks for understanding the position and experience of women in either fishing or farming communities have proved unhelpful and inappropriate. Studies of women in farming communities in Britain and Ireland, while sensitive to regional and local differences, have tended to generate generalised statements about the gradual disengagement of women from agricultural labour in the nineteenth century under the impact of increasing mechanisation, specialisation and the acceptance of the ideology of domesticity which frowned upon women's labour and especially physical work undertaken in public.[46] Historical literature on women in Scottish rural society is still in its infancy and is dominated by analysis of lowland agriculture which indicates a pattern similar to that suggested for England, that is a steady decline in the numbers of women engaged in rural occupations.[47] Our knowledge of the shape and trends of women's agricultural work in the Highlands and Islands is even sparser. However, it is unlikely that models based on the Gàidhealtachd would be applicable to Shetland given the marked differences in religious and moral culture, and in demographic and migration patterns. The power of the Free Church in the Western Isles has no real equivalent in Shetland, for instance. The limited research that has been published on women in the Western Isles portrays them as 'reliant on men for their status, protection and power, and having little control over their own lives'.[48] Judith Ennew, in her 1980 study of the Western Isles, writes that 'In the Hebrides there are few career opportunities for women and little perception of the possibility of a female role which is not tied to the domestic sphere.'[49] Gender roles are portrayed as quite separate, manifested in same-sex association and in gendered spatial knowledge as well as in the more obvious work roles.[50] These portrayals of women in rural Highland communities bear little relation to the position of Shetland women.

Studies of fishing communities, of which there are many in Scotland and elsewhere in Europe, although tending to portray them as the domain of men, have recently acknowledged women's role. Early studies stereotyped the women of fishing villages as 'fish-wives' or 'herring-lassies' or as passive members of the household and community, portrayed as waiting and weeping for their absent menfolk rather than engaging in productive activity.[51] More recently, though, the importance of women to the whole fishing operation and the organisation of the 'joint maritime household' has been recognised in diverse places, from Iceland to Newfoundland, including Scotland.[52] In maritime communities men's absence has focused attention on the 'greater dependency on women to control land-based food production, greater role differentiation amongst males/females ... and a greater economic independence for women.'[53] And the gendered construction of these communities has been explored, highlighting not only the roles of women but also the ways in which notions of appropriate roles for men and women in wider society have little purchase in the lives of fisher families. Of course there is no archetypal maritime community; fishing communities exhibit a variety of practices and work roles. Hence, the character of women's work in these communities was equally varied. Fishing at sea is almost universally a male occupation, and fishermen and their work culture are often seen as the crucible of the fishing community.[54] Yet participation in land-based work tends to be much more varied in terms of the types of work undertaken – fish processing, fish sales, book-keeping, bait digging, agricultural labour and domestic and emotional support to name just a few – and the value ascribed to it.[55] Shetland's mixed economy of fishing, crofting and hosiery does not lend itself to easy categorisation, but this is not to say that it is unique or that there are not comparable communities elsewhere in Europe or farther afield. Indeed, it is the rather similar fishing and farming regions of the Nordic counties (Norway, Sweden, Finland and Iceland), the warmer climes of northern coastal Portugal and the more distant coastal communities of Newfoundland that suggest alternative ways of understanding gender roles and relations in Shetland beyond the models erected for elsewhere in the British Isles. And it is primarily – although not exclusively – anthropologists and ethnologists who have pioneered a combination of material and symbolic approaches to help us understand not only what women (and men) do in such communities, but also how power, authority and value are differentiated between the sexes.[56] Thus, it is not sufficient to apply generalised notions of sexual difference and gender hierarchies to particular social, economic, cultural and historical contexts. Women's status is not easily read from simple models of the sexual division of labour.[57]

Anthropologists have encouraged us to make comparisons of cultural practices across space. A number of studies of what might be classified as maritime and mixed fishing and farming communities in the Nordic countries, Portugal and the eastern seaboard of Canada have highlighted features of gender relations and the position of women that are applicable to Shetland too.[58] The absence of men at sea, the central presence of women within the household so that it may be described as 'woman-centred', the importance of women's productive labour either on the farm, in the home or in paid employment, the necessity also of women's social and reproductive labour and the concomitant independence of women are all distinctive features of these particular communities. These have profound implications for actual work roles and for the ways in which relations between the sexes are constructed, experienced and represented. Women in these communities were undoubtedly attached to the domestic sphere, and this would commonly imply their subordination within a society which valued 'public' activities over those defined as private.[59] But anthropologists have shown that in these types of communities women's socially reproductive role – as bearers and nurturers of children but also as workers in the household and outside, as maintainers of kinship relations and so on – are cultural practices which constitute the bedrock of the formation of gendered practices. Thus in the fishing communities of the East Neuk of Fife, fishermen's wives appear to outsiders as oppressed, dependent and 'irrationally attached to an outmoded wifely role' on account of their 'preference for domesticity'. But, as Byron and Chalmers show, these women regard themselves as the opposite of the subordinate domestic wife, as 'being in charge of domestic decisions while their husbands are away, they see themselves as having more independence and autonomy than other women.'[60] And in northern Portugal, in the face of a dominant ideology of female subordination, women's role as independent producers gave them an authority and autonomy which conflicted with the roles expected of them.[61] However, in the maritime communities of present-day southern Finland, although women have a sense of themselves as more independent than wives of shore-based workers, this is tempered by the sense of responsibility and loneliness.[62]

Another strength of the anthropological literature is the privileging of women's voices. Anthropologists and ethnologists observe and engage with their subjects, becoming 'participant observers' in the field or ethnographic observers in cultural production. Historians, on the other hand, tend to work at one remove from their subjects, using documentary materials to interpret the past through the eyes or the pens of those who recorded behaviour and events. However, such is the strength of women's narratives in Shetland, and such is the importance of women's place within narratives on Shetland identity that the historian is duty-bound to take the personal or the autobiographical as the entry point into any analysis of women in Shetland's past. It is only through an understanding of women's sense of self – both in the past and in the present – that we can approach an inclusive and democratic representation of women in Shetland's past.

The turn to the self, to personal narrative in the form of autobiography, oral history and other forms of personal testimony, has transformed the writing of social history, but it has been an especially powerful force in women's and gender history and in the related disciplines of anthropology and ethnology. In all of these fields, women's voices had been silenced, and the interpretive models constructed to explain human behaviour in the past and the present were constructed around androcentric perceptions. Placing women's testimonies at the heart of one's analysis alters the perspective radically. As Sally Cole states, in the context of her historical-anthropological study of women in a Portuguese fishing community: 'life stories give us as outsiders access to women's subjective experiences and present women as social actors constructing their own lives in ways that empower them and employing strategies to achieve goals that they define within their particular historical and social contexts.'[63]

Cole's study demonstrates to the historian how personal testimony may be used to challenge the construction of women that has prevailed in the anthropological and historical literature. In these Portuguese communities, as in Shetland, women were the numerically preponderant sex, but they also had a strong sense of themselves as producers or workers as opposed to reproducers. Once one grasps that the wife-mother-homemaker paradigm is not the only way to think about women in the nineteenth century then it is easy to accommodate women's voices into an alternative narrative which challenges that centred upon the male producer-female reproducer model. In Shetland a popular narrative of otherness has facilitated this kind of accommodation. In the 1970s, as the community was struggling to deal with the influx of 'foreign' workers and the economic changes, references to women's equality with men in the crofting-fishing past, to the respect for women's work within the community and to the contrast between gender relations in Shetland (egalitarian) and those pertaining on the Scottish mainland where, it was implied, women were put upon and subordinate to men, were incorporated into a distinctive Shetland identity.

Personal testimony, mainly that of women, is at the core of my book. I have placed women's subjectivities at the heart of my analysis because it is only through listening to women speak – directly in oral history interviews or indirectly through testimonies recorded by legal clerks, church elders and so forth – that we can begin to reconstruct a narrative of the past that they would recognise. Women's consciousness is 'rooted in their subjective experiences of the material and cultural conditions of their lives'.[64] Personal testimony allows us to hear women interpret their experiences and use these experiences to construct their identities.

In researching and writing this book I recognise that I have contributed to the circulation of a myth of Shetland women in the past. The historian can never stand outside the process of the reconstruction of the past; indeed, she is implicated in the production of narratives which contribute to a myth system, which in turn is re-used and recycled. Shetland is a society highly conscious of its own role in the construction and interpretation of its histories. The past is a living place, continually consumed and reproduced for internal and external consumption. The historian from outside Shetland can not stand apart from this process for long, especially if she is determined to engage with narrative formation in the present as much as in the past. Like the anthropologist who becomes part of the story, my presence in Shetland and my demonstrable interest in Shetland women influenced the story I have to tell.

This book is a dialogue between Shetland women of the past and those of the present. The dialogue occurs within a framework of myths – ideas about Shetland, its past and the place of women in this past. The voices of women of the distant past are resurrected and retold by the voices of women in the present, and my role has been to provide a narrative form to these disparate subjectivities in order to provide another reinterpretation of Shetland's past from a woman's point of view.

Notes

1 Capt. Craigie (1849) in N. Kendall, *With Naught but Kin behind them: The Shetland of its Early Emigrants* (Melbourne, Brown Prior Anderson, 1998), p. 154. The comment was made with reference to women's road-making skills.
2 Shetland Archive, Lerwick (SA), D 1/135: unidentified newspaper cutting, c.1897.
3 'Shetland Island Britain Series', *Observer Magazine*, 20 July 1980, p. 1.
4 *Northern Ensign*, 25 April 1861.
5 SA, D 1/135: *Shetland Times*, 5 Nov. 1898. Gaelic was never spoken in Shetland, where the local language was Norn, derived from Norse.
6 B. Smith, 'The development of the spoken and written Shetland dialect: a historian's view', in D. J. Waugh (ed.), *Shetland's Northern Links: Language and History* (Edinburgh, Scottish Society for Northern Studies, 1996), pp. 30–43.
7 W. Moffatt, *Shetland: The Isles of Nightless Summer* (London, Heath Cranton Ltd, 1934), pp. 34–5.
8 See C. G. Brown, *Up-helly-aa: Custom, Culture and Community in Shetland* (Manchester, Manchester University Press, 1998).
9 S. Hibbert, *A Description of the Shetland Islands* (Edinburgh, Constable, 1822), p. 96.
10 Edward Charlton (1832) in Kendall, *With Naught but Kin*, p. 52.
11 E. Standen, *A Paper on the Shetland Islands* (Lingfield, Mill Print, 2000, orig. 1845).
12 SA, D 1/135: *Chicago Daily News*, Oct. 1927.
13 Revd John Brand (1701) in Kendall, *With Naught but Kin*, p. 39.
14 Thomas Preston (1744) in D. Flinn, *Travellers in a Bygone Shetland: An Anthology* (Edinburgh, Scottish Academic Press, 1989), p. 87.
15 SA, D 1/134: *The Scotsman*, 16 Feb. 1885.
16 SA, D 1/134: *The Scotsman*, 16 Feb. 1885.
17 SA, D 1/135: Dr Edward Westermarck, 'A summer in Shetland' (unattributed, undated: probably *Shetland Times*, c.1898).
18 SA, D 1/135. A similar belief that the inhabitants were the last remaining speakers of a pure form of Irish Gaelic was held by visitors to the Blasket Islands off the south coast of Ireland. See C. Moreton, *Hungry for Home: Leaving the Blaskets: A Journey from the Edge of Ireland* (London, Viking, 2000).
19 SA, D 1/134: *Ladies' Journal*, 3 Oct. 1891.
20 SA, D 1/135: *Singapore Free Press*, undated.
21 SA, D 1/134: *Chambers' Journal*, 21 Oct. 1889. On the 'picturesque' see A. Gilroy, 'Introduction', in A. Gilroy (ed.), *Romantic Geographies: Discourses of Travel 1775–1844* (Manchester, Manchester University Press, 2000), pp. 1–15, here pp. 4–5.
22 SA, D 1/135: *The Scotsman*, 2 Sept. 1903.
23 A. Conan Doyle (1880) in Kendall, *With Naught but Kin*, p. 41.
24 H. D. Smith, *Shetland Life and Trade 1550–1914* (Edinburgh, John Donald, 1984), pp. 10–28 and 93–153.
25 Brown, *Up-helly-aa*, pp. 104–12.

26 See Brown, *Up-helly-aa*, pp. 139–51.

27 See J. Squires, 'Re-visiting "internal colonialism" – the case of Shetland', *Shetland Economic Review* (Lerwick, Shetland Islands Council, 1993), pp. 1264–9.

28 See, for instance, S. Macdonald, *Reimagining Culture: Histories, Identities and the Gaelic Renaissance* (Oxford, Berg, 1997), a study of a community on Skye; J. Nadel-Klein, *Fishing for Heritage: Modernity and Loss along the Scottish Coast* (Oxford, Berg, 2003), which looks at east-coast fishing communities; and A. Strathern and P. J. Stewart, *Minorities and Memories: Survivals and Extinctions in Scotland and Western Europe* (Durham, NC, Carolina Academic Press, 2001) which focuses on Ayrshire and Dumfries and Galloway.

29 R. Samuel, *Theatres of Memory*, vol. I: *Past and Present in Contemporary Culture* (London, Verso, 1994), p. 139.

30 For a discussion of the relationship between locality and identity see A. P. Cohen, 'Belonging: the experience of culture', in A. P. Cohen (ed.), *Belonging: Identity and Social Organisation in British Rural Cultures* (Manchester, Manchester University Press, 1982), pp. 1–17, here p. 4.

31 See Nadel-Klein, *Fishing for Heritage*, pp. 171–212.

32 R. Byron and G. McFarlane, *Social Change in Dunrossness*, report for Shetland Islands Council (1979), p. 49.

33 See A. P. Cohen, *Whalsay: Symbol, Segment and Boundary in a Shetland Island Community* (Manchester, Manchester University Press, 1987).

34 J. Gray, 'Open spaces and dwelling places: being at home on hill farms in the Scottish Borders', in S. M. Low and D. Lawrence-Zúñiga (eds), *The Anthropology of Space and Place: Locating Culture* (Oxford, Blackwell, 2003), pp. 224–44, here p. 224.

35 Cohen, *Whalsay*, pp. 115–16.

36 Cohen, *Whalsay*, pp. 115–16.

37 Interview with Agnes Leask, 20 March 2002.

38 Cohen, *Whalsay*, p. 115.

39 Interview with Agnes Leask.

40 For a discussion of the choice of 'remote' areas for study by anthropologists see E. Ardener, '"Remote areas": some theoretical considerations', in A. Jackson (ed.), *Anthropology at Home* (London, Tavistock, 1987), pp. 38–54.

41 J. Ennew, *The Western Isles Today* (Cambridge, Cambridge University Press, 1980); P. G. Mewett, 'Associational categories and the social location of relationships in a Lewis crofting community', in Cohen (ed.), *Belonging*, pp. 101–30; Mewett, 'Exiles, nicknames, social identities and the production of local consciousness in a Lewis crofting community', in Cohen (ed.), *Belonging*, pp. 222–46; Macdonald, *Reimagining Culture* (on Skye); R. Fox, *The Tory Islanders: A People of the Celtic Fringe* (Cambridge, Cambridge University Press, 1978).

42 All kirk-session records and the records of the sheriff court are held in Shetland Archive, Lerwick, whereas those sources for most other parts of Scotland are kept in the National Archives in Edinburgh.

43 S. Delamont, *Appetites and Identities: An Introduction to the Social Anthropology of Western Europe* (London, Routledge, 1995), pp. 84–5.

44 This is not to say that out-migration is not an issue. Many young people still leave Shetland to pursue higher education, and the 2001 census recorded a demographic decline.

45 The book was published as L. Abrams, *The Making of Modern Woman: Europe 1789–1918* (London, Longman, 2002).

46 See N. Verdon, *Rural Women Workers in Nineteenth-Century England: Gender, Work and* Wages (Woodbridge, Boydell Press, 2002); J. Bourke, *Husbandry to Housewifery: Women, Economic Change and Housework in Ireland 1890–1914* (Oxford, Clarendon Press, 1993).

47 See R. Anthony, *Herds and Hinds: Farm Labour in Lowland Scotland, 1900–1939* (East Linton, Tuckwell Press, 1997); T. M. Devine, 'Women workers, 1850–1914', in T. M. Devine (ed.), *Farm Servants and Labour in Lowland Scotland 1770–1914* (Edinburgh, John Donald, 1984), pp. 98–123.

48 A. C. Frater, 'Women of the Gàidhealtachd and their songs to 1750', in E. Ewan and M. M. Meikle (eds), *Women in Scotland c.1100–1750* (Edinburgh, Tuckwell Press, 1999), pp. 67–79, here p. 78. See also in the same collection D. U. Stiùbhart, 'Women and gender in the early modern western Gàidhealtachd', pp. 233–49.

49 Ennew, *The Western Isles Today*, p. 79.

50 Ennew, *The Western Isles Today*, pp. 80–3.

51 J. Nadel-Klein and D. L. Davis, 'Introduction: gender in the maritime arena', in J. Nadel-Klein and D. L. Davis (eds), *To Work and To Weep: Women in Fishing Economies* (St John's, Memorial University of Newfoundland, 1988), pp. 1–17.

52 R. Byron, 'The maritime household in northern Europe', *Comparative Studies in Society and History* 36 (1994), pp. 271–91; Nadel-Klein and Davis (eds), *To Work and To Weep*; P. Thompson, 'Women in the fishing: the roots of power between the sexes', *Comparative Studies in Society and History* 27 (1985), pp. 3–32.

53 M. E. Smith, 'Comments on the heuristic utility of maritime anthropology', *The Maritime Anthropologist* 1 (1977), pp. 2–8, here p. 4.

54 J. Nadel-Klein, 'A fisher laddie needs a fisher lassie: endogamy and work in a Scottish fishing village', in Nadel-Klein and Davis (eds), *To Work and To Weep*, pp. 190–210, here pp. 191–2. See also Cohen, *Whalsay*, in which he defines the community almost solely in terms of male work and culture.

55 There are exceptions. See S. Cole, *Women of the Praia: Work and Lives in a Portuguese Coastal Community* (Princeton, NJ, Princeton University Press, 1991) on a Portuguese village where some women did regularly go to sea. Female fishing also appears to have been accepted amongst the Sami of northern Norway. See G. Thorvaldsen, 'Coastal women and their work roles', in H. Sandvik, K. Telste and G. Thorvaldsen (eds), *Pathways of the Past* (Oslo, Novus, 2002), pp. 139–51, here pp. 144–5.

56 See H. L. Moore, *Feminism and Anthropology* (London, Polity, 1988), p. 30.

57 For an extensive discussion of this issue in a comparative context see D. L. Davis and J. Nadel-Klein, 'Terra cognita? A review of the literature', in Nadel-Klein and Davis (eds), *To Work and To Weep*, pp. 19–50, here pp. 37–8 and 48–50.

58 See, for example: Byron, 'The maritime household in northern Europe', pp. 271–90; C. Brettell, *Men who Migrate, Women who Wait: Population and History in a Portuguese Parish* (Princeton, NJ, Princeton University Press, 1986); Cole, *Women of the Praia*; C. McGrath, B. Neis and M. Porter (eds), *Their Lives and Times: Women in Newfoundland and Labrador* (St John's, Killick Press, 1995).

59 U. D. Skaptadóttir, 'Housework and wage work: gender in Icelandic fishing communities', in G. Pálsson and P. Durrenberger (eds), *Images of Contemporary Iceland:*

Everyday Lives and Global Contexts (Iowa City, IA, University of Iowa Press, 1996), pp. 87–105, here pp. 89–90.

60 R. Byron and D. Chalmers, 'The fisherwomen of Fife: history, identity and social change', *Ethnologia Europaea* 23 (1993), pp. 97–110, here pp. 108–9.

61 Cole, *Women of the Praia*.

62 H. Hagmark, 'Maritime and seafarers' wives in the Åland isles in the 20th century', unpublished paper, 2001.

63 Cole, *Women of the Praia*, p. 40.

64 Cole, *Women of the Praia*, p. 41.

2

Stories

The old wives' tale might be stuff and nonsense, but it too could yield a harvest in corn and gold, if you stroked it smooth and combed it through. (Marina Warner, *From the Beast to the Blonde*, p. 25)

Narrative

ONE CHILLY DAY in the spring of 2001 I sat down with Mary Ellen Odie in the Old Haa at Burravoe on the island of Yell to talk about women in the past. In response to my questions about the economic and cultural position of women in Shetland history Mary Ellen told me a series of extraordinary stories about individual women who have come to exemplify the condition of Shetland womanhood. There was the woman who suffered distress following the disappearance of three of her sons at the whaling in Greenland and the suicide of a fourth son overcome with grief. We talked of Louisa Guthrie, whose husband was drowned in the fishing disaster of 1832, and of Nelly Kitty, whose sweetheart was drowned in the same storm and who married a whaler instead. She told me the story of Janet Rusland, who survived alone with the help of her neighbours and who was convicted in the sheriff court for potato theft, and of Betty Green, who carried her mother-in-law on her back in a straw basket or kishie. Then there were May Moar and Grace Petrie, both of whom were awarded Humane Society medals for rescuing fishermen from their storm-wrecked boats. And finally Mary Ellen related the story of Barbara Brown, the 'Bride of Vigon', who ran off with another man on the day before her wedding, and Barbara's mother Merran, who was imprisoned by her mad master and had to 'do a midnight flit', escaping out of her window down knotted sheets and fleeing by boat to the neighbouring island of Fetlar so she could marry her sweetheart.[1] All of these stories were told to me by a woman who has lived in Shetland all of her life and who is a memory bank of women's history. Their importance is immense.

Shetland identity is unusual because unlike most of western culture, it is strongly feminine. It is founded upon narratives of the past which incorporate a series of complementary archetypes of Shetland womanhood: the tragic woman, the heroic woman and the crofting woman. For over two centuries these archetypes have, singly and collectively, performed two functions in Shetland. First, they have constituted models of ideal femininity upon which Shetland women have drawn in the construction of their own sense of self. And second, they have acted collectively to project women as pivotal to the whole identity and culture of the Shetland archipelago. The perspective of this uniqueness from outside Shetland society illuminates the vigour of the feminine in the island's sense of itself, both now and in the more recent past. It is a place in which women's worlds of the imagination resonate strongly in the experiences of both women and men. Shetland culture is strongly female.[2]

The exploration of this culture starts with storytelling and personal identity. In this chapter we look at women and gender relations in the nineteenth and twentieth centuries through examination of the construction of historical myth. In later chapters we will look at economic and demographic factors that underpinned the materiality of women's dominance of culture. But we start with how Shetlanders imagine themselves.

There is no central or singular understanding of the Shetland woman. It is a composite construction made up of three 'idealised discourses' – the tragic, heroic and crafting woman – which can only be understood within a larger 'myth system'. The myth system is that of Shetland culture, the source of history, place and language, upon which Shetlanders – both men and women, young and old – draw as individuals to construct a sense of themselves. Every item of culture, every song, poem, dialect word, photograph and so on, is understood only in the context of a wider cultural system or backdrop, called by the poststructuralist theorist and philosopher Roland Barthes the 'myth system'.[3] The Shetland myth system that has become the framework within the islands for understanding and interpreting Shetland history consists of several key elements which can be summarised thus. Shetland is a community that represents itself in terms of its Norse heritage and its economic structure. These two factors more than any other are used to distinguish Shetland from elsewhere in the United Kingdom. It was primarily a fishing community with a dependence upon crofting as a secondary occupation, and it is this combination of work on the land and at sea that has come to structure narratives of the past. Shetland inhabitants express their identity and their ethos within this framework, which encompasses features such as long male absences, distinctive gender roles, the croft as a way of life, the importance of kinship and community and recognition of a distinct cultural heritage.[4] The three associated archetypes of Shetland womanhood – the tragic woman, the heroic woman and the crofting woman – are essentially indigenous ideal types and thus must be understood within this broader myth system.

The tragic woman was skilfully portrayed by one of Shetland's famous daughters. Christina Jamieson (1864–1942), resident of Lerwick, prolific writer and founder of the Shetland Women's Suffrage Society, penned a perceptive piece in 1910 which still stands as an insightful comment on the condition of Shetland womanhood. In Shetland:

> The women adore the men. The whole interest, effort, ambition, pathos and tragedy of their lives centre on the men, whose lives are so precarious. There is no mother or aunt or sister or wife or daughter who does not lavish the utmost affection, the most unselfish and unexacting devotion, on the men folk; who never go forth to their business on the deep who the women feel in every fibre of their frames that it may be for the last time – they may never come back. This dread is a sub-current of the whole course of their lives, to which it imports an intense and religious pathos.[5]

This was an island community where men were primarily engaged in seafaring occupations. The inherent dangers of seagoing at this time, as well as the more specific risks associated with the kind of open-boat fishing conducted for much of the nineteenth century, resulted in a significant death rate amongst men of working age, hence Christina Jamieson's observations. A series of fishing disasters – in 1832, 1881, 1887 and 1900 – along with the everyday wastage of men lost at sea created a culture of loss, poignantly described in the *Shetland News* shortly after the Delting disaster of 1900, when twenty-two men drowned:

> Fifteen families have been bereft of their bread-winners. In one case, the family left – that of James Cogle, Toft – consists of the widow, and seven children. The oldest son, Gilbert, who is 19, has been at sea. He returned home on hearing of the disaster. The oldest girl, Mary (17) is subject to fits, and not able to do much for herself. The other children's ages range from 14 down to 2. This family are very poor. The croft is a very small one, and can keep only one or two animals . . . The saddest case of bereavement is that of the Nicolson family at Firth. There are two houses on the croft, built end to end.

Here Charles Nicolson and his four sons and son-in-law, John Hay, lived together . . . The sons were four fine young fellows, careful and active, of a happy disposition, and general favourites. They had the best boat in the place, and were comfortably off. Only three weeks before, one of the daughters, Maggie, had been married to John Hay. It may be imagined how terrible is their bereavement – six men taken out of one house, and only three sorrowing women left! Their distress will evoke a widespread sympathy.[6]

Fictional representations of Shetland women similarly dwell on the woman's love for a man and her heartache at seeing him leave for the fishing with the knowledge that he may never return to marry her. The popular stories of the Unst-born writer Jessie Saxby (1842–1940), a contemporary of Christina Jamieson, often featured a newly married young woman pining and waiting for a young man in the knowledge that the sea claimed so many lives of seafaring men, or she described the plight of the widows and orphans left behind.[7] In Saxby's 'The brother's sacrifice', published in 1876, she tells the story of Britta Ingster. Britta married her childhood sweetheart, but his death at sea left her a young widow with a son to bring up alone:

To pay the rent and retain the home which *he* [her husband] had provided for her, and which held so many tender associations, was the great ambition of Britta's life; but hard times came when there was no fish on the coast, and no corn or potatoes in the field, and Britta had often to send her little boy supperless to bed, while she sat till the small hours plying her knitting needles, the produce of which was all she had to depend on for tomorrow's dinner. She worked hard and long, and never murmured, but she could not keep the wolf from the door . . . She had no relations, and her neighbours had enough troubles of their own this season; besides, Britta was modest and sensitive, and she could not bear to parade her poverty before the eyes of her kind but rude-minded neighbours.[8]

And in her collection of short stories *Heim-Laund and Heim-Folk*, Saxby returned to this motif in the story of the newlywed and young mother May Hectorson who, reflecting on the power of the weather and the sea to impact upon her community, looked out to sea and sighed, ' "There's aye *some* puir women need pray when the winds blaw sair." "Yea lass" replied her elderly neighbour, "when *wir ain* is safe at hame we forget the sorrow that comes frae the sea tae mony a sister's fireside. The Lord mak' wis mair pitiful!" '[9] The theme of tragedy in the lives of young women is taken up much later in Jenny Brown's film *The Rugged Island: A Shetland Lyric*, filmed on Shetland in 1933.[10] The story centres on a young couple, Andrew and Enga, engaged to be married. When Andrew goes away to sea Enga waits and worries for him and spends her time going about the croft work until his return. The womenfolk in the film, although constantly engaged in croft work, are portrayed as focusing much of their energy upon the men in their lives.

But the discourse of the tragic woman does not develop into self-pity. Indeed, as Christina Jamieson observed, the tragedy of absence, loss and widowhood was not allowed to succumb to despair, for 'the household of women toils on. The central interest of their lives is gone and they are poorer' yet 'neither they nor anyone for them seems to notice that for the actual necessities of life they have never been dependent on the men.'[11] For Jamieson the tragedy of the Shetland woman's lot was not solely that she lived for an ideal that was so often cruelly snatched away, but that women's 'constant industry and self-dependence' was not sufficiently recognised, either by their menfolk, who took their women for granted, or by the state, which had refused to entrust women with the franchise.[12]

The second discourse on the Shetland woman can be found in depictions of what may be described as 'heroic' women. These are strong women who overcome the odds to survive in a harsh environment and who have come to symbolise Shetland, the way of life and its distinctiveness, both for outsiders and for generations of Shetlanders. Archetypes of the heroic woman abound. The most feted beyond Shetland is Betty Mouat. Betty was in most ways an unremarkable Shetland woman, who became nationally famous for her lone drift to Norway on the sailing vessel the *Columbine* in January 1886, when she was fifty-nine years of age.[13] Betty lived the typical life of a Shetland woman. Unmarried, she contributed to the household income by her fine knitting, which she exchanged for goods in Lerwick's stores under the barter or truck system. It was on one of her boat trips to Lerwick from her home at Levenwick, to sell shawls and seek medical advice regarding a recent stroke, that Betty was carried out to sea. A heavy swell swept the skipper and his crew overboard, leaving Betty to drift off alone. Sustained by just a bottle of milk and two biscuits, Betty survived eight days and nine nights before the *Columbine* ran aground off the Norwegian coast. She was attached to a rope and hauled ashore by local fishermen.

Betty Mouat's story soon reached the British and continental press, and in 1886 her own account of the voyage was printed in *The Scotsman*, where it was said that 'at no period of her trying experience does she seem to have given way to anything like violent grief, but rather . . . endured her dreadful trial . . . with remarkable calmness and resignation, if not with fortitude.'[14] Her arrival in Edinburgh occasioned tremendous interest; reportedly hundreds of people – mostly ladies – queued to see her at 8 Hermitage Terrace, and she received offers to appear as a curiosity in public exhibitions. Her return to Shetland was also greeted by crowds on the dockside. Betty Mouat's experience fascinated a nation unacquainted with the hard lives of Shetland women, and she came to encapsulate the image of the Shetland heroine, an uncomplaining stoic woman, economically and emotionally self-sufficient, a stark contrast to the image of the dependent and passive woman so prevalent in Victorian Britain. Her importance as an iconic character for Shetland womanhood and Shetland distinctiveness is still celebrated. Two books have been devoted to her story, visitors to Shetland can visit her grave in Dunrossness churchyard, and her former cottage in nearby Scatness has been preserved as a camping böd.[15]

Two women who, in separate incidents, saved the lives of men doomed to drown are further exemplars of this heroic archetype. May Moar and Grace Petrie were ordinary crofting women, and both received official recognition for their acts of heroism in the form of medals for bravery.[16] Of Grace's actions in 1856 (accompanied by her father and sister-in-law) the *Shetland Times* remarked that 'here we have the noblest instincts of our nature in their fullest energy. What are the highest titles worth in comparison with the simple names of these large-hearted and daring women and men.'[17] May Moar (sometimes known by her maiden name of Hectorson), who carried out a similar feat in 1858 off the coast of Yell, was immortalised in a popular story by Jessie Saxby, 'A daughter of sea-kings'. When a four-oared boat capsized in a storm in the sight of May and her neighbours, May went to the rescue. She was lowered over a rocky precipice with fishing line and a rope and proceeded to haul in the exhausted men. ' "If some o'you will guide weel this rope", said May Hectorson decisively, and dashing from her face her woman's tears. "I'll gang ower the banks" (precipice) "and save the men, wi' God's help." '[18] All of these women were commemorated and held up as icons of Shetland womanhood, a status aided by their typicality as well as their exceptional deeds. All three, Betty Mouat, Grace Petrie and May Moar, are still portrayed today – in official representations and popular memory – as exemplars of Shetland women in the past.[19]

The third discourse most commonly used to frame and understand women in Shetland's past is that of the crofting woman.[20] Within this fishing-crofting community women were often left to run the crofts alone for at least part of the year. The female crofter was tough, hard-working and independent, and it was this role above all others that gave Shetland women their reputation for 'being in among things'.[21] The female crofter has come to assume a degree of symbolic power in Shetland, as the authentic sign of a past which is also revered for its simplicity and its gender equality. In photographs, museum exhibits and educational films the crofting woman achieves a symbolic status unequalled by other occupational groups. In popular memory, crofting women are celebrated and revered for their ability to do what is described as 'men's work'. The comment that 'da women den could do laek men' sums up the modern perception of Shetland women in the past.[22] They are represented as resourceful, skilful and unique, and the female crofter represents much that is admired about the resilience of Shetlanders in the past as well as a leitmotif for many things that are perceived to be distinctive about Shetland society, in particular its gender egalitarianism. Today, the idealised image of the female crofter woman may be appropriated to provide a powerful and empowering model for women. On the other hand it may also inhibit or constrain alternative narratives of the past. As Jack argues, the 'perpetuation, and celebration, of this singular dominant cultural ideal effectively denies the possibility of positive alternative histories.'[23]

These idealised discourses – of the tragic woman, the heroic woman and the crofting woman – must be understood within the context of the material reality of women in Shetland. This was a woman's world – a place where women dominated demographically and where women played a central economic role and had an independent economic identity. These material circumstances informed women's sense of self and contributed to the tendency for women narrators to place women at the centre of their stories and to narrate stories about a world of women. Men were not only physically absent from the islands for much of the time; they are also fascinatingly absent from the worlds depicted by women in their oral testimony and their storytelling. Female storytellers empower women's place in the history of Shetland by placing them at the centre of their narratives. Thus when a present-day Shetland crofter spoke to me about how she built her croft house in the 1950s and the means by which she 'scraped by', she was speaking with the authority of a woman who was confident about her ability to be independent, and this, in turn, was informed by her understanding of women's role in crofting in the past and her present position as president of the Shetland Crofting Foundation.[24] And when Mary Ellen Odie told the story of her great-great-grandmother Nelly Kitty, a woman whose sweetheart drowned before she could marry him, she invoked the images of the tragic woman and the heroic crofting woman. With no men left in the village to do the physical work, 'Nelly sowed the oats for the whole village you see, and she took the boat and went to the fishing to catch something to eat just like a man would . . . So she was quite a woman.'[25] Her story of Nelly Kitty is framed by the wider discourses on women in Shetland's past and at the same time contributes to a particular way of understanding women's historical role in these islands.

However, these discourses on the Shetland woman were not all indigenous, and some are relatively recent. In the nineteenth century the crofting woman was often pitied by visitors to the islands. Her weather-beaten face, rough hands, hardy disposition and economic self-sufficiency were not traits to be praised by those more comfortable with discourses on the dependent, domestic woman in Victorian society. Representations of the heroic and the tragic woman, on the other hand, were a product of more complex influences in the nineteenth century. A combination of reports written by visitors to the islands, romanticised representations of island life by Shetland and non-Shetland writers and novelists, and the reproduction of these discourses in the local and national press and the pulpit resulted in the creation of a caricature of Shetland womanhood that combined a romantic heroism with tragedy and resilience. The writings and more particularly the sketches of Frank Barnard, a London-based artist and visitor to Shetland, typify this romantic genre.[26] In more recent times, an intensified idealisation of the female crofter and her status as an iconic symbol of Shetland distinctiveness was arguably a consequence of Shetlanders' reaction to the social, economic and cultural changes wrought by the oil industry in the 1970s. As a recent historian of Shetland women argues, 'an acknowledgement of communal subjectivities provides a window on the way in which society wishes to view itself. It also provides a window on the ways in which members of a society wish to present themselves to others.'[27] So we must weave together two narrative threads – the mythic and the material – in order to tell a story of Shetland women in the past.

Sagas

The mythic belief in the strength, resilience and power of Shetland women may have its deepest roots in the stories of the Norse peoples – or Vikings – who settled in Shetland in the ninth century. The Norse were a seafaring people of Scandinavian origin. Although often stereotyped as 'marauding pagan warriors' who spent long periods away from their homesteads, many were accompanied by women on their voyages to the previously uninhabited or sparsely inhabited lands of Greenland, Iceland, Faroe and northern Scotland including Shetland. The Icelandic sagas are detailed narratives, originating in the thirteenth century, that purport to present a historically based picture in fictional form of Viking life in Iceland between the ninth and the eleventh centuries. In these stories, Viking-age women – both those who stayed on the homesteads and those who went to sea – are represented as strong, even dominant, intelligent, independent and determined. These are women such as Unnr the Deep-Minded, who left Norway for Scotland and then, once her ship was built, set sail for Iceland, where she settled and became a powerful woman in her own right.[28] The sagas probably tell us more about the preoccupations of the thirteenth-century Icelanders than about the historical reality of the Viking age, and, to take this further, it is likely that the Sagas were presented to the nineteenth-century reading public in new versions, in ways that reflected contemporary concerns.[29] In nineteenth-century industrialising Sweden, for example, preoccupations with patriotism and a harking back to a time when the Nordic peoples were united and strong informed a re-writing of the history of the Viking age. With the rise of nineteenth-century domestic ideology, a stereotype of the Viking woman as high in status and head of the household emerged, bolstered by those who campaigned for women's emancipation: 'The master of the house shared his power within his house with the housewife . . . She ruled the house according to her own will; she was in charge of the locks and keys.'[30]

In a context in which men were often away, women's economic power may have been enhanced, a theory supported by the relatively high proportion of female graves from the Viking period discovered in Norway.[31] According to one nineteenth-century Scottish interpretation of the sagas, the Viking age 'gave the women a sense of responsibility and freedom of management . . . the women acquired calmness and soundness of judgement, and the Sagas show they were given a very free hand in the management of affairs.'[32] In one Shetland version of a tale known as the story of 'the women who keepit der tongues atween their teeth for eens', women played a key role in liberating themselves and their menfolk from the tyranny of the Danish invaders. Following a raid on Unst, the invaders enslaved those at home and planned to capture the men when they returned from the sea. The women, however, 'did not tamely submit' to their captors. One night, after much secrecy and planning, the women murdered the invaders, who had been drugged with strong drink. The tale is otherwise known as the story of women who could keep a secret – evidently a notable accomplishment for women, who in nineteenth-century society were more likely to be characterised as gossips and loose talkers. To celebrate and commemorate their victory, the wife of the household was to take the seat at the 'best and high-end o' the Bord'. 'One imagines', writes Jessie Saxby, 'that this domestic revolution may have inaugurated the Viking Age in Shetland . . . our women won for their Northmen their freedom and their homes!'[33]

In nineteenth-century interpretations it was said that under Norse rule Shetland women were skilled craftswomen and household managers. 'The position of the women-kind was very honourable in those days . . . The mistress of a household was no mere ornamental figure-head, but a mainspring in whose default all affairs were at a standstill.'[34] But this female-dominated society was short-lived. With the rise of Scottish influence, especially from around the fifteenth century, the position of women allegedly deteriorated as they were forced to work to pay taxes and to undertake heavy outdoor labour. This situation improved only in the eighteenth century when the advent of the whaling industry brought more money to the islands and women began to produce hosiery for the market. At the end of the nineteenth century, observers commonly harked back to the 'golden age' of the Norse era to explain the prominent role of women in crofting and the economy in general. Women, it was said, held sway both indoors and out 'and seem in a fair way to return to the honourable state of the women of the Odal time, from whom they inherit their simple industrious habits and wholesome contempt of luxury.' According to this writer in 1899, Shetland women had no need of advocates of women's rights because they were already in charge of their affairs and are 'quite able to do the work of men'.[35] Thus, as Cohen observes, 'mythological distance lends enchantment to an otherwise murky contemporary view . . . myth is beyond time', making the past 'impervious to the rationalistic scrutiny of historians . . .'[36]

The romanticisation of the Viking age and the elevation of Norse womenfolk to the status of heroines, with a position in society equal to if not greater than that of their menfolk, owes much to nineteenth-century Shetland writers and folklorists. Leading amongst them were Jessie Saxby and her brother the Revd. B. Edmonston, who endeavoured to present a picture of a romantic Shetland with a distinct culture traceable to the Norse era. The picture they painted was a fictional recreation of the past and a legitimation of the present informed by an intellectual engagement with the world of the sagas and of the Norsemen who settled in Shetland and created the foundations of its culture of survival.[37] By the first half of the nineteenth century Norn – the language of the Norse – had disappeared apart from remnants evident in the Shetland dialect, Norse Udal law had been superseded by Scots law, most property was now owned by Scots landlords, and the Scottish Presbyterian church was well established. However, by the second half of the century Shetland intellectuals were busy promoting a Norse romantic revival, the most dramatic and long-lasting result being the festival of Up-helly-aa, a calendar custom consciously modelled on the symbols of the Viking age. But Norse romanticism could also be used to rethink interpretations of the position of women in nineteenth-century Shetland, turning what appeared to be a picture of subordination and exploitation in to one that portrayed women as equal to men and possessing considerable autonomy. In the twenty-first century the stereotype or myth of the independent, powerful Viking woman and her legacy to Shetland women of the modern age is still to be found, for example, in the literature of the Shetland writer Margaret Elphinstone, whose novel *The Sea Road* is a retelling of the sagas with a woman – Gudrid – at the heart.[38]

Why is it important to know all of this? Because these ways of thinking about Shetland women have shaped the way in which they are represented and perceived in modern times, and have influenced the ways in which Shetland women themselves construct narratives of their lives and histories. The myth of the powerful, independent Norse woman legitimates a telling of stories which have women as actors at the heart of the narrative. Female storytellers who use these motifs and frames of reference have, to paraphrase the novelist Angela Carter, 'a wish to validate their claim to a fair share of the future by staking their claim to their share of the past'.[39]

Old wives' tales

Norse myths and tropes are present throughout the popular cultural construction of Shetland identity. Since the 1890s, popular images of the Vikings as raiders and conquerors have been presented in ritual form each year at the festival of Up-helly-aa; Norse place-names have been revived, and dialect poetry and popular literature loosely based on the Norn language are encouraged to flourish. Yet no complete Norse tales or ballads or heroic sagas have survived in the Norn language in Shetland despite the vigorous attempts by Shetland intellectuals from the 1870s onwards to revive Shetlanders' consciousness of their Norse heritage.[40] Storytelling in the islands tends, therefore, to be local or domestic in theme, featuring the sea, the trows (or fairies) and common everyday matters woven into fantastical narratives, moral tales and romantic yarns.[41] 'Mother had a lot of stories that she had been told when she was a child', recalled the oral respondent Jessie Sinclair; 'of course it was all trows.'[42] 'Often it was women who told the best tales, fairy stories and things', recalled Mary Ellen Odie. 'And Mary [Manson] was particularly good and so was Jean Thompson, they were the two nautical ones.'[43] Though we know very little about the transmission of oral culture in Shetland in the past, the little evidence we have points to folktales in their oral form being passed on by women. Karl Blind, who published extensively on Shetland folklore, remarked in 1896 that 'women are often the chief holders of popular tales', noting that Shetland was curious in this respect.[44] Shetland's distinctive female storytelling tradition may be associated with the demographic situation in the nineteenth century whereby women significantly outnumbered men and the pattern of work which took men away from home for long periods. A similar situation has been observed in the case of Galicia in Spain, where the combination of fishing and farming meant that women were prominent in the workforce and where authority in the family rested with the mother.[45]

In the twentieth century, though, collectors of folk narratives and oral tradition, especially those from outside Shetland, have tended to focus their attention primarily upon male storytellers, whose tales have been recorded and translated into literary form in the name of cultural preservation. The words and the stories of local Shetland men such as Tom Tulloch, Bruce Henderson and Jeemsie (James) Laurenson may now be heard unchanged on tape by future generations, and these purveyors of Shetland oral culture have had their status affirmed by intellectual recognition.[46] No female storytellers in Shetland have been granted such legitimacy outside the islands.

Indeed, the very label 'storyteller' has a very particular meaning for ethnographers, denoting a person who can relate a well-known tale in a particular style for an audience. The teller is as important as the tale because he or she has a mastery of form and language which conveys a story using particular conventions and motifs. There are, of course, female storytellers who conform to this scholarly definition, including some in Shetland, but a widening of the definition of 'storyteller' by feminist scholars permits the inclusion of many more women who have a story to tell. Gossips, 'old wives', fireside fairy-tale tellers, the 'Mother Gooses' of tale-telling – all have been rediscovered and rehabilitated by feminist writers in the fields of literature, anthropology, ethnology and folklore studies.[47] Women's historians have adopted eclectic methodologies in order to 'rescue' or hear women's voices and have especially turned to oral history – essentially the telling of stories about the past. Other kinds of texts as well, such as witchcraft narratives and judicial declarations by female defendants in court, have been analysed as stories or narrative texts. The notion of the 'silent woman', the woman who was advised to hold her tongue, the woman whose father or husband spoke on her behalf, has been challenged since the 1970s by historians and anthropologists who want to hear women's 'dangerous' or 'seductive' tongues. The 'old wives' tales', so long associated with ignorance, superstition and backwardness, have been reconstituted as valuable indicators of domestic life and of the everyday. Whether women tell a fairy-story, a magical tale or a story from their past, they are creating and re-creating narratives that are as legitimate as the well-known stories recorded and fixed for posterity in the archives or published as 'authentic' folklore.

Oral histories can be part fairy-tale, part autobiography, part domestic narrative, but they are always transmissions of social memory and, like all good oral narratives, are a commentary on the present as much as a retelling of the past.[48] Oral histories may be 'memories' of events in the past but they are also narratives of a culture.[49] These narratives are shaped by the narrator's experience and also by her relationship to discursive constructions of the past. These are mediated through popular literature such as newspapers, local magazines and journals, fiction, popular and academic history, community heritage presentations and so on. In Shetland all of these elements are particularly salient. Shetlanders today have an active interest in and reverence for their own history. Most Shetland households own books on Shetland history, and many subscribe to popular and literary magazines produced in the islands, notably the *New Shetlander* and *Shetland Life,* which publish items on history and literature and promote dialect prose and verse. The local newspapers regularly feature items of historical interest, especially in the summer, when Shetland is home to scores of archaeologists. Moreover, Shetland has a vibrant indigenous museum and archive culture, not just in Lerwick but also on the islands in the form of locally run heritage centres such as those on Fetlar and Yell, and more substantial exhibits such as the Unst Boat Haven. The Shetland Family History Society has an active presence, recording and transcribing reams of genealogical data, and in 2001 participated in a large BBC-filmed project using DNA tracing to authenticate the importance of Nordic origins in the Shetland people.

Oral respondents shape their stories about the past with reference to all of these public representations of history and culture, although they are not determined by them. Personal testimonies are inter-subjective; in the words of the women's historian Penny Summerfield 'it is thus necessary to encompass within oral history analysis and inter-pretation, not only the voice that speaks for itself, but also the voices that speak to it, the discursive formulations from which understandings are selected and within which accounts are made.'[50] Female respondents in Shetland draw upon the prevalent 'myths' of Shetland women – the tragic, the heroic and the crofting woman – but, at the same time, those myths may provide women respondents with a platform to speak and may promote a willingness to place themselves, or women in general, at the heart of their stories. In short, the discourse on the strong, inde-pendent Shetland woman can be empowering for present-day Shetland women. It provides female storytellers with a legitimising framework for their own stories, but it does not determine the stories they tell.

However, this myth may also have negative consequences, espe-cially for some, particularly younger, women, whose experience bears little relation to that of the idealised or stereotypical Shetland woman portrayed in the popular media. For instance, the ideal of the heroic female crofter who was equal to her man is a powerful and potentially empowering image. But it attains that status only if the narrator is able to compare her own role with the idealised image in a favourable light.[51] With Shetland changing so much since the 1970s, many women may be unable to use the idealised or mythical past as a means of bolstering their own identity. However, it may be employed as a frame for inter-preting the experience of previous generations of women. For instance, when I interviewed Netta Inkster, the daughter of a renowned female storyteller, she had little difficulty in recounting her mother's life within the discourse of the heroic, crofting woman, but she did not construct her own life in the same way. Of her mother, a crofter all of her life, she said: 'it would have been hard definitely looking at it nowadays but she just seemed to flow through it and no bother, I mean she just, everyday she got up early morning – she was hardly ever in bed – and on top of all this knitting had to get the weekend messages – had to be sitting there and knitting.'[52] Her mother had been a fine hand-knitter, and one of her lace shawls had been sent to Princess Mary. Beside her mother, Netta told me, she felt 'so inadequate when I think of what she used to do and what I have to do now.' This self-condemnation seemed harsh as Netta had undertaken hard paid work in the 1970s servicing the oil workers, which allowed her to build a comfortable modern house in place of her family's largely unmodernised croft house. So the dominant discourses on Shetland womanhood privilege the experience of the archetypal female crofter, but no comparable contemporary oil-industry heroine has emerged in popular or public discourse. Hence the mythical Shetland woman remains embedded in the past.[53]

Performance

It has been observed that women's tale-telling differs from that of men in terms of genre and purpose. Men have a tendency to adopt the heroic epic genre, whilst women are more likely to create lyric tales or fairy-tales. Women's storytelling may be magical or romantic, featuring female protagonists; it may be educational in the form of a moral tale or critique of social conduct; or it may be autobiographical.[54] And in terms of style it has been said that women's tales have a tendency to be grounded in everyday life, characterised by description drawn from female experience. 'The special social and everyday conditions of the life of a woman . . . have placed their imprint on the tales which were related by women', states a Russian collector of fairy-tales.[55] Though the experiences of Shetland show that there has been a place for the heroic woman, women's tales also often have an educational or disciplinary purpose, imparting lessons for survival.

Personal narratives are products of the inter-subjective relationship between the narrator or subject and the audience (whether in the form of storytelling or the oral history interview). The way in which a narrative is told is influenced by the composition of the audience and the expectations held by both sides. The content and form of a story told to a family member may differ markedly from that told to an academic researcher, for instance. Moreover there are, at any one time, a number of performative models on offer to the narrator. The majority of oral history interviews take place in the home of the subject, or at least in a semi-private setting conducive to an intimate conversation. However, many interviewees assume that what is expected of them is a public performance. Today, oral history is so frequently seen as an integral part of media representations of the past that respondents may assume that their narratives belong in the public domain and hence may feel 'under pressure to perform for a stranger as a narrative subject . . . as the subject and hero of a narrative aiming to communicate an experience laden with signification.'[56] This performative aspect of the oral history interview can be manifested in many different ways. Some respondents will make elaborate preparations of the interview setting; others may present pre-prepared scripts or articulate a concern that the story being told conforms to what is required by the interviewer. Richard Bauman defines performance as 'an aesthetically marked and heightened mode of communication, framed in a special way and put on display for the audience.'[57] In Shetland, a particular performance model that may be adopted is what I describe as the storytelling mode, a confident and practised narrative style whereby the subject takes control of the 'interview' in an assertion of authority. In this context the performative mode adopted is to some extent determined by the 'script'; that is, the story or narrative requires a certain form and style in order that it is heard in the appropriate way.

I want to focus on three oral narratives with Shetland women to illustrate these points about genre and performance. The first narrator is Mary Manson. She was interviewed in her home in 1982 at the age of eighty-five by a local historian and folklorist, Robbie Johnson. Also present were a geologist from Liverpool and two others, possibly Mary's husband and a district nurse. Mary Manson lived all her life on a croft at West Sandwick on the island of Yell. She was most likely interviewed because of her encyclopaedic knowledge of local families and genealogy, but she was also known in Shetland as a storyteller. The second narrative is the interview that I conducted with Mary Ellen Odie in 2001. Mary Ellen was identified to me as a local expert on Shetland women. She is also an active local historian who curates a local heritage centre on Yell. Mary Ellen Odie has lived all her life on Yell and has an intimate knowledge of local families and customs. The third narrative is an interview I conducted in 2002 with Agnes Leask in her own home with her husband present. Agnes, born in 1934, comes from a family of crofters and works a croft with her husband in Weisdale on the Shetland Mainland. These three narratives will be analysed in turn for what they can tell us about the relationship between experience and discourse, between the voice that speaks for itself – the personal testimony – and the voices that speak to it – the discursive formulations.

Mary Manson, Mary Ellen Odie and Agnes Leask adopt similar performative styles for their narrations. All three possess an authority which is expressed in a particular narrative format. To the twenty-first-century ear, these narratives bear more resemblance to a pre-modern storytelling mode than to a modern oral history interview. For some decades now we have been familiar with the media culture of the question-and-answer interview designed to elicit information. However, the form preferred by these female subjects strikes one as emanating from a different time and a different place. Both Mary Manson and

Agnes Leask adopt a narrative style which privileges the subject over the interviewer. Both women speak in long monologues largely uninterrupted by the interviewer. Their frequent use of the first-person narrative bolsters the idea of the storyteller being a special person who possesses particular knowledge and insight. This form of narrative is based on a cultural tradition that the spoken word possesses an authenticity to which written texts cannot aspire. The spoken voice is taken to be interior and superior to other formats. Thus, the format adopted by each of these women is not arbitrarily chosen.[58] They have learned to narrate a story in a particular style or form which avoids chronological organisation and which rather takes particular moments and experiences as narrative devices.[59] Thus when the interviewer poses the question 'Now what was that story aboot dee midder?', Mary Manson proceeds to narrate a very long and detailed story from her family history which describes a journey made by her mother to fetch a cure from a wise-woman. This is a story that she has certainly told several, perhaps many, times before.[60] Agnes Leask told me a number of stories which related to her experiences of crofting but which were not directly prompted by my questions. The stories of how she rebuilt her croft house, of how she learned to milk the cows and about how she cured a sick calf, were all narrated in great detail with no direct prompting or questioning. Mary Ellen Odie's stories are drawn from her memory and her family's memories of life on Yell and from cases drawn from the archives, and these too were narrated in the absence of specific prompts by the interviewer.

All three narrative performances draw upon traditions of 'storytelling' (as opposed to autobiographical chronological narratives). In Shetland, as in other parts of Scotland, storytelling was (and is) an art requiring the acquisition and demonstration of a particular technique and observing certain conventions or rules. Shetland stories in particular tend to rehearse a number of traditional themes and maintain certain conventions, such as the use of direct quotation or speech and the introduction of significant detail at dramatic moments.[61] Stories in general have a particular power, particularly in the hands of a skilled storyteller who can 'move into the way others remember the past and change it merely by introducing an unexpected detail into an unfamiliar account.'[62] The fact that it is women who are the narrators adds another dimension to the analysis. The myth of the heroic Shetland woman in history is combined with the power of the storytelling mode to produce legitimising accounts of Shetland society in the past and the present in which women have a central place.

The narratives related by these women are not primarily tales of the imagination but are stories crafted from autobiographical memory and the cultural past. From the magical narrative of Mary Manson to the autobiographical narrative of Agnes Leask, these tales are all distinguished by the use of domestic detail or context, their groundedness in the specificity of the everyday life of Shetland and their use as narratives of cultural survival. It may be said that women's oral and written narratives possess three functions: the transmission of social memory, the maintenance and reification of the heroine myth and the validation of women's place in Shetland history and thus, by extension, their place in the present.

Mary Manson's story conforms to the magical or fairy-tale format of narrative, but her tale of a journey by two girls to fetch a cure from a wise-woman also has the character of a morality tale containing messages about boundaries of community. As a storyteller Mary Manson is a purveyor of women's knowledge and culture, what has been described as a 'memorial guardian'.[63] She narrates a tale about a journey undertaken by her mother and another young girl from Yell to fetch a cure or potion from a wise-woman called Merran Winwick who lived at Muness on the island of Unst. She describes the details of the journey, the food they ate (bustin broonie, a kind of bannock or flat loaf), the help they received, the state of their feet when they reached their destination, the house in which the wise-woman lived and the experience of the girls while they waited for the cure to be prepared.

> I mind Mammy saying it was a fine bed at she had, she had a tatted rug and a feather bed and of course, then a days it was likely supposed tae be a wonderful bed, onywye they got aff o dem and they got intae this bed and she drew the door across the front. So you can keen what they were likely tinkin', locked in a dis black prison, didna know what was going to happen after that, so anyway, she left them in yunder and she guid out, and she was a braw while away, and at last they heard her comin in, but it had tae be kinda light, at had tae be the spring do sees at she could see, anywye, daylight coming up or something, but they heard her coming in and they heard her starting to get the fire up, it was a fire in the middle of the floor and they heard her gettin doon the peats and gettin this fire going, and a pouring a water and a rattling of pans and tins and all this, and then after a while they fan the smell o' lik dis roots, lik a strong smell of roots boiling, so Mammy said they could lie no longer for they were never fallen asleep, she got up and she tried, there was a chink in the door, and she got up and she tried tae peep and see what was going on and she said that the old wife was sitting ower the heartstane wi' all this pots and pans and a great pot hanging in the crook, boiling with this mixture.[64]

The Mary Manson story has all the ingredients of the classic fairy-tale: young girls on a transformative journey, a 'witch', magic potions, taboos (the girls were not permitted to look at the mixture or to let the bottle touch the ground), suspense and juxtapositions of light and dark, young and old, good and evil. And yet this story is primarily about Shetland values and culture. In the space between the girls leaving home and returning we enter an imaginary world populated by good people and potentially bad people; the teller creates a world which offers a commentary upon the nature of island culture: the sense of community and mutual obligation (expressed in the help and hospitality the girls received). The story has what Angela Carter calls a normative function, reinforcing the ties that bind people to one another. Repeated references to the folk who helped them on their way and particularly the food they received contrast with Mary Manson's reflections earlier on in the interview about the kind of society she lives in where such reliance on folk is unnecessary.

> Weel, I canna mind when it would have been, but onywye I should think the difference noo, an yet we're never thankful enough, two nurses and two doctors here in Yell, and you just need tae feel a pain or anything, lift the phone and call the Doctor and he's here afore you get the phone laid doon, at the door tae see what's wrong wi' you, and then tae think aboot the old folk, what a life they had if anything was the matter with them, aha.

The wise-woman is the marginal figure in the story, marking the boundary between the safety of home and the unknown of the 'Northered' (literally the area north beyond Yell but also implying a magical place) and that between the everyday and the supernatural.[65] And then of course we have the happy ending. The girls get home safely, the medicine cures the cousin, she goes on to marry and have nine children, and everyone lives happily ever after.

It is no coincidence that this story centres on female protagonists who are given the opportunity to demonstrate their skills. This, too, is a common feature of the fairy-tale, and Angela Carter notes that such characterisations may well have their origins in the society from which they originate.[66] Passivity was not an option for women in economically marginal societies: rather they needed wit, cleverness and resourcefulness to survive. Such women are often sent on epic journeys; they are required to use their intelligence to solve riddles or to escape the clutches of monsters. Carter suggests that the fairy-tale offered an opportunity for women to exercise their wit in societies characterised by contempt for women. Perhaps the epic journey undertaken by these two girls and their resourcefulness in bringing home the medicine is a comment upon women's own perception of their place in Shetland society, both in the past and in the present. Here we may recall Christina Jamieson's observations on her kinswomen who endured the 'harsh indifference of men to women they have ceased to need' and who alone 'maintain continuous life in the isles'.[67]

Mary Manson's narrative invokes, on the surface at least, a very different world from the one in which she (and her listeners) are materially situated. Her narrative evokes the fairy-tale, but she does not begin her story with 'once upon a time'; her story is not primarily a tale of the imagination, but a conjuring up of a lost world brought to life and made 'authentic' by the use of dialogue and local detail. Mary Ellen Odie also tells vivid stories of Shetland heroines but, unlike Mary Manson's narrative, which brings the past into the present, Mary Ellen's stories are about a past which she 'knows' through her life on Yell and her immersion in the history of the island. Mary Ellen adopts a different narrative form to that of Mary Manson. She weaves together personal memories and family stories with documented history. In the following conversation about the 'hungry gap' – the period of time after the last year's grain ran out and before the new grain was harvested – Mary Ellen brings into her account supportive evidence of a doctor (Thomas Irvine) and a royal commission (the Napier Commission of 1883), woven into her own and family evidence in the manner of scholarship.

> But that hungry gap must have been such a frightener. And one thing in relation to women that I certainly know affected the people in North Yell particularly we have Thomas Irvine's very poignant note at the end of the list of names of people, was the potato famine it happened just the second year after the Irish, and North Yell got a really bad blight. It was then that the . . . meal roads of North Yell were introduced seriously after that year. But then the meal roads had to be introduced just before when the hungry gap had really widened in the late 30s, that was a bad bad time. It comes out, I tell you where it comes out quite graphically is in the Napier Commission where people describe what it was like to be, to have your last meal and then know that after that it was just the bare essentials. My great-granny knew how to cook a starling, do you believe that? . . . Her man was drowned and she was really left destitute, 1851. And they caught starlings in a gun? It was just a kind of set up with a stick and a net, when they went in the poor things it collapsed and they got the starlings. And they cooked limpets and whelks and all that. So that was always sort of a by word when

we thought mam was being a bit mean . . . and she says I never had to eat whelks like Granny did.[68]

Mary Ellen's authority is derived from her family history and her interest in Shetland women of the past, bolstered by researched references to authenticating 'official' sources. Her stories are entertaining but also educational and autobiographical and always rooted in the realities of material life in Shetland. She speaks as if she knows the women she describes, and in one sense she does; her archival research has brought them to life so that the past lives in the present. Her story of Janet Rusland typifies this kind of narrative.

> There was just one female that survived alone in the nineteenth century that I know of and that was Janet Rusland. And she came to a cousin who was my something's grandfather and he gave her a plot of land just outside the . . . dykes for her to cultivate. And Janny's house is still to be seen and Janny's byre and her park and she actually survived like that with help from neighbours. But she couldna have lived without help, impossible. But that woman was one of the few felons that I've found. They were taken up for thieving potatoes at Sellivoe . . . it's in the sheriff records. And therefore her description which is something you need to hone in on is the police description of prisoners . . . have you seen it? Janny Rusland as we call her . . . I mean it was the middle of the last century, the century before that, she was tiny with brown eyes and her sister was 5 feet 5 with blonde hair.[69]

Janet Rusland appears with her sister in the Shetland prison register for 1870. Both were tried for potato theft but while her sister was acquitted Janet was convicted and punished with ten days' hard labour. Janet is recorded as standing 5 foot $2^{1}/_{2}$ inches tall with brown eyes and hair and 'little reading'; her sister was blonde.[70]

Like Mary Manson, Mary Ellen Odie adopts a heroic narrative when speaking about women in the past. Mary Ellen's narrative is peppered with stories of women who demonstrated their bravery, their stoicism, their strength, their impetuosity or their bloody-mindedness, from the story of Barbara Brown, the 'Bride of Vigon', to the recognised heroines of sea rescues, May Moar and Grace Petrie. These are stories which serve to fix in the memory of the listener an image of the autonomous or independent Shetland woman of the past, and they mirror the well-established discourses on Shetland womanhood. However, at the same time these stories serve to validate the position of the narrator and of Shetland women in general. For Mary Ellen Odie, social memory is a process of recovering and communicating the past.

For Agnes Leask, my third storyteller, the past is autobiography and a way of life – crofting – which may be resurrected in a modern context. Her narrative is characterised by a series of stories about the past which have a bearing on the present difficulties experienced by Shetland crofters and which place into relief the conditions under which crofters work today. And although Agnes is too knowledgeable about the realities of the crofting way of life to romanticise it, she does use stories about crofting in the past as a form of what Geertz termed 'sentimental education' to express what it means to be a Shetlander.[71] 'Of course in those days, same as the present day, you had to have an income outwith your croft. The croft was your home and your way of life, your own food for your table, if you were lucky a few beasts to sell in the autumn to pay the rent and that sort of thing.'[72] The crofting way of life symbolises community for Agnes. Speaking about the tendency of people nowadays to move away from the crofts she said: 'And even with children growing up . . . living in smaller communities like that, you were often bunched together, [were] more integrated with older people, they learn the values of life . . . children, they are not learning the same values, and this is what I see diminishing, this crofting tradition.' For Agnes, the past still exists in the form of material survivals – the archaeological remains of long-abandoned crofts – and in her memory of the crofting year and the struggle to make a living. Her detailed narratives documenting the building of her croft house, the calving of cows, the story of a sick calf, the work involved in bringing the peats from the hill, show Agnes to be a keeper of social memory and a practitioner of the art of storytelling in the form of oral history which serves to preserve knowledge of crofting as a way of life in the past and the present. And although she does not dwell particularly on women's position, Agnes's own life experience is testament to the centrality of women to the continuation of a crofting lifestyle in modern Shetland. She was a hands-on presence on the croft throughout her childhood and adulthood, and she contributed essential supplementary income to the family in the 1950s and 1960s:

> And at that time there was practically no work in Shetland at all and Davy [her husband] sort of did odd jobs with his tractor for folks roundabout, neighbours roundabout. It wasn't a great deal of money coming in but we sort of scraped by and then of course there was a farm at the end of the road there, and there was a bigger farm further up the valley and they were always looking for casual labour, so in amongst weeding me own tatties I'd go there whenever they needed casual labour – cabbages, tatties, single turnips, or working the peats

because they used to hire in gangs of women to do the peat work. And it all helped to tide us over. When nothing else was available Mother and I would go and gather winkles . . . and then in the evenings in the wintertime I'd do hand-knitting . . . I bought the knitting machine and once I got the knitting machine, got orders, firms were giving out orders because it was sort of cottage industry then. Then we were more or less financially secure, as long as I could churn out about a dozen jumpers in the week. That would put our bread on the table for the week, and then of course we had our own vegetables, our own lamb and mutton.[73]

As president of the Shetland Crofting Foundation, Agnes Leask was well acquainted with government policy on crofting, subsidy schemes and new initiatives because, as she said, 'I have always been so determined to keep crofting going. I've sorta kept pace with all the developments . . . '.[74] Agnes's narrative is more than a reconstruction of her memory of the past. Her description of the crofting way of life – 'communal working at its best' – is also a means of making a political comment on the predicament of Shetland crofting culture today. The self-sufficiency of the past is contrasted with the cost today of slaughtering lambs, the refusal of the spinning mills to buy the coloured wool of Shetland sheep and the introduction of payments for conservation measures on crofts. Agnes Leask is a storyteller, but her stories have an overt contemporary message. Whereas in the past her stories about superstitions, folk-cures and the relationship between humans and the environment may have transmitted knowledge and essential skills for survival, today they serve more to amplify what has been called 'the predicament of culture' – when people like Agnes, in order to defend their right to live a particular way of life, have to re-create and emphasise 'tradition'.[75] Old storytelling forms are used to engage with new problems concerning survival of a culture or way of life.[76]

What these three storytellers have in common is an authority to speak which is derived from experience and knowledge and from their role as carriers and transmitters of social memory. Mary Manson's authority was legitimised by her performative role as a storyteller as well as her knowledge of and belief in the authenticity of the tale. Mary Ellen Odie's authority rests upon her family's history on Yell, a legacy of stories passed down through the generations and an active interest in the reclamation of women from the archives. Agnes Leask has lived the crofting way of life she describes, and speaks from a political position of some power. All three women also dramatise women's skills in their stories, a feature which appears to be a characteristic of women's storytelling in communities with a matriarchal culture or a predominance of women.[77] By telling stories Shetland women are engaging in a process which constructs a series of dialogues about women in the past. These stories are shaped but not determined by discursive narratives of the past which place women at the centre of things and which ascribe to women the skills of survival in a hard, unremitting culture. Alternative narratives which place women in a lesser or subordinate light are rare.

Some may detect a contradiction in the juxtaposition of my assertions that women narrators draw on discursive formulations of Shetland womanhood to frame their stories (a structural approach) and, at the same time, that their storytelling is a creative and performative engagement with the present in which they reconstruct the past in order to say something about their existing cultural condition (a dialogic approach).[78] However, it seems to me that Shetland women use precisely the discursive formulations of archetypal Shetland womanhood to stake a claim to speak, about both the past and the present. Their authority is drawn, in part, from a widespread acceptance in Shetland society that women in the past played a prominent role in the economy and society. However, this does not necessarily shackle or constrain their oral performance. The only structural constraint imposed on their narratives was imposed by the interviewer and, as the anthropologist Cruikshank and others have demonstrated, in a society possessing strong narrative conventions or oral traditions, respondents are able to assert their authority on the process.[79]

Life history narratives are different from archival sources in their flexibility and their ability to range across time. They are 'cultural documents' which have as much to say about the present as about the past.[80] For some historians this elasticity is problematic; it precludes using oral testimonies as one would use any other document. In the context of Shetland, however, the use of personal testimony helps us to traverse the interpretive landscape through the eyes – or voices – of women. Life history narratives incorporate myth, meaning and metaphor. In Cruikshank's words, oral tradition should not be interpreted as 'evidence about the past but as a window on ways the past is culturally constituted and discussed'.[81]

Conclusions

From the late nineteenth-century popular fiction of Jessie Saxby to the modern novels of Margaret Elphinstone, the mythic ideal of Shetland womanhood has had a profound resonance. Today it still acts as a legitimating image for women conscious of the pace and depth of change in the islands. The heroic crofting woman provides an unchanging and sufficiently distinctive ideal at times when the traditional structures of everyday life have been undermined. The discourse on the mythic Shetland woman is a metaphor for much that has been lost since the time when visitors alighted on the islands and remarked upon the distinctive role undertaken by the womenfolk. But it is also a commentary upon the ways in which women today construct their identities. As feminist scholars have pointed out, female narratives deal with 'woman's condition and with the collective representations of woman as they have been shaped by the society with which the women being interviewed must deal.'[82]

Women have recently been described as keepers of social memory or 'memorial guardians'.[83] Female writers and narrators transmit social memory about the place of women in Shetland, which may in large part be described as 'female knowledge' and which privileges the female voice and female actors. The stories told by nineteenth-century writers like Jessie Saxby, by modern-day storytellers and by respondents in oral history projects are composites: they combine social experience and memory, autobiography and historical materiality. As such, women's stories offer a multi-sensory encounter which captures the interplay between gender, discourse and experience. In the chapters that follow, we explore the link between these representations and their material foundations. We see how the image of the woman as an agent of survival was founded on an economic and demographic reality.

Notes

1 Interview with Mary Ellen Odie, 4 April 2001.

2 See, for example, 'Mutiny in the isles', *Daily Record*, 6 March 2002. An article reporting the establishment of the first women's networking forum remarked, 'the women who live there are a force to be reckoned with. And, in the business stakes, Shetland sisters are most definitely doing it for themselves.'

3 R. Barthes, *Mythologies* (London, Vintage, 1993), esp. pp. 109–58.

4 See Cohen, *Whalsay*, pp. 82–4, for a discussion of the concept of 'ethos' in one Shetland community.

5 C. Jamieson, 'The women of Shetland', *The New Shetlander* 177 (Hairst, 1991), pp. 31–3, here p. 31.

6 *Shetland News*, 12 Jan. 1901.

7 For example, J. M. E. Saxby, 'Minister of Daalsaitor', in Saxby, *A Camsterie Nacket: Being the Story of a Contrary Laddie Ill to Guide* (Edinburgh and London, Oliphant Anderson and Ferrier, 1894), in which six women are told their husbands have been

lost in a fishing disaster and about Lowrie, an orphan brought up in the manse. See also the poems 'Lost at the haaf' and 'Home at last', in J. M. E. Saxby, *Lichens from the Old Rock: Poems* (Edinburgh, William P. Nimmo, 1898).

8 J. M. E. Saxby, 'The brother's sacrifice', in Saxby, *Daala-Mist: Or, Stories of Shetland* (Edinburgh, Andrew Elliot, 1876), p. 44.

9 J. M. E. Saxby, 'A daughter of sea-kings', in Saxby, *Heim-Laund and Heim-Folk* (Edinburgh, R. and R. Clark, 1892), p. 6.

10 *The Rugged Island: A Shetland Lyric*, directed by Jenny Brown (1934), Scottish Film and Television Archive, Glasgow.

11 Jamieson, 'The women of Shetland', p. 31.

12 Jamieson, 'The women of Shetland', p. 33.

13 There are two accounts of the Betty Mouat story: R. Grant, *The Lone Voyage of Betty Mouat* (Aberdeen, Impulse Books, 1973); T. M. Y. Manson, *Drifting Alone to Norway* (Shetland, Nelson Smith Printing Services, 1996). See also 'Betty Mouat', in E. Ewan, S. Innes, S. Reynolds, R. Pipes (eds), *Biographical Dictionary of Scottish Women* (Edinburgh, Edinburgh University Press, 2006).

14 SA, D 1/134: *The Scotsman*, 24 Feb. 1886.

15 Grant, *The Lone Voyage*; Manson, *Drifting Alone to Norway*.

16 On Grace Petrie see M. S. Robertson, *Sons and Daughters of Shetland 1800–1900* (Lerwick, Shetland Publishing Company, 1991).

17 *Shetland Times*, 19 July 1879.

18 Saxby, 'A daughter of sea-kings', *in Heim-Laund and Heim-Folk*, p. 11.

19 See www.shetland-museum.org.uk/collections/culture/may_moars_medal.htm (consulted 14 Nov. 2002).

20 For a full discussion of the impact of this discourse on representations of the past as well as constructions of the identity of contemporary crofting women see C. A. H. Jack, 'Women and crofting in Shetland from the 1930s to the present day', PhD thesis, University of the Highlands and Islands Millennium Institute, 2003.

21 SA, 3/1/123/1: John Gear.

22 SA, 3/1/124/1: Katie Inkster.

23 C. A. H. Jack, 'Shetland women and crofting from the 1930s to the present day: recreating their pasts', unpublished paper, London, 2001.

24 Interview with Agnes Leask.

25 Interview with Mary Ellen Odie.

26 F. Barnard, *Picturesque Life in Shetland* (Edinburgh, George Waterston & Sons, 1890); www.shetland-museum.org.uk/collections/culture/frank_barnard.htm (consulted 2 March 2004).

27 Jack, 'Shetland women and crofting', p. 2.

28 See J. Jesch, *Women in the Viking Age* (Woodbridge, Boydell Press, 1991), chapter 6.

29 Jesch, *Women in the Viking Age*, pp. 200–2.

30 Hylthén-Cavallius (1868) quoted in E. Arwill-Nordbladh, 'The Swedish image of Viking age women: stereotype, generalisation, and beyond', in R. Samson (ed.), *Social Approaches to Viking Studies* (Glasgow, Cruithne Press, 1991), pp. 53–64, here p. 53.

31 L. H. Dommasnes, 'Women, kinship and the basis of power', in Samson (ed.), *Social Approaches to Viking Studies*, pp. 65–73, here p. 67.

32 SA, D 1/135: *The Scotsman*, 4 Sept. 1899.

33 J. M. E. Saxby, *Shetland Traditional Lore* (Edinburgh, Grant & Murray, 1932), pp. 92–3. See also G. F. Black, *County Folklore*, vol. III: *Orkney and Shetland Islands* (orig. 1903; reprint Felinfach, Llanerch Publishers, 1994), p. 220.

34 SA, D 1/135: *The Scotsman*, 4 Sept. 1899.

35 SA, D 1/135: *The Scotsman*, 4 Sept. 1899.

36 A. P. Cohen, *The Symbolic Construction of Community* (London, Tavistock, 1985), p. 99.

37 See Brown, *Up-helly-aa*, pp. 17–19.

38 M. Elphinstone, *The Sea Road* (Edinburgh, Canongate, 2000).

39 A. Carter (ed.), *The Virago Book of Fairy Tales* (London, Virago, 1990), p. xvi.

40 The exception is 'The Hildina ballad', a long poem recorded in Foula in 1774. It is reproduced in Norn and in English in J. J. Graham and L. I. Graham (eds), *A Shetland Anthology: Poetry from Earliest Times to the Present Day* (Lerwick, Shetland Publishing Company, 1998), pp. 1–11.

41 E. Marwick, *The Folklore of Orkney and Shetland* (Edinburgh, Birlinn, 2000), p. 15.

42 SA, 3/1/179: Jessie Sinclair.

43 Interview with Mary Ellen Odie.

44 K. Blind, 'Shetland folklore and the old faith of the Scandinavians and Teutons', *Saga-Book of the Viking Club* 1 (1896), pp. 163–81, here p. 165.

45 On Galicia see M. Rey-Henningsen, *The World of the Ploughwoman: Folklore and Reality in Matriarchal Northwest Spain* (Helsinki, Academia Scientiarum Fennica, 1994).

46 The School of Scottish Studies, Edinburgh University, has recorded and preserved the words of these men, and they have all had an issue of the Scottish folklore magazine *Tocher* devoted to them.

47 See M. Warner, *From the Beast to the Blonde: On Fairy Tales and their Tellers* (London, Vintage, 1995); Carter, *The Virago Book of Fairy Tales*; N. Wachowich, *Saqiyuq: Stories from the Lives of Three Inuit Women* (Montreal and Kingston, McGill Queen's University Press, 1999); J. Cruikshank, *Life Lived Like a Story: Life Stories of Three Yukon Native Elders* (Vancouver, University of British Columbia Press, 1990).

48 The oral histories used in this study are a combination of interviews conducted by myself and the more numerous collection of interviews conducted by others since the 1970s and held in Shetland Archive.

49 See Cruikshank, *Life Lived Like a Story*.

50 P. Summerfield, *Reconstructing Women's Wartime Lives: Discourse and Subjectivity in Oral Histories of the Second World War* (Manchester, Manchester University Press, 1998), p. 15.

51 See Jack, 'Women and crofting in Shetland', pp. 226–36.

52 Interview with Netta Inkster, 9 April 2001.

53 Similarly, there is no available heroic discourse for women who work in the fish-processing industry either here or in other fishing communities. See Nadel-Klein, *Fishing for Heritage*, pp. 88–91.

54 L. Dégh, *Narratives in Society: A Performer-Centred Study of Narration* (Bloomington, IN, Indiana University Press, 1995), p. 66. See also J. Cruikshank, 'Claiming legitimacy: prophecy narratives from northern Aboriginal women', *American Indian Quarterly* 18:2 (1994), pp. 147–67.

55 Sokolov (1938) quoted in Dégh, *Narratives*, p. 69.

56 Chanfrault-Duchet quoted in Summerfield, *Reconstructing Women's Wartime Lives*, p. 22.

57 R. Bauman, 'Performance', in R. Bauman (ed.), *Folklore, Cultural Performances, and Popular Entertainments* (Oxford, Oxford University Press, 1992), pp. 41–9, here p. 41.

58 See Personal Narratives Group, 'Forms that transform', in Personal Narratives Group (ed.), *Interpreting Women's Lives: Feminist Theory and Personal Narratives* (Bloomington, IN, Indiana University Press, 1989), pp. 99–102.

59 On the differing narrative styles employed by men and women see Cruikshank, *Life Lived Like a Story*, p. 3. Also see L. Stanley, 'From self made women to women's made selves? Audit selves, simulation and surveillance in the rise of public woman', in T. Cosslett, C. Lury and P. Summerfield (eds), *Feminism and Autobiography* (London, Routledge, 2000), pp. 40–60.

60 Indeed, other Shetland storytellers refer to Mary Manson's narration of this story. See SA, 3/1/55/2: Henry Hunter.

61 Marwick, *The Folklore of Orkney and Shetland*, pp. 161–2.

62 N. Z. Davis, *Women on the Margins: Three Seventeenth Century Lives* (London, Harvard University Press, 1995), p. 7. See also P. Morrow, 'On shaky ground: folklore, collaboration and problematic outcomes', in P. Morrow and W. Schneider (eds), *When Our Words Return: Writing, Hearing, and Remembering Oral Traditions of Alaska and the Yukon* (Logan, UT, Utah State University Press, 1995), pp. 27–51. More generally see M. de Certeau, *The Practice of Everyday Life* (Berkeley, University of California Press, 1984).

63 See J. L. Nelson, 'Gender, memory and social power', *Gender & History* 12:3 (2000), pp. 722–34, here p. 732.

64 SA, 3/1/77/2: Mary Manson.

65 See Warner, *From the Beast to the Blonde*, pp. 181–3.

66 Carter, *The Virago Book of Fairy Tales*, p. xiii.

67 Jamieson, 'The women of Shetland', p. 31.

68 Interview with Mary Ellen Odie.

69 Interview with Mary Ellen Odie.

70 SA, 1/8/1: Lerwick Prison criminal register, 1837–78.

71 C. Geertz, 'Deep play: notes on the Balinese cockfight' in C. Geertz (ed.), *Myth, Symbol and Culture* (New York, Norton, 1971), pp. 1–37, here p. 27; and see the discussion of the meaning of the croft in Cohen, *Whalsay*, pp. 98–110.

72 Interview with Agnes Leask.

73 Interview with Agnes Leask.

74 Interview with Agnes Leask.

75 James Clifford quoted in N. Wachowich, 'Getting along: life histories as adaptation to changing social climates in the Arctic', unpublished paper, 2002, p. 3.

76 See J. Cruikshank, 'Myth as a framework for life stories: Athapaskan women making sense of social change in northern Canada', in R. Samuel and P. Thompson (eds), *The Myths We Live By* (London, Routledge, 1990), pp. 174–83.

77 See Cruikshank, 'Myth as a framework', p. 180.

78 For an explanation of these approaches from an anthropological perspective see A. Barnard, *History and Theory in Anthropology* (Cambridge, Cambridge University Press, 2000), pp. 8–10.

79 See Cruikshank, *Life Lived Like a Story*, pp. 2–3.

80 Cruikshank, *Life Lived Like a Story*, p. 3.

81 Cruikshank, *Life Lived Like a Story*, p. 14.

82 M.-F. Chanfrault-Duchet, 'Narrative structures, social models and symbolic representation in the life story', in S. B. Gluck and D. Patai (eds), *Women's Words* (London, Routledge, 1991), pp. 77–92, here p. 78.

83 Nelson, 'Gender, Memory'; E. van Houts, *Memory and Gender in Medieval Europe 900–1200* (London, Macmillan, 1999).

3

Place

As I looked around, women came peering curiously out, their fair hair floating in the wind ... Numbers of women were passing to Lerwick from the distant moss, their creels packed with peats and busy knitting at the same time. (Shetland Archive, D 1/135: *Dundee Courier*, 31 January 1893)

Women in the landscape

WOMEN DOMINATED THE SHETLAND LANDSCAPE in the nineteenth century. They outnumbered men, particularly amongst the age groups active outdoors, and this made them much remarked upon by commentators. Women were highly visible and highly productive, which made for a sharp contrast to most other places in Britain. This contrast extended from a material occupation of the landscape and its economy to a discursive dominance. Elsewhere in the British Isles women of the middle and increasingly the working classes were discursively confined to those spaces deemed appropriate by the ideology of domesticity: the home and parlour, the servants' quarters, the factory.[1] The house was woman's sole 'natural' space because of its association with women's roles in the home and family. Men were free to inhabit more 'public' spaces beyond the physical and ideological boundaries of the home. But visitors to Shetland were struck by women's seemingly ubiquitous presence in their field of vision, that is in the public sphere. Everywhere they looked they saw women: in the fields, on the hill, in the streets. The women viewed by these travellers seemed exotic, the racial 'other', the markers of difference which helped them to reaffirm their ideas about hierarchies of culture back home. Representations of women have commonly been used to symbolise boundaries between cultures. They represented the 'inviolate centre' (of the family, the community or the nation) as well as the 'symbolic border guards', patrolling the imaginary line between the familiar and the strange.[2] As a woman's place, Shetland itself then came to represent the 'other'.

Until the middle of the century the women portrayed in these accounts were observed dispassionately as if they were merely curiosities or tourist attractions. They were part of a landscape, commented upon for its bleakness, its beauty and its differentness from the more tamed environments to which most travellers were more accustomed. 'In this wild country', remarked a surgeon on alighting from a whaling ship in 1856, 'women carry the fuel for the fire, and . . . the land is turned up by women delving it with spades.'[3] Women were ever present in the frame of view. The scientist James Wilson in 1841 noted 'droves of women proceeding on their never-ceasing journey to the mosses in the hills for peats, with their cassies or straw baskets on their backs, and knitting eagerly with both hands.'[4] In later decades, female writers superseded such observations with value judgements about appropriate gendered behaviour. By the 1880s it was the condition rather than the mere presence of women that became the benchmark for highlighting the 'backwardness' of Shetland in comparison with the British mainland. The prominence of women in the Shetland economy, and their physical

1   Three women carrying kishies of peats from Gremista to Lerwick, 1901

labour, shocked visitors to the islands. According to one observer who visited Shetland in the 1880s:

> ... the chief burden of labour on the land is left to the women. To them – the women – life must be hard and dreary enough, for the country is without any of those pleasant attractions to which we who live in more southern climes are accustomed. . . . Work, work, work, and hard work too. Peat is the common fuel used in town and country, and you may daily see, trudging along the roads towards town, scores of peasant women, each carrying on her back a 'creel' of wicker work piled high with peat, which they first dig and then sell for a few pence. This is not all, for whilst they bend under their heavy burdens, their fingers are always busy plying their knitting needles. I this morning passed a batch of six women in a row, each struggling under a load of peat, each knitting away for dear life, and all six in a busy chorus of small talk, thus exercising three useful functions at one and the same time. There must be something radically wrong in society when a grandmotherly old woman is obliged to trudge along the hard road, bare footed and bent double under a load of fuel, carried for miles to market all to help keep the family pot-a-boiling! How I did wish she would stop me and ask for help. But she didn't. How mean I felt afterwards for not having stopped her! But most assuredly the Shetland women work harder than the men.[5]

The sight of women engaging in physical labour in public appeared to offend the eyes of these educated travellers, who may not have been acquainted with the sight at home. Although women across Britain had commonly been employed in field labour, by the end of the nineteenth century a combination of agricultural improvement, enclosure and the prevalence of domestic ideology meant that it was now relatively rare to find women engaging in such physical work in public. Women's position as workers in Shetland 'indicated but a low state of civilisation'.[6] Cutting and carrying peats, working the land and gutting fish were activities deemed unwomanly or unfeminine. But the sight of women working also drew sympathy. According to the 'Lady Correspondent' of the *Dundee Advertiser* in 1898, the peasant women she encountered upon her 'holiday in Ultima Thule' 'look overdriven and weighed down with unremitting labour.'

> The women do most of the work of the croft, digging the ground with their long, narrow spades in the spring three in a row, and carrying the manure on their backs in the 'caeshies'. When I asked why the crofters didn't club together and get a pony for this rough work, the cynical retort was – 'What are the wives for?' . . . I must confess

that the sight of those patient, toilsome women always made me inclined to get angry with somebody.[7]

Similarly, an American visitor to the islands in 1887 was driven to suggest that something practical be done 'by the wealthy classes in Shetland to lift the poor peasant women from the humiliating drudgery to which many of them are compelled to submit, and place them where they may share in those advantages which are calculated to refine and ennoble their sex.'[8]

However, it was not just the appearance of women doing hard physical work that shocked visitors. It was the apparent indolence of the men that made women's labour so hard to stomach at a time when the chief components of ideal masculinity were productive male labour and the protection of domestic womanhood. The majority of able-bodied men in Shetland made a living from the sea, either as fishermen or as merchant seamen, and thus were absent from home for long periods of time. Shetland men, like men in other seafaring communities, were treated as precious, perhaps because they and their womenfolk were ever conscious of the fragility of life at sea.[9] They fulfilled the masculine role at work, but this was rarely observed by visitors. Rather, what they saw conflicted with all notions of masculinity pervasive in European society – both the ideal breadwinner and the anti-ideal, the violent, drunken heathen.[10] When Shetland men came home, it was said that they treated their womenfolk like servants. According to Alexander Trotter, a surgeon on a visiting whaling ship:

> In this wild country, women carry the fuel for the fire, and . . . the land is turned up by women delving it with spades. I am told too that the Shetland men generally go a six months trip to sea . . . As soon as they come home like true gentlemen they live on their money setting their wives and daughters to cultivate their little bit of land: their own lazy lordships standing giving orders with their hands in their pockets. Even now you may see sailors and their wives coming into the town, the wives almost invariably carrying the husbands' trunks and boxes slung on their backs; his supreme highness walking alongside quietly smoking his pipe or maybe riding on a pony to keep him from the trouble of travelling and perhaps hurting his very delicate and valuable feet.[11]

At this distance we might suspect these visitors of exaggeration but as late as the 1940s the same story was told by an elderly crofter. 'We women carried our men's sea-chests to the ports. I myself have walked to Lerwick with a heavy trunk on my back, and that is twenty miles from here.'[12] Tales like this were common enough. Accompanying a report on the general election in the *Daily Chronicle* in 1910, under the headline 'Shetland wives', the journalist recounted an incident he experienced while visiting the islands. 'A [Shetlander] came into the bar parlour to sell the landlords a pair of socks which his wife had knitted. "She has been a good wife to me", he said. "She has brought me seven children, and I have not had to do a day's work since I married her." '[13]

What shocked visitors to Shetland – visitors who were over-whelmingly middle-class and educated, steeped in the ideology of ideal domestic womanhood and separate spheres – was the apparent absence of the sexual division of labour and appreciation of separate gender roles prevalent elsewhere in Britain. Shetland women were carrying out tasks which elsewhere would have been undertaken by men. At the same time they knitted hosiery which brought much-needed income (in the form of goods) into the household and they carried out all the domestic tasks. It was this combination of roles that flummoxed outsiders. It was what one American journalist termed the 'Shetland paradox', 'for in the Shetlands the women are the best men'.[14]

The outdoor work undertaken by women was not only inappropriate work for females according to many visitors; it also ruined their looks. 'But few of the country women are beautiful', remarked the Revd James Catton, a Methodist minister in Shetland in 1835; 'their mode of living and labouring injures their health, shape and complexion, many of them are of a very sallow complexion and haggard look.'[15] And Samuel Hibbert was hardly less complimentary in 1822 when he argued that it was the men who 'cause a more than ordinary portion of labour, fatal to the preservation of a delicate and symmetrical form, to devolve upon the poor females.'[16] Physical labour outdoors and constant exposure to peat-fire smoke transformed 'fresh supple young girls, with their bobbed hair, silk stockings and short skirts' into 'listless, leathery old crones', according to the American journalist Negley Farson.[17]

Outsiders' surprise and implicit criticism of the position of women in Shetland can be understood against a background of nineteenth-century mores regarding separate gender roles. The criticism was not of women working per se, but rather of the kinds of work women under-took. Knitting – a form of employment widely regarded as 'woman's work' and an activity seen as suitable for women on account of their alleged manual dexterity, their tolerance of monotonous labour and their association with the domestic sphere – was praised as a local handi-craft which could be carried out without damaging a woman's physique or her domestic diligence. 'They seem to knit by instinct', commented a female writer in 1898, 'going to or returning from the hill, gossiping at their doors, resting in the sunshine, their fingers are never still.'[18] Knitting, it was implied, complemented women's domestic activities whereas croft work detracted from their femininity.

Shetland's otherness, its difference from mainland Scotland, has always struck visitors, but the markers of that difference have not remained constant. Today, visitors are most likely to comment upon the isolation of the place, the relative absence of trees, the remarkable bird life and the appearance of relative prosperity in contrast with other Scottish rural communities. Few would comment on the place or position of women, and those that do tend to remark upon the reversal of the nineteenth-century situation, noting the good fortune of Shetland women living in a place with so many single men![19] In the nineteenth century it was women – their role in the economy and their active presence in the life of the islands – who symbolised that difference so powerfully. However, it was not the visitors alone who defined difference. Their observations were subsequently taken up and reinterpreted by Shetlanders themselves seeking to promote a distinctive Shetland identity. It is this period of Shetland's history, from the late eighteenth century to the First World War, that provides a template or a framework for present-day inhabitants to envisage and understand their past and their present. The difference that had been equated by outsiders with backwardness and the perceived subordinate position of women in the nineteenth century was transformed into a difference that celebrated Shetland women's active and equal role in contrast with 'Scottish' women, who were portrayed by some Shetlanders as dominated by their menfolk. However, this pride in women's role has its roots in the material realities of Shetland life. The images painted by nineteenth-century visitors were shaped by their own predilections, but what they saw was not a tourist attraction. It was day-to-day life and work in all its banality.

Life and work

The dominant images of Shetland women promulgated by nineteenth-century visitors to the islands – of women returning from the hills bearing baskets on their backs laden with peat, simultaneously knitting, of women working on the croft, and of women waiting for and on their fishing menfolk – gave the impression that women were fully implicated in the economic life of the community. But in fact women were marginal to the main economic activity of fishing. Shetland was a society characterised by fishing *and* crofting as two mutually dependent activities. Thus the economic roles of men and women were similarly interwoven.

The 'Auld Rock', as Shetland has often been known, squats virtually treeless in the rough North Atlantic, its rocky coastline indented with fjord-like voes which provide safe harbour and respite from the energy-sapping winds. Sitting at the same latitude as parts of Greenland, Shetland nevertheless has a climate milder than one might imagine, although it is undoubtedly very windy and the growing season is relatively short. The soil is poor for the most part – the hectarage of peat bog far surpassing the amount of land suitable for cultivation – and the climatic conditions make this a barely suitable place to practise agriculture, resulting in a reliance on livestock.[20] Even today the main crops are potatoes and cabbage, with some wheat and barley. Nineteenth-century agricultural improvements had little positive impact on the amount of arable land available. By the 1930s less than 5 per cent of Shetland was given over to arable cultivation, compared with almost 40 per cent in neighbouring Orkney.[21] Thus Shetlanders have never been able to live from the land alone; they were known as fishermen who used the land to supplement their livelihood, in contrast with inhabitants of Orkney, who were farmers with a boat. 'With a few exceptions, every farmer is a fisherman, and every fisherman a farmer.' In 1841 the compiler of the entry for Northmavine parish in the *New Statistical Account of Scotland* aptly remarked:

> During the summer season, therefore, when the men are at sea, the crops, cattle, &c. are left to the care and management of women and children, who, I dare say, do the best they can. But it is to be supposed, that, if a division of these two employments could be effected in some way or other, the land would be improved and cultivated to better advantage, than it has hitherto been.[22]

Fishing, crofting and knitting provided the economic backbone, albeit an extremely insecure one, for the majority of inhabitants of the scattered settlements of rural Shetland throughout the nineteenth century and well into the twentieth. The relatively prosperous Shetland that may be observed today, with its modern Scandinavian-style houses, enviable roads and community facilities, is a very recent development consequent upon the oil-industry boom of the 1970s and its continuing economic legacy. But until the 1960s, Shetland was a poor place in almost every measurable economic and social indicator.

The majority of the rural population, then, at least until the First World War, made a living from the land and the sea, but Shetland's peculiar tenancy relationships made conditions here unique in the British Isles. Until the beginning of the eighteenth century tenancy agreements in Shetland were remarkably free, and tenants benefited from fixed rents and an ability to engage with the market. However, following the crisis-riven 1690s, when Shetland was afflicted with famine, disease, cessation of trade and impoverishment, a new form of tenancy arrangement was brought into being by the merchants and lairds.[23] 'Fishing-tenure' was a form of bondage, reminiscent of feudal landlord–tenant relationships, whereby tenants and their families were obliged to fish for the landlords and to give most of their produce from the sea and often from the land to the landlord in payment of rent. The landlord set the rent and often fixed the price of fish too below the market rate. Landlords, some of whom were also merchants dealing in fish, grain and all other necessary goods, would advance the men and their families fishing gear and provisions, which were also to be paid for from the fish harvest. In 1839 the landowner Arthur Nicolson signed the following agreement with 26 of his tenants on the island of Papa Stour.

> Sr A. Nicolson agrees to set his lands at the same rent . . . He farther agrees to advance to the tenants fishing materials at prime cost and to contract with a merchant or merchants to receive the tenants produce, and to credit them for the same, deducting only a small commission for his trouble and risk. The tenants on the other hand engage faithfully to deliver their produce to such a contractor at the rates agreed for by Sir A. Nicolson on their behalf, and that under a penalty of ten shillings whenever such agreement shall be contravened by them by their disposing of their produce to others than the contractor, the said penalty to be paid to the contractor and recovered by him. Tenants persisting in this practice will be warned and summarily removed from the property.[24]

Tenants were obliged to take shares in the larger boats introduced by the landlords, which took men further out to sea for the haaf or deep-sea fishing and kept them away from home for longer periods. And finally female hosiery producers were ensnared in a system of barter-truck whereby local produce, including hosiery, was exchanged for shop goods. Most tenants then existed in a cashless or barter economy in which it was easy to become ensnared in debt.

The land worked by the tenants was mostly so poor that it was impossible to make an independent living from it. And landowners exacerbated the condition of their tenants by subdividing the farms into outsets – small enclosures situated on the common grazing land – to house more fishermen in order to increase their income from the sea.

'The soil in Shetland is no farther valuable in the estimation of the proprietors than as it furnishes settlement to fishers', commented one nineteenth-century writer.[25] In other words, landlords could not make a living from tenants' land rent on account of the poor living the land provided and so they relied upon income from the sea. Any tenant who sought to sell his or her fish elsewhere was liable to be threatened with eviction. The result was that tenants became ensnared in debt to the merchant-landlords with no redress. The population of the islands increased from around 15,000 in 1755 to more than 29,000 in 1831. This resulted in overpopulation, exhaustion of the land and widespread indebtedness. Farms were too small and not sufficiently productive to support a family, and there was little incentive for tenants to improve their holdings. Exacerbating the poor situation of tenant farmers were two waves of clearance in the 1820s–1840s and the 1860s–1870s. Townships were cleared, and scattalds, areas of common grazing or pasture without which most farms were not viable, were confiscated for sheep rearing. By the middle decades of the nineteenth century land-ownership was concentrated in very few hands. As Smith remarks, 'Shetlanders had no direct access to their own means of subsistence.'[26]

For most of the nineteenth century, the lives of most rural Shetland inhabitants were centred upon the township. A township was defined by a local sheriff as:

> a collection of cottages built of stone and generally straw-thatched, surrounded by feal dykes [peat or turf enclosures] which separate the township from its hill-pasture or scattald. In front of the cottages are the town-maills – a piece of ground always left uncultivated, and on which are tethered the stock required by the crofters for their domestic use. Lower down are the kail-yards [cabbage patches] of the cottagers, and patches of arable growing crops of bere, potatoes or oats, always unfenced and sometimes held in a runrig.[27]

From the early 1800s under the fishing-tenure system, landlords customarily built dwelling houses on their land for their tenants, and the tenants were obliged to construct outbuildings and to maintain them. Most croft cottages were of the two-roomed but-and-ben style. The but end was the main living space with a central fire, a hole in the roof for the smoke and a collection of furniture and cooking utensils whilst the ben end generally housed the sleeping space of the householders and might act as a best room for receiving visitors. Attached to these two rooms was the byre housing animals.[28] Visitors to the islands at the beginning of the nineteenth century frequently remarked upon the poor living conditions of rural inhabitants. Sarah Squire, a Quaker who travelled to Shetland in 1835, was rather aghast at the apparently dirty accommodation offered to her on her travels, noting in her diary that 'there was no place in Sandness where we could have had comfortable lodgings for the people were very kind, but the habits and manners in some of the country places are so connected with the absence of cleanliness that I consider it a great privilege we have in general been comfortably provided for.'[29] With a living density of over six persons per household in most rural parts of Shetland at this time, Miss Squire was fortunate perhaps to be so accommodated.[30] By 1900, as the fishing-tenure system disappeared and crofters with fixity of tenure built and improved their own croft houses, the rural housing stock began to improve but, according to evidence presented to the Royal Commission on Housing in Scotland in 1913, the rural districts still contained houses deemed uninhabitable on the grounds of public health (although the practice of keeping a cow in the house was 'practically a thing of the past').[31]

Each farm or household had a byre and a barn and sometimes other buildings for animals or crops as well as plantiecrues – stone enclosures on the hill for the propagation of cabbage and kail seedlings before the small plants were transferred to the kailyard.[32] Most tenants had the right to cut peat from the hill for fuel. The townships were close-knit communities within which all members were dependent upon one another and obliged to share the resources of the land and the sea. And yet tenants had clearly delineated individual rights of access to and use of different types of land, sometimes widely scattered around the township in small strips where runrig operated, although, as land was sub-divided and outsets created on the scattald, it became impossible to operate the runrig system to be fair to all tenants. By the first decades of the nineteenth century runrig had become uncontrollable, although it took until the twentieth century to disappear altogether.[33] Township inhabitants jealously guarded ownership and use of plantiecrues, peat banks and stacks, kailyards and so on. When the resources for food, fuel and clothing were so poor and in such short supply in an economy largely driven by barter of goods, it is not surprising that conflict some-times characterised township relations as much as reciprocity.

By contrast with the rural townships, Shetland's main town of Lerwick was, in the nineteenth century, a bustling commercial centre and port. In 1821, 2,224 inhabitants or 8.5 per cent of the population of Shetland lived here; by 1871 the number was 3,655 or 11.7 per cent and growing. In the summer months the resident population was swollen by hundreds of fishermen, gutters, coopers and others associated with the fishing industry, some from other parts of Shetland and others from across Scotland. Lerwick was a cosmopolitan town. Since the seventeenth century it had offered a haven for ships at anchor, and this made it a crossroads for traders, travellers and seamen from across northern Europe as well as a magnet for rural Shetlanders. Some visitors, like the author Wilkie Collins, who accompanied his artist father to Shetland in 1842, saw Lerwick through rose-tinted glasses: 'The quaint grey houses of the town; the absence of a single carriage or cartroad through any part of it; the curious mixture of Dutchmen, Shetlanders and soldiers from the garrison, passing through the narrow, paved lanes of the place, presented that combination of the new and the picturesque.'[34] Not all visitors were so charmed, however. 'The streets were narrow and strewed with refuse', commented Christopher Thomson in 1847.

> Companies of sailors, the greater part of them reeling drunk, were parading about as if the island belonged to them. At the time when the Greenland sailors call here, particularly on the passage out, these islands are kept in a state of fermentation. The retailers of whiskey, the shop-keepers, fortune-tellers, and the loose females, which even here are found in numbers keeping a sharp look out upon the cash and whiskey of the sailors.[35]

By the 1900s Lerwick was still a busy thoroughfare, enlivened by the herring fishery and its associated activities, which more than doubled the size of the town in the summer months. When the Revd David Johnstone arrived there around 1910 he remarked upon the hustle and bustle of a commercial sea port:

> Hither the people are drawn every day from the remotest parts of the mainland and from the outlying islands. All the year round there is more or less of stir in this main street. From the early spring time, when the whale ships bound for Greenland arrive to make up their complement of men, until the end of the fishing season, there is a constant influx of strangers swelling the tide of traffic. As the summer approaches, Dutch, Prussian and French fishing smacks crowd into the harbour, all seeking the herring harvest so plentiful in these waters. The foreigners from these vessels all make Commercial Street their chief promenade ... These Hollanders take their walks abroad in groups or crews, fair haired men and boys crowd along, talking, laughing, jesting and always smoking ...[36]

In many respects Lerwick was a microcosm of Shetland but it was also singular in character. Lerwick was metropolitan, combining the atmosphere of a major sea port with the ostentation of a provincial town and the squalor of an industrial city. It was to Lerwick that visitors gravitated for accommodation and entertainment, and for Shetlanders it was a commercial centre, a hiring place, a hub for buying and selling and an amusement centre. It housed the municipal authorities and the sheriff court. It also contained some of the worst housing conditions in Scotland by the second half of the century. The town's growth as a population and commercial centre had not been accompanied by improvements in the housing infrastructure for the labouring classes. At the north end of the town at Gremista were some of the worst houses in Shetland, 'simply wooden erections, neither wind nor water-tight. They stand on bad sites with no drainage, and the surroundings of them are filthy in many cases; they are surrounded with all manner of refuse, fish offal, and refuse of every description.'[37] Packed into the narrow lanes that radiated uphill from the docks were numerous overcrowded rooms accommodating short- and long-stay tenants. Many of the inhabitants of these were single women. In 1881 in Navy Lane, which wound its way up from Commercial Street to the more prosperous Hillhead, numerous unmarried and widowed women lived cheek-by-jowl in rented accommodation, making a living by letting rooms to female lodgers and knitting hosiery.[38] The overcrowding in the lanes of Lerwick persisted until after the First World War. Margaret Shearer, a former health visitor in the town, recalled how 'the lanes of course were the worst. I found the lanes terrible. Burns Lane was very bad at that time. Big block building wi crowds o folk in each room . . . I wis calculating once that there were 72 folk in the building wi just 4 doors an it was a 3 storey building . . . and then you would get 6 bairns in a bed maybe at a time.'[39]

By the mid-nineteenth century the population of Shetland had risen to more than 30,000. The increase was in part a result of the fishing-tenure system; lairds and merchants encouraged young couples to settle on outsets in order to increase the number of fishermen in their employ. But many tenants married too early, before they possessed the material means to maintain a croft and the relentless subdivision of land threatened the viability of farms. By the 1880s fishing-tenure was almost finished, undermined by the growth of the herring fishing industry. When the Napier Commission arrived to take evidence regarding croft rents in Shetland in 1883, fishermen-crofters were not afraid to state their grievances openly. By contrast, in 1872 when the Truck Commission had arrived in Shetland to investigate the operation of barter-truck in the knitting and fishing industries, few complaints about the inequities of fishing-tenure had been expressed. In 1883, though, those called to give evidence lined up to demand security of tenure, fair rents and the right to improve property without fear of rent increase.[40] None, apart from the Foula men, complained about fishing-tenure. The Crofters' Commission fair-rent tribunals in 1889 and 1892 also contributed greatly to crofters' sense of security.[41] Moreover, the herring fishery, which experienced a boom from 1897 onwards, the growth of offshore cod fishing and the improvement in communications between Shetland and the Scottish mainland, offered choices to Shetland men and women who did not wish to be tied to a fishing-tenure agreement or to a Shetland-based fishing-crofting lifestyle.

By 1900 the most pernicious elements of the fishing-crofting system had disappeared, and men who had previously been tied to their lairds in a fishing-tenure relationship were now free to be independent fishermen. For women, though, there was no such transformation. Their menfolk continued to make a living from the sea in the herring fishing, the whaling vessels or the merchant marine and continued to work away from home for long periods. Women remained at home on the croft, and it is difficult for the historian to discern any qualitative change or improvement in their lives, especially since women's primary productive activity – hand-knitting – continued to be dominated by the barter-truck system. This system was highlighted in all its complexity by the 1872 Truck inquiry commissioned by the government. However, the enquiry did not bring to an end to the system, and even the 1887 Truck Amendment Act failed to quash a barter system which was embedded in Shetland life and which continued beyond the First World War.[42] As the historian of the Shetland knitting industry Linda Fryer notes, 'knitting . . . lagged behind the fishing industry and experienced a very protracted transition from a barter to a cash economy.'[43] The significance of this failure to reform the most important productive activity undertaken by women becomes clear in the context of Shetland's demographic profile.

Surplus women

For the whole of the nineteenth century there were appreciably more women than men in the Shetland Islands. This was a marked imbalance paralleled in very few places in Europe. Figure 3.1 illustrates the excess of women over men in the islands for almost 200 years. In 1821 there were 121 women for every 100 men; in 1861 the ratio peaked at 143:100; by 1901 it was still as high as 127:100. The figures were taken in early April each year, before the season for men departing for the fishing,

and so they underestimated the true sex imbalance in the April–
September period. There was nowhere else in Scotland with such a
disparity in the proportions of men and women. In comparison with
the average sex ratio in Scotland as a whole, Shetland's demographic
experience was remarkable, at least from 1841 onwards, as Figure 3.2
demonstrates. Even in Dundee, a city habitually described by historians
as 'a woman's town' on account of the number of women who migrated
there to work in the textile industry, the ratio was 130 women to every
100 men in 1871. If Dundee was a woman's town, Shetland was even
more a woman's island.[44] In Orkney, another island community with a
high degree of male emigration, the sex ratio was considerably lower,
with 117 women to every 100 men in 1871, and in the far north of the
country in the counties of Caithness, Sutherland, Ross and Cromarty
and Inverness, the sex ratio never rose above 118:100.[45] As *The Scotsman*'s
correspondent rightly observed in 1885, this state of affairs had a profound impact upon social relations in the islands and, further, upon
the ways in which structures of power were perceived and experienced.
'The fact that Shetland has 135 females to every 100 males – 4 females to
every 3 males – is, of itself, evidence of a very extraordinary state of
society in those islands . . . and this unusual number of females must
have a great effect on all social relations.'[46]

Figure 3.1 Male–female population of Shetland, 1801–2001

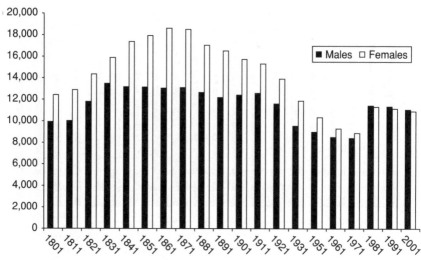

Source: *Census of Scotland*, 1851–2001; Fryer, *Knitting by the Fireside*, p. 182

Already, at the start of the nineteenth century, women significantly outnumbered men. How long the imbalance had existed, and at what degree, is not known. The most likely reasons for this are threefold: the much higher propensity of men to migrate, the long-term absence of men from their homes on account of the nature of the fishing industry and associated sea trades, and a high death rate amongst men at sea. Migration was undoubtedly a significant factor. From 1831 until 1861 approximately 1,500 men emigrated each decade, compared with around 500 women. Between 1861 to 1871 the number of male migrants is estimated at 1,470 compared with just 631 females, and the vast majority of men who left their home were between the ages of 15 and 30. The consequences of the migration of this particular stratum of men for the gender ratio amongst those left behind were stark. In 1861, when the demographic imbalance was at its peak, in the age cohort 20–29, there were 230 women for every 100 men. Indeed, in the census years 1861 and 1871 the discrepancy in this age cohort in particular was dramatic. By comparison, in Orkney the ratio within this age cohort was 125 women to every 100 men in 1861 – still a stark sex imbalance but less remarkable than that further north.[47] By 1891 the sex imbalance in Shetland was

Figure 3.2   Number of females per 100 males in Shetland and Scotland, 1801–2001

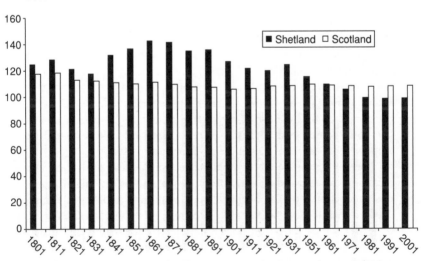

Source: *Census of Scotland*, 1851–2001; B. R. Mitchell and P. Deane, *Abstract of British Historical Statistics* (Cambridge, Cambridge University Press, 1962), pp. 8–9; Fryer, *Knitting by the Fireside*, p. 182

somewhat less marked across all age cohorts – 135 women to every 100 men (although in the 20–29 age group there were still 146 women to every 100 men) – but it was not until the mid-twentieth century that the ratio stabilised at a level closer to the Scottish average.

In contrast with men's propensity to leave Shetland, women were far less willing to leave home despite entreaties to do so. Following the destitution years of the 1840s strenuous attempts were made to encourage single Shetland women to emigrate to Australia. In 1850, William Kingston, a prominent promoter of the 'right type of emigrant', praised Shetland women as 'moral, very industrious, cleanly in their habits, accustomed to work in the fields, and when not so engaged to manufacture hosiery. They are religious, simple in their tastes, they speak English, and the appearance of them is most pleasing.'[48] In spite of these paeans of praise, only nineteen women left the islands in 1850. During the decade 1871–81 an increase in the number of female migrants was noted: more than 1,700 migrated, compared with more than 2,100 men, but during the 1880s the gender discrepancy widened again.[49] In the 1890s it was still observed that nothing would encourage Shetland women to migrate south for work, despite demand from the linen manufacturing districts. 'Roundly, there are three females to every two males in these islands and although it has been shown that girls who are expert as knitters may readily earn from 7s 6d to 20s a week in Dunfermline, Kirkcaldy or Perth, yet even this temptation is insufficient to induce them to leave their cabins and hillsides.'[50] Why this should have been the case is difficult to explain. Across the northern counties in general women were as likely as men to migrate from their county of birth to elsewhere in Scotland or to England. Shetland women's experience of the world beyond Shetland was much more limited than that of their seafaring menfolk, and they had fewer opportunities to leave, at least in the decades before the rise of the herring fishery. But, as will be shown later on, women had a central place in Shetland culture that both empowered them and limited their willingness to leave.

One of the consequences of the reliance on the sea was the high loss of men to sea life and an early death. Seafaring was the most dangerous occupation, and the Shetland open-boat haaf or deep-sea fishing exposed men to unparalleled risk. Drowning at sea was the chief cause of death amongst men of working age. In 1881 74 Shetland men died as a result of accident or negligence, most likely drowning at sea. This was the second highest figure in Scotland after Aberdeen. The equivalent number for females was 3.[51] A number of fishing disasters wiped out whole communities of men of working age. In 1791 around 50 heads of families were lost from Northmavine and Fetlar, whilst in 1832 17 boats and their crew of more than 100 men were lost from communities from Unst to Nesting during a frightful storm. In July 1881, 58 men in 10 boats, most of them from small communities around the north of Yell, perished at sea, leaving numerous widows, children and other dependants. And in December 1900 22 men drowned from the Delting area north of Lerwick, leaving 15 widows, 47 children and many other dependants.[52] Week in, week out, the sea was relentless in taking a steady toll of men, so unpredictable were the waters around the islands. Typical was the plight of Thomas Goodlad from Burra Isle, who drowned in 1907 along with two crew in a boat crossing the short distance from Burra to Scalloway – a journey today of a few minutes by car across a road bridge. He left a widow and nine children.[53]

Moreover, those who joined the whaling vessels and the merchant marine were often away from home for months or years at a stretch. In the 1860s up to 700 men left for the Greenland whaling every year, and when the whaling industry declined at the end of the century the merchant navy took its place, with up to 3,000 Shetland men permanently employed in this industry.[54] This was a society, then, which took a heavy toll on its population, a point not lost on the MP for Shetland and founder of the P&O shipping line, Arthur Anderson, in 1851:

> The great disparity [in the sex ratio] has been produced by the almost universal predilection of the men for seafaring occupation, which impels great numbers of them to quit the islands, and enter into the sea service in the more southern parts of the kingdom, where they generally settle for the remainder of their lives. It is further caused by the hazardous nature of the chief occupation of those who remain, the prosecution of the fisheries in open boats, in which many perish almost every season.[55]

The consequences of an imbalanced sex ratio may be both structural and cultural. The impact on social structures is relatively easy to measure. A surplus of one sex has implications for the marriage rate, the average age at marriage and the number of celibates or 'never married', and hence also for the fertility rate. The propensity of men of marriageable and working age to migrate and the consequent impact upon the sex ratio, particularly in the under-40 age cohort, severely limited women's marriage prospects. For Shetland women in the marriageable age group, their chances of finding a marriage partner were markedly weakened during the middle decades of the century and did not improve significantly until well after the turn of the century.[56]

Between 1851 and 1951, as Figure 3.3 illustrates, the marriage rate in Shetland was consistently lower than the Scottish average. In 1861 there were 6.8 marriages per 1,000 of the population in Scotland but only 5.3 in Shetland. By 1901 the relative figures were 7.0 and 5.0. In fact a discrepancy remained in the relative marriage rates until the 1960s.[57] Moreover, the mean age at marriage was higher in Shetland than the Scottish average. In 1861 almost 20 per cent of Scottish men aged between 16 and 29 were married. The equivalent figure in Shetland was 8 per cent.[58] Amongst women 25 per cent of Scots were married before they were 30, but in Shetland only 16 per cent did so. By 1901 the tendency for both sexes to marry late was still in evidence – very few of those under the age of 20 had married – thus questioning the conventional wisdom that the system of fishing-tenure encouraged early marriage. But in the age cohort 30–39, 45 per cent of females were still unmarried, compared with 32 per cent of men of the same age. By the age of 50, Shetland men were far more likely to be married than women. Indeed, as Figure 3.4 shows, men's marriage opportunities were consistently more favourable than those of women.

One of the clearest indications of the consequences of the sex imbalance on women's marriage chances is the discrepancy between the

Figure 3.3   Marriage rates in Shetland and Scotland, 1851–1961

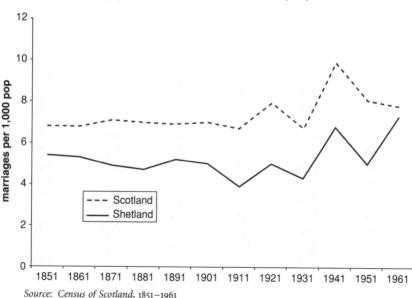

Source: Census of Scotland, 1851–1961

percentages of women and of men who never married. In the 45–54 age group the discrepancy between the marriage fortunes of men and women in the islands is clear. In comparison with their English counterparts a significantly higher proportion of Scottish women never married; in 1861 this was around 20 per cent, or one in five. In Shetland, the proportion of never-married women was significantly higher than the Scottish average and, furthermore, higher than the proportion in the crofting counties.[59] In the period 1861–1921 more than one in three women between the ages of 45 and 54 had never married, with 1881 as the peak year, when 38 per cent of women in this cohort remained single. If a woman had not married by the age of 45 she was unlikely ever to tie the knot, owing to her inability to conceive. By contrast, men in Shetland were as likely to marry as men elsewhere in Scotland. In 1891 only 15 per cent of the 45–54 age group had never married, compared with a marginally lower Scottish average of 13 per cent. The marriage fortunes of those Shetland males who stayed at home compared favourably with those of men elsewhere in Scotland.

Figure 3.4 Unmarried men and women in Shetland, 1861–1911: percentages of total men and women aged over fifteen years

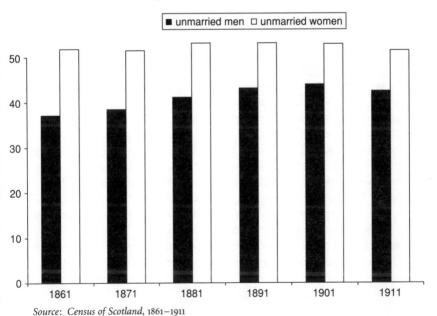

Source: Census of Scotland, 1861–1911

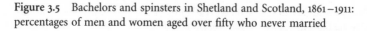

Figure 3.5 Bachelors and spinsters in Shetland and Scotland, 1861–1911: percentages of men and women aged over fifty who never married

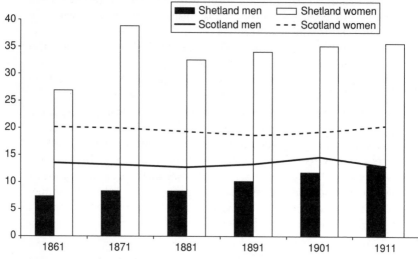

Source: *Census of Scotland*, 1861–1911

If we look at the numbers of never-marrieds amongst the over-50 age group we can gain a more detailed picture of the discrepancy in the marriage prospects of men and women and the worsening situation over time for women's marriage opportunities. As Figure 3.5 demonstrates, a far higher proportion of women in the over-50 age group – almost 40 per cent in 1871 – had never married, in contrast with the significantly lower numbers of men, suggesting that men's opportunities for marriage did not significantly decline with age.

In comparison with the Scottish average, and indeed in comparison with figures for Britain as a whole, the proportion of spinsters in Shetland was remarkable. In 1881 there were more than 6,000 women without a husband, or 28 per cent of the female population over the age of 15. This figure is significantly higher than the estimates of between 9 and 18 per cent calculated for various places in Britain from the sixteenth to nineteenth centuries.[60] Throughout the second half of the nineteenth century the discrepancy between the experiences of women in Shetland and in Scotland as a whole remained wide, as Table 3.1 illustrates. As the proportion of Scottish women who were married stayed more or less constant at around 43 per cent, the proportion of Shetland women who married fell slightly while those who did not rose. By

Table 3.1   Marital status of women (aged fifteen and over), Scotland and
Shetland, 1861–1911 (percentage of total)

	unmarried		married		widowed	
	Scotland	Shetland	Scotland	Shetland	Scotland	Shetland
1861	44.3	51.8	43.1	35.9	12.7	12.3
1871	43.2	51.5	43.9	36.1	12.9	12.5
1881	43.0	53.1	44.4	33.5	12.6	13.4
1891	44.2	53.1	43.8	34.1	11.9	12.8
1901	44.5	52.9	44.3	34.3	11.3	12.8
1911	44.0	51.5	45.2	36.4	10.8	12.1

Source: Census of Scotland, 1861–1911

Note: totals may not add up to 100 owing to the rounding of percentages

1901 Shetland was the Scottish county with the highest percentage of spinsters amongst women over the age of 15. At 52 per cent this was markedly higher than the Scottish average of 44.5 per cent and higher even than that of the county of Forfar (which included the 'woman's town' of Dundee), where 47 per cent of women were spinsters.[61] Moreover, the proportion of married women in Shetland in the over-15 age group in 1901, 34 per cent, was significantly lower than the Scottish average of 44 per cent. Permanent celibacy was a likely experience for a high proportion of Shetland women right through the nineteenth century.

A low marriage rate and a high average age at marriage for women, as well as a relatively high occurrence of widowhood in a woman's childbearing years, resulted in a low birth rate. In rural Scotland, and more especially in the crofting counties, the high proportion of women who never married (between one-fifth and three-tenths between 1851 and 1911) and the decline in male nuptiality during the second half of the nineteenth century resulted in a fertility rate significantly below the Scottish average.[62] In Shetland in 1855–60 the birth rate per 1,000 of the population was 27; the average for Scotland was 34. By the end of the nineteenth century the disparity was much greater, with Shetland's birth rate in 1896–1900 at 20.2 compared with 30 for Scotland as a whole.[63] What is perhaps surprising, however, is the extremely low illegitimacy rate in Shetland. Historians have generally argued that illegitimacy tends to be high in societies with a late age at marriage and a 'surplus' of women over men. But in Shetland, where both of these factors were present, the argument can not be sustained. The illegitimacy rate was consistently low for the whole of the nineteenth century. In 1861 there were 4.3 illegitimate births per 100 births in Shetland, whereas the Scottish average was 9.2 – albeit disguising a wide range, from the low rates of the counties of the far north – Orkney, Sutherland, Caithness – to the much higher rates recorded in counties like Dumfries, Wigtown, Aberdeen and Banff.[64] By 1901 the respective figures were 3.7 and 6.3. Indeed, Shetland consistently had one of the lowest rates of illegitimacy in Scotland; so notable was the apparent infrequency of an illegitimate birth that in 1885 one observer remarked that 'this is evidence of a very high standard of morality'.[65] At the very least it would appear that limited marriage prospects for women did not encourage or condone extra-marital sex.

Societies with a large proportion of singletons, whether unmarried or widowed, tend to exhibit particular patterns of household formation. The proportion of more complex households, containing more than two generations or a combination of close and extended kin, as well as single-person households, is likely to be higher than usual in order to accommodate the number of individuals who are not incorporated into conjugal units. On the island of Yell, for example, an analysis of 183 households listed in the 1851 census identified 95 simple family households consisting of husband and/or wife with their children, 15 'solitaries' consisting of a man or woman living alone, and 72 complex households containing two or three generations and a variety of kin, from mothers and fathers, sisters and brothers to nephews and nieces, grandchildren, in-laws and sundry others.[66] Not unusual was the Robertson household from Greemister, Mid Yell, which contained the head, 28-year-old Bartle Robertson, a fisherman and farmer, and his wife Elizabeth. They lived with Bartle's elderly mother and father, his 33-year-old spinster sister Margaret and bachelor brother Laurence, a 72-year-old unmarried aunt and a 9-year-old nephew who was presumably Margaret's illegitimate son.[67] Such a household thus incorporated two unmarried women who may have had difficulty securing accommodation elsewhere and making a living alone.

Generalised European models of family formation and household structure have been found wanting for their failure to incorporate regional differences, but research into the relationship between household size and structure and the economy on a local basis has been more helpful.[68] The precise nature of household formation is closely tied to the available economic opportunities in the local context, as a study of coastal communities in southern Finland indicates. Here, the 'polyculture of the archipelago', a mixed economy of fishing, farming and domestic handicraft production not unlike that of Shetland, required 'many hands with many skills' in order to undertake tasks at the same time. Hence the extended or multiple household was a functional necessity.[69] Thus a household structure that facilitated the operation of multiple tasks was one which incorporated a range of persons of different ages and both sexes. This kind of structure was ideal in a society with a relatively high proportion of unmarried women. In Shetland, where the number of unmarried and widowed females was high, and where female emigration was comparatively low, it must be assumed that there were a number of possibilities for single women to survive, by contributing to another household. The alternative was for these women to support themselves alone. Certainly the proportion of female-only households (that is, consisting of one or more unmarried or widowed females) was notable. Almost one-quarter of elderly households (defined as containing at least one person of sixty years or older) on the islands of Yell and Unst were female-only by 1891, and amongst these the majority consisted of just one or two persons.[70]

In such demographic circumstances it is not surprising to find a high percentage of female-headed households. In 1851, 24 per cent of households across the whole of Shetland were headed by women, an average that hides a wide disparity between the town of Lerwick, which at 41 per cent contained the highest proportion, to the island of Whalsay, which had the lowest at 12 per cent.[71] In all parishes around half of these female household heads were widows and most were aged over 45 years. For instance, on Yell 27 per cent of the total households were headed by women, and of these 51 per cent were widows and 20 per cent were unmarried. Their median age was 49. An analysis in South Mainland in 1861 shows that 25 per cent were headed by females, 37 per cent of whom were widows and 32 per cent unmarried. Within this group, 37 per cent of the households were all-female containing either lone females (18 per cent) or groups of related women, typically a widow and her adult daughters or two unmarried sisters. For instance at Luster in Dunrossness, a 98-year-old widow, Ellen Goudie lived with her two unmarried daughters, Janet aged 60 and Isabella 48, and her 19-year-old granddaughter, also Isabella, who was presumably the illegitimate child of one of the daughters. Ellen and Isabella were paupers, but Janet and the younger Isabella earned a living by spinning and knitting.[72] A small distance away at Clumly the unmarried Flaws sisters – Catherine aged 67, and twins Margaret and Janet aged 49 – lived under one roof as spinners.[73]

How did unmarried and widowed women survive in an economy dominated by that most male of occupations – fishing? The prevailing system of tenancy for most of the century, based on a fishing contract with the landlord, marginalised unmarried women and widows. A woman might have managed to run a croft, but without a man to fish she would not be able to pay her rent. Thus the plight of unmarried women and widows without adult sons was often pitiful. In 1851 in the South Mainland district there were 145 female heads of household – 18 per cent of all householders. Seventy-nine or 55 per cent of these were widows, and 43 or 30 per cent were unmarried. Sixteen or 37 per cent of the unmarried female heads were designated paupers; 15 made a precarious living by knitting and spinning. Of the widows, however, just 11 or 14 per cent were paupers; the rest were described as cottars, crofters or farmers, knitters or spinners. There was even one merchant amongst them.[74] Widows, although traditionally regarded as amongst the most impoverished in rural communities, may have benefited from inheriting a tenancy or their husbands' businesses. Spinsters, on the other hand, possessed little capital; the tenancy of a croft would have been hard to get without a man to fish. In these circumstances it was not uncommon to find unmarried women living on the outskirts of townships on outsets. Such was the position of the three unmarried Nicolson sisters – Cecilia aged 52, Ann aged 54 and Barbara 44 – who in 1851 farmed an outset of five acres on the edge of Dale township in Tingwall parish.[75]

By 1881, 20 years after the population peak and the year when the sex imbalance was most marked, Shetland's womenfolk were more likely than their counterparts anywhere else in the British Isles to head their own household and to live for a significant part of their adult lives without an adult male. All-female households were common, with many containing no adult males at all. In Lerwick, though, the female household head was ubiquitous, accounting for 44 per cent of all heads of household in 1881 (compared with an average of 31 per cent for Shetland as a whole in that year). Lerwick was a woman's town. Women accounted for 57 per cent of the population here, and of those women over the age of 15, one half or 49 per cent were unmarried, leaving 30 per cent married and 18 per cent widows.[76] Lerwick, then, probably more than anywhere else in Shetland (and perhaps in the whole of Europe), was a place where lone women could live and work independently. Here, in contrast with the rural parishes, the availability of cheap rented accommodation and the diversity of the employment opportunities must have enabled unmarried women and widows to survive, and thus the town acted as a magnet for women from rural parishes across Shetland. Only 18 per cent of widows in the town and 26 per cent of unmarried women had been born in Lerwick, suggesting that the town offered these categories of women an opportunity to earn a living and live a life independent of the constraints of the fishing-crofting lifestyle. Not all unmarried women would have relished a life as part of someone else's household. In Lerwick women lived and worked in close proximity with other women. Some parts of the town were dominated by women and by female-headed households. In Church Lane, for instance, one of the narrow lanes off Commercial Street, 38 or 62 per cent of the households were headed by women. Amongst these, 25 contained singleton females and the majority contained no adult males. At 7 Church Lane, which contained five female-headed households, there lived Grace Morrison, a fisherman's widow, with her three children and two lodgers; 76-year-old Elizabeth Smith, who was unmarried, lived on her own and made a living as a knitter; a widow, Ann McPherson, also a knitter, resided with her two adult children; 19-year-old Ann Grant lived with her mother-in-law, both knitters, presumably whilst her husband was at sea; and 40-year-old Jane Blance, a spinster, knitted for a living and took in an unmarried lodger, 56-year-old Ann Peterson, who worked as a nurse.[77]

Many of these women were working in a makeshift economy, knitting, taking in lodgers, working as servants, as laundresses and dressmakers. Widows, elderly spinsters and single mothers could find a niche in this bustling town servicing the transient population and the resident middle class, and they were always able to resort to knitting, the occupation of necessity for more than half of Lerwick's widows in 1881, as Figure 3.6 demonstrates. Similarly, the unmarried woman could find a range of employment options in Lerwick that were not present in the rural districts, notably work in the domestic service sector and in retail business. Whilst hosiery occupied the majority of unmarried women throughout Shetland including Lerwick, those who chose to live in the town worked in a wider range of occupations than their rural sisters, with domestic service and retail work available as alternatives to hosiery production. By contrast, in Dunrossness for instance, unmarried and widowed women were more heavily concentrated in hosiery production (45 per cent) and in general and farm service (25 per cent).

The cultural consequences of the sex ratio imbalance, the impact on people's behaviour and experience, are more difficult to quantify. Olwen Hufton has written that 'All women lived in societies in which marriage and motherhood were regarded as the norm, spinsterhood and infertility as a blight, and in which the notion of the family economy, of the family as a composite unit permitting the sustenance of the whole, was axiomatic.'[78] She suggests that women who lived outside the family were inhabiting a kind of 'twilight existence'. Similarly, Miriam Slater

Figure 3.6 Occupations of unmarried women and widows in Lerwick, 1881: percentage in each occupational group

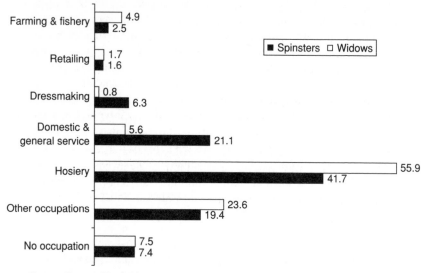

Source: *Census of Scotland*, 1881

argues that spinsterhood condemned a woman to 'a lifetime of peripheral existence . . . a functionless role played out at the margins of other people's lives without even that minimal raison d'être – the possibility of bearing children.'[79] But in communities where a surplus of women in the population had become the norm and where women were able to be economically productive, it is likely that marriage was not regarded as the only respectable or desirable way to live. Societies with a high proportion of spinsters and widows in the population were characterised by a great variety of household models and a widening of the concept of the family economy to incorporate clusters of females of various ages.[80]

Social and attitudinal changes associated with a high proportion of females in the population are not easy to identify. However, one might speculate that issues such as the relative status of the married to the unmarried, the value placed upon women's virginity and chastity, the economic power of women and the potential for their enhanced status in such a society might assume a different hue in Shetland in the context of continuous demographic imbalance.[81] As one visitor to Shetland noted, 'only in the matter of number is woman "superfluous"'.[82] In all other respects women occupied a central place and played a crucial role in economic and social life. However, all of these possibilities must be

examined in a specific cultural context. Societies with a female predominance in the population may develop along 'matricentric' or
woman-centred lines, as is the case in parts of Portugal.[83] In the northwest of that country, the economic conditions and the religious climate
combined to permit a positive culture of spinsterhood, where female
celibacy was preferable to unmarried motherhood, and where women's
work on the land provided them with access to a world beyond the
household. Unmarried women developed strong kinship bonds and
effective working relationships with other women. In other societies, like
Shetland, the marginal economic conditions, the system of landholding
and the disciplinary morality of the Protestant church meant that
spinsterhood was never a particularly enviable state, far less an honoured
one. But neither was marriage a guarantor of financial security and
respectability for women. The high mortality rate amongst fishermen
meant that early widowhood was a strong possibility, and the economic
position of a widow, especially if she had children, was no better than
that of her unmarried counterpart. In these circumstances, spinsterhood, marriage and widowhood were all part of a continuum for women
and none of these became the defining element of their identity.

In her study of a Portuguese parish with a long tradition of female
preponderance in the population, Caroline Brettell suggests that permanent spinsterhood was not a source of stigma for women. She argues
that unmarried women were regarded as an economic asset by their
parents, that such women could gain respectability by their incorpora-
tion into another household, and that women who did not marry had a
greater freedom outside the household.[84] In short, single women had
a defined place and role within the community. In Shetland, however,
the economic circumstances were so much more marginal that a single
woman was always likely to be in a precarious position because the
balance between her being an asset to a household and a burden was
extremely fine. However, a single woman could contribute economically and in kind to another family. As Mary Ellen Odie explained:

> Yes well you see they had a lot many children, it was good to have
> help with the mothering, for the seventh or eighth child wasn't getting
> much of a share, with the best mother in the world they don't so I
> do think the maiden aunt was mmm. I remember once scolding
> my nephew I think it was and my grandfather said ya, a young sow
> was never good wi grises, that's what they said, they called young
> pigs grises (laughs) and I thought it was a big insult. He laughed
> and he didn't think I would take it at an insult and there I can
> remember it yet. But on the whole I think the maiden aunts were

good . . . desperately sad for them, but they just, this was their family, they were staying with family. It's nothing new in Shetland, absolutely nothing new.[85]

Unmarried women played an essential role in fishing-crofting families where the husband fished and the wife ran the croft while he was away at sea, or in households lacking an adult male. They cared for the younger children, and their work – usually hand-knitting or farm labouring and, during the herring season, working at the gutting – brought crucial resources in material goods and cash into the family. Despite the ubiquity of the spinster here in Shetland and elsewhere in northern Europe where the proportions of never-married women have always been relatively high, her position has often been interpreted as unfortunate or marginal. But this assessment does not take account of the central role played by these women in marginal communities and the ability of spinsters and widows to form viable households.

Conclusions

Shetland was a woman's place in terms of its demography and its economy. Visitors to the islands were not hallucinating; they did see a society populated by active toiling women. There were not merely more women than men for the whole of the century: women were key to the island economy. These circumstances had concrete consequences for household structures and family dynamics as well as individual life courses. But they also impacted upon the ways in which women themselves constructed their identity in nineteenth-century Shetland and upon how the history and identity of Shetland has been represented since. However, the subjective and material consequences for women of these demographic conditions were not, as some have argued, a 'subjective sense of powerlessness', but rather a sense of individual self-worth and value.[86] In the absence of men, women's expectations were altered and power relations shifted.[87] In the following chapters we will pursue the question of how these material and demographic conditions came to shape gender relations in Shetland in the context of work relations, female culture, the moral order and finally women's power. The fact is that Shetland had an astonishing demography, perhaps almost a unique one. And that material difference had cultural consequences of great moment. Women were on top in the numbers game, and the ideology of domesticity and separate spheres did not and could not fit into their lives.

Notes

1 See S. Mills, 'Written on the landscape: Mary Wollstonecraft's *Letters Written During a Short Residence in Sweden, Norway and Denmark*', in A. Gilroy (ed.), *Romantic Geographies: Discourses of Travel 1775–1844* (Manchester, Manchester University Press, 2000), pp. 19–34, here pp. 24–6. See also D. Massey, *Space, Place and Gender* (Cambridge, Cambridge University Press, 1994).

2 A. McLintock, *Imperial Leather: Race, Gender and Sexuality in the Colonial Contest* (New York, Routledge, 1995), pp. 24–5; N. Yuval-Davis, *Gender and Nation* (London, Sage, 1997).

3 A. Trotter (1856) in Flinn, *Travellers in a Bygone Shetland*, p. 197.

4 J. Wilson (1841) in Flinn, *Travellers in a Bygone Shetland*, p. 50.

5 SA, D 1/134: *Barnet Press*, undated.

6 SA, D 1/134: *Northern Ensign*, 25 April 1861.

7 SA, D 1/135: *Dundee Advertiser*, 9 Sept. 1898.

8 *Shetland Times*, 1 April 1888.

9 A similar attitude is reported in other parts of Scotland. See, for example, D. Macdonald, *Tales and Traditions of the Lews* (Edinburgh, Birlinn, 2000) where 'men were precious' and women undertook the drudgery (p. 102).

10 On ideals of masculinity in nineteenth-century Britain see J. Tosh, *A Man's Place: Masculinity and the Middle Class Home in Victorian England* (New Haven and London, Yale University Press, 1999).

11 A. Trotter (1856) in Flinn, *Travellers in a Bygone Shetland*, p. 79.

12 W. P. Livingstone, *Shetland and the Shetlanders* (London, Thomas Nelson & Sons, 1947), p. 171.

13 SA, D 1/135: *Daily Chronicle*, 1910 (no exact date).

14 SA, D 1/135: *Chicago Daily News*, Oct. 1927.

15 Revd J. Catton (1835) in Flinn, *Travellers in a Bygone Shetland*, p. 135.

16 Hibbert, *A Description of the Shetland Islands*, p. 23.

17 SA, D 1/135: *Chicago Daily News*, Oct. 1927.

18 SA, D 1/135: *Dundee Advertiser*, 9 Sept. 1898.

19 'Desperately seeking love – look to Lerwick', *The Herald*, 30 Nov. 2001.

20 I. A. Morrison, 'The Auld Rock: the physical environment as an element in the interplay of continuity and change in Shetland's history', in D. J. Waugh (ed.), *Shetland's Northern Links: Language and History* (Edinburgh, Scottish Society for Northern Studies, 1996), pp. 84–9.

21 A. Fenton,*The Northern Isles: Orkney and Shetland* (East Linton, Tuckwell Press, 1997), p. 2.

22 *The New Statistical Account for Scotland*, vol. XV (Edinburgh and London, William Blackwood & Sons, 1845), p. 78.

23 B. Smith, *Toons and Tenants: Settlement and Society in Shetland, 1299–1899* (Lerwick, Shetland Times Ltd, 2000), pp. 70–3.

24 SA, D 24/69/5: Minute of agreement between Sir A. Nicolson and tenants, 1839.

25 Quoted in Fenton, *The Northern Isles*, p. 56.

26 Smith, *Toons and Tenants*, p. 80.

27 Charles Rampini to the Crofters' Commission, 1883, quoted in Smith, *Toons and Tenants*, p. xi.

28 Fenton, *The Northern Isles*, pp. 161–6.

29 SA, D 1/83: Journal of Sarah Squire, Quaker, kept during a religious visit to Shetland, Orkney and the north of Scotland, 1835. With typed transcriptions by Marjorie Dell.

30 Fenton, *The Northern Isles*, pp. 157–9.

31 *Royal Commission on Housing in Scotland*, Shetland evidence, 1913, lines 11,842–3 and 12,326.

32 Fenton, *The Northern Isles*, pp. 101–5.

33 Smith, *Toons and Tenants*, pp. 29–31.

34 W. Collins (1842) in Kendall, *With Naught but Kin*, p. 53.

35 C. Thomson (1847) in Kendall, *With Naught but Kin*, p. 52.

36 SA, 1/134: 'The old rock: Shetlandic sketches', *The Beacon* (undated, probably c.1910).

37 *Royal Commission on Housing in Scotland*, Shetland evidence, 1913, line 11,838.

38 *Census of Scotland* (Edinburgh, HMSO) (hereafter census), 1881: Lerwick.

39 SA, 3/1/112: Margaret Shearer. See also W. R. Steele, 'Local authority involvement in housing and health in Shetland c.1900–1950', MPhil thesis, University of Strathclyde, 1992.

40 British Parliamentary Papers, 1 C (1st series) 3980 I–IV: *Royal Commission of Inquiry into the Condition of Crofters and Cottars in the Highlands and Islands of Scotland* (Napier Commission), 1884. See, for example, the evidence given by John Omand, Mid Yell, lines 18,807 ff.

41 Smith, *Toons and Tenants*, p. 78.

42 L. G. Fryer, *Knitting by the Fireside and on the Hillside: A History of the Shetland Hand Knitting Industry c.1600–1950* (Lerwick, Shetland Times Ltd, 1995), pp. 51–64.

43 Fryer, *Knitting by the Fireside*, pp. 50–1.

44 E. Gordon, *Women and the Labour Movement in Scotland 1850–1914* (Oxford, Oxford University Press, 1991), p. 142.

45 Census, 1871.

46 SA, D 1/135: 'The people of the Shetland Isles', *The Scotsman*, 16 Feb. 1885.

47 Census, 1861.

48 W. Kingston (1850) in Kendall, *With Naught but Kin*, p. 169.

49 Figures in J. M. Brock, *The Mobile Scot: A Study of Emigration and Migration 1861–1911* (Edinburgh, John Donald, 1999), appendix 13, p. 369.

50 SA, D 1/134, *Newcastle Chronicle* (undated, probably 1894).

51 *Registrar General for Scotland Annual Report, 1881* (Edinburgh, HMSO, 1881), pp. 52–3.

52 SA, D 1/357/3: Shetland Fishermen's Widows' Relief Fund, minutes of meeting of Directors, 5 Jan. 1901.

53 SA, D 1/357/6: Shetland Fishermen's Widows' Relief Fund, applications for relief.

54 Smith, *Shetland Life and Trade*, pp. 158–9.

55 A. Anderson, 'Female population of Orkney and Shetland' (1851), in Kendall, *With Naught but Kin*, p. 220.

56 Census, 1861.

57 In 1961 the marriage rate for Scotland was 7.8; in Shetland it was 7.3.

58 Census, 1861.

59 M. Anderson, 'Why was Scottish nuptiality so depressed for so long?', in I. Devos and L. Kennedy (eds), *Marriage and Rural Economy: Western Europe since 1400* (Brepols, Turnhout, 1999), pp. 49–84, table 2.6, p. 79.

60 B. Hill, *Women Alone: Spinsters in England 1660–1850* (New Haven and London, Yale University Press, 2001), pp. 10–11.

61 Census, 1901.

62 See Anderson, 'Why was Scottish nuptiality so depressed for so long?', pp. 58–60.

63 M. Flinn (ed.), *Scottish Population History from the 17th Century to the 1930s* (Cambridge, Cambridge University Press, 1977), pp. 338–9, table 5.3.1.

64 On high illegitimacy rates see A. Blaikie, *Illegitimacy, Sex and Society: Northeast Scotland 1750–1900* (Oxford, Oxford University Press, 1993).

65 Only Clackmannan, Dumbarton, Partick, Coatbridge, Kirkaldy, Hamilton and Motherwell recorded lower illegitimacy rates than Shetland in 1901 (census, 1901). SA, D 1/134: *The Scotsman*, 16 Feb. 1885.

66 Calculated from the 1851 census for Yell.

67 Census, 1851: Mid Yell.

68 See, for example, P. Laslett and R. Wall (eds), *Household and Family in Past Time* (Cambridge, Cambridge University Press, 1978).

69 See B. Moring, 'Household and family in Finnish coastal societies 1635–1895', *Journal of Family History* 18 (1993), pp. 395–414, here p. 408, and B. Moring, 'Marriage and social change in south-western Finland, 1700–1870', *Continuity and Change* 11 (1996), pp. 91–113.

70 Yell had 38.9% one-person households and 50% two-person households in 1891; Unst had 42.2% one-person and 35.9% two-person households. See B. Heenan, 'Living arrangements among elderly Shetlanders in the parishes of Lerwick, Yell and Unst between 1851 and 1891', in A. H. Dawson, H. R. Jones, A. Small and J. A. Soulsby (eds), *Scottish Geographical Studies* (Dundee and St Andrews Universities, 1993), pp. 218–28, here pp. 224–5.

71 Calculated from the 1851 census.

72 Census, 1861: South Mainland.

73 Census, 1861: South Mainland.

74 Census, 1851: South Mainland.

75 Census, 1851: Tingwall.

76 The marital status of the remaining 3 per cent was unstated in the census.

77 Census, 1881: Lerwick.

78 O. Hufton, 'Women without men: widows and spinsters in Britain and France in the eighteenth century', *Journal of Family History* 9 (1984), pp. 355–76, here p. 355.

79 Slater quoted in P. Sharpe, 'Dealing with love: the ambiguous independence of the single woman in early modern England', *Gender & History* 11 (1999), pp. 209–32, here p. 210.

80 Hufton speaks of 'spinster clustering' but clusters of widows were also common.

81 See the models suggested in M. Guttentag and P. F. Secord, *Too Many Women? The Sex Ratio Question* (London, Sage, 1983).

82 SA, D 1/135: *Ladies' Field*, 21 Sept. 1907.

83 See Brettell, *Men who Migrate*, p. 265.

84 Brettell, *Men who Migrate*, pp. 130 ff.

85 Interview with Mary Ellen Odie.

86 Guttentag and Secord, *Too Many Women?*, p. 20.

87 See C. Brettell, 'Male migrants and unwed mothers: illegitimacy in a northwestern Portuguese town', *Anthropology* 9 (1985), pp. 87–110, here p. 105.

4

Work

Q: Do you do anything else in the way of working for your living than
 by knitting these articles?
Andrina Simpson: Yes, I am married.
(*Commission to Inquire into the Truck System, Second Report
(Shetland), 1872, Evidence, line 326*)

Producing

THE DECEPTIVELY SIMPLE reply given by the Lerwick knitter Andrina Simpson upon being asked whether she did anything else in addition to knitting to make a living speaks volumes. For Shetland women marriage meant induction into a fishing-crofting household wherein their role was as producers as much as reproducers. When the United Kingdom Truck Commission visited Shetland in 1872 for the purpose of investigating the persistence of truck in the islands, it uncovered a picture of women's work that had largely disappeared elsewhere in the British Isles. The commission focused on the fishing and hand-knitting industries, for it was in these employment sectors that truck was most entrenched. The evidence, collected over several days, provides a comprehensive insight into the character of trade and exchange in hosiery, fish, foodstuffs and dry goods. It also presents an unequalled view of the nature of women's work in Shetland towards the end of the nineteenth century. The women who gave evidence were candid and direct and provided the commissioner with detailed descriptions of the operations of the truck system as well as a very personal perspective on their identity as workers.

Historians of women's work in northern Europe have tended to argue that women's role in agricultural labour altered in the nineteenth century in terms of the numbers involved and the types of work undertaken, consequent upon structural changes in agricultural production and the pervasiveness of discourses of domesticity which situated women in the home. The family or household-economy model of production and reproduction, whereby work and domestic life were co-dependent and wherein all family members contributed work of equal value (although usually incorporating a sexual division of labour), was gradually and unevenly superseded by a different kind of family unit characterised by the separation of home and work, what is termed the family wage economy.[1] Within this model, most commonly identified in the context of industrialisation, domestic production took second place to wage labour outside the home, and female labour was subordinate to male breadwinning. During the transition from the household economy to the family wage economy in the rural context, female labour on the land was subject to constraints imposed by technology and by ideology which resulted in fewer female agricultural workers and their concentration in sectors regarded as low-skilled and poorly paid such as hoeing, weeding and haymaking.[2]

According to the census of 1861, 52 per cent of employed females in Shetland worked on the land; 32 per cent were engaged in the hosiery, textile and clothing trades (mostly as knitters); 17 per cent were employed in domestic service and associated trades.[3] These figures did not include female dependants, including more than 3,000 'wives', many of whom almost certainly worked on the croft or farm or engaged in some form of paid or unpaid productive activity. These three sectors remained the dominant areas of female employment on the islands until the twentieth century, supplemented by the rise of the herring industry from the 1880s, which provided seasonal gutting work for women. By 1901 more than two-thirds of employed females were identified in the census as workers in the hosiery and textile occupations, just 8 per cent worked in domestic service, and agriculture employed a mere 15 per cent.[4] However, so-called female dependants were excluded from the occupied category. Indeed, in 1901 more than 6,000 females over the age of 10 years were recorded as unoccupied yet the likelihood is that most of these, even the very young and the very old, would have contributed to the household economy. By 1911 women's contribution to agriculture was once again better recognised by the census takers. This sector provided work for 34 per cent of Shetland women identified as occupied, the hosiery and textile industries employed 45 per cent, and just 8 per cent were defined as working in the service industry.[5] Again, though, almost 6,000 women were recorded as unoccupied.

Viewed from the statistics, women's work in Shetland has a profile not dissimilar to that elsewhere in rural Europe. It was concentrated in a small number of sectors, the jobs women undertook were often described as domestic in character, allied to what were typically female roles in the household, and these sectors were characterised by low pay.[6] In many other respects, though, working women in Shetland did not resemble their counterparts in other parts of the British Isles. Firstly, they commonly engaged in physical outdoor labour at a time when much agricultural work had been deemed unsuitable for women elsewhere. In England a Royal Commission on Agriculture in 1843 regarded field work as too heavy for women and certainly unfeminine, and from the middle of the century women's farm labour was declining.[7] Secondly, the ideology of domesticity which ideally located a woman within the home in a reproductive rather than productive capacity had no purchase in rural Shetland, where the home was simultaneously a place of work and of home life and where the two were intimately related. The census did not record the constant, everyday croft work which was undertaken by most women outside Lerwick, whether they had another occupation or not. Nineteenth-century discourses on womanhood associated ideal femininity with the economically unproductive woman. Shetland women, however, were continuously implicated in the market as producers and consumers, at least until the inter-war years. The unproductive female had no place here except amongst the very small Lerwick middle class. The image of the Shetland woman as crofter, knitter or domestic servant – and often all three at once – provides a glimpse of the complicated and sophisticated role played by women in the economy of the islands. Visitors often commented upon the multiple tasks undertaken by women here and they were shocked by the physical and outdoor nature of their labour, but few really appreciated women's central place in a complex web of market relationships.

Women's position in the nexus of production was central to their identity in these islands. Notwithstanding the constraints of female employment opportunities here, women's role in autonomous production and trade in goods placed them at the heart of social relations in the townships and in Lerwick, and women's direct and active involvement in productive and market relations provided them with access to spaces and opportunities which were receding for women elsewhere in the British Isles. In short, Shetland women's participation in the formal economy – in farming, hosiery production, the fish processing industry and a range of other jobs – bucked the trends evident elsewhere. Whereas in England, Ireland and some parts of Scotland, female agricultural labour was declining as a result of the introduction of new technology and the increasing observance of notions of female dependence and domesticity, in Shetland there is no evidence that women's active role in the economy was decreasing or that women were forced to rely upon what has been described as an 'economy of makeshifts'.[8] Rather, women here did both. Makeshift was a necessary corollary to paid work at all times.

The Shetland economy has traditionally been dominated by the sea. Throughout the sixteenth, seventeenth and eighteenth centuries Shetland was a nodal point for northern European trade, mainly in fish but also in salt, tea, tobacco, gin, livestock and woollen goods with the other North Atlantic and North Sea trading states as well as the Baltic ports and Scotland and England to the south.[9] Much of this trade was dominated by German merchants, but by the end of the eighteenth century Shetlanders' reputation as a seafaring people meant that the islands had become a recruiting station for the Greenland whale fishery and the merchant marine and navy. These were employment sectors monopolised by men. By contrast, women's work was land-based and mostly home-based, constrained by the limited natural resources and by the prevalent climatic conditions. Crofting and farming, hand-knitting and other forms of textile production were the prime areas of employment for females in a fishing-crofting economy.

Early in the nineteenth century attempts to diversify into small-scale manufacture employing females were short-lived. Attempts to introduce linen manufacture in the eighteenth century failed, and a straw plaiting venture met a similar fate. At its peak in 1809 the straw plaiting industry employed up to 200 women in factories in Lerwick and Dunrossness, but straw of the quality required for plaiting could not be produced in Shetland. The high cost and unreliability of imports of raw material from England meant that such a venture had difficulty in achieving viability here. By contrast, in Orkney straw plait manufacture employed up to 2,000 women at its peak in the 1840s using home-grown straw, although here too production ceased by the 1870s.[10] But it was not just the unreliability of raw material supplies that caused the demise of this industry. Labour was not easy to secure, causing Thomas Ogilvy, the manager of one of the Lerwick factories, to seek legal redress on the grounds that 'many of [the female employees] deserted the employment after having been carefully taught the business and went over to others of a similar profession on the slightest pretence.'[11] The fact that the women were employed at piece rates according to the quality of the goods they produced may have informed their decision to switch employers. The death knell of the industry, though, was not due to the unreliability of the workforce but was precipitated by a reduction of import duty on foreign-made articles, making Shetland-produced goods uncompetitive.[12] Thus in 1841 it was remarked that in Lerwick:

> The women in this, as in other parishes, are a good deal employed in knitting stockings, mitts, and other articles of hosiery. There was formerly a straw-plait manufactory; but, for several years, it has been dropped. There is an attempt at present making by Messrs Hay and Ogilvy, to establish a herring-net manufactory; and there can be no doubt of the propriety of thus securing employment on the spot in the manufacture of an article, the weaving of which is so simple, and so easily acquired, and which is now much used in the district.[13]

The only other industry of any real significance employing women was kelp manufacture. Kelp is the product of seaweed burning and was used in the production of soap, iodine and glass and as an alkali in bleaching. The production process involved wading into the sea to collect the tang (coarse seaweed) with a large fork called a taricrook, spreading the seaweed to dry on the grass, and then burning it in a kelp kiln until the kelp formed a smooth substance. The kelp was then left to harden until it could be broken up and transported.[14] The work was filthy, hard and tedious, often carried out by women and children at the shoreline. Although the raw material was relatively plentiful, production in Shetland flourished on a significant scale only from the 1780s until the 1820s, a period when alternatives to kelp – salt and barilla – were prohibitively taxed or unobtainable owing to wartime blockades. In contrast, kelp production in Orkney provided a considerable income. By the middle of the nineteenth century few were employed in the kelp industry in Shetland, mainly on Bressay and the northernmost islands. Thereafter seaweed was more likely to be spread on croft land as a fertiliser, and women's work in the manufacture of kelp came to an end.

The short-term nature of employment in straw plaiting and kelp manufacture only serves to emphasise the limited range of opportunities for women's wage earning in Shetland. Alternatives included farm or domestic service, agricultural labouring and, to a lesser extent, shop work. Women were sometimes employed to carry peats down from the hills as well as in a variety of manual occupations such as setting and heaping potatoes, singling turnips, delving and manure carrying, a job for which Barbara Coutts received 7d in 1859 from James Williamson of Mid Yell.[15] But, with the exception of the herring gutting, which took off in the 1880s, most women made a living within a make-shift, non-cash economy dominated by agriculture and hosiery production. Shetland was a cash-poor society as a result of the dominance of barter-truck in goods and services, and women's labour and trade in goods lay at the heart of this system. In these islands women's work and their need to engage with the market on an everyday basis implicated them in a complex set of economic and cultural relationships which has left as a legacy the image of the productive Shetland woman.

Crofting

The dominant and idealised image of the Shetland woman has become synonymous with the female farmer and crofter. In a community so dependent upon fishing it is perhaps surprising that the idea of the croft bears such a symbolic weight and that women's work on the croft should come to signify for present-day Shetlanders the essence of the Shetland way of life. It is an image that sharply contrasts with the Scottish Highlands, where crofting has been more closely associated with masculine identity.[16]

'Crofting' refers to a form of subsistence farming in the Highlands and Islands of Scotland that developed from the late eighteenth century. It emerged with the break-up of inland common-farmed settlements in the wake of the Jacobite rebellion of 1745–46, over-population and official disapproval of Gaelic language, religion and culture, followed in the early nineteenth century by landlord clearance to make way for more lucrative economic activities such as sheep rearing and the management of sporting estates. Crofting was thus an economy of survival, characteristically consisting of mixed farming on marginal coastal land, with very small amounts of arable and greater portions of pastoral land, augmented by fishing, kelp making, spinning, weaving or other cottage industries. But crofting was also a culture of resistance, and grew in Highland mythology as a way of life that distinguished a Gaelic-speaking community, increasingly puritan in its religion, from anglicised and absentee landlords.[17] But in Shetland, without Gaelic culture and with even more barren agricultural land, crofting was uniquely fishing first with farming second. Here, the dominant agricultural system until the middle of the nineteenth century was based on townships with runrig, sub-divided fields and common grazings or scattalds, as opposed to the discrete agricultural holdings associated with crofting elsewhere. It was this system, which co-existed with fishing-tenure, that obliged tenants to fish for the landlord or the merchant and to deliver the fish harvest in payment of rent. Crofting developed later in Shetland than in mainland Scotland, mostly in the mid- and later nineteenth century following two phases of clearance, but it was no less an economic system of survival in which the people invested a sense of cultural resistance and identity. By the time of the 1886 Crofters' Holdings Act, which provided security of tenure, fixed fair rents and shifted power from landlords to the state, crofting as an agricultural activity had a firm footing in Shetland. Notwithstanding the relatively late development of crofting as a discrete agricultural activity in Shetland, the term 'crofting' is used as a universal shorthand to refer to a range of agricultural practices and a way of life in the nineteenth century. Indeed, crofting is regarded as a 'structure of social organisation', a means of interpreting the past in the present so that it carries a symbolic or explanatory significance that transcends economic definitions.[18] Hence, here I will use the term 'crofting' loosely to refer to the variety of small-scale subsistence agriculture practised in Shetland throughout the nineteenth century.

Visitors to the islands in the nineteenth century invariably remarked upon women's intense and, as it appeared to them, demeaning physical activity outside in all weathers. 'Almost all the work done on the land is done by the women', reported a minister from the south-west of Scotland who visited Shetland in 1861.

> They not only do all the work of the home, besides their achievements in knitting all sorts of hosiery, but they do the ploughing and the harrowing as well. He had actually seen women in Zetland harnessed to harrows. The women cut the peats and bring them home, carry out the manure to the fields, plough the fields with wooden ploughs drawn by little oxen – in fact they do the whole outdoor as well as indoor work.[19]

Hailing from Dumfriesshire, this writer was unlikely to have witnessed women undertaking such outdoor work on his home turf, and thus his surprise at conditions in Shetland was heightened. But he was not alone in expressing amazement at the sight of women working out of doors. 'Most of the work on the crofts of the peasantry is done by the weaker sex; for here . . . "the woman is the better man"', remarked a contributor to a popular journal in 1883.[20] 'It is not a little astonishing to notice the active part taken by women in the Shetland economy', commented a contributor to the *Ladies' Journal* in 1891: 'With the husband at sea, the whole care and work of the croft and household devolves upon the wife, and this is no child's play. Not only does she dig and plant out the whole ground herself with such help as she may get from her family, but she looks after all the livestock and otherwise attends to her own work proper about the house and croft.'[21]

It is this depiction of the female crofter that has come to assume a degree of symbolic power in Shetland as the authentic sign of a past which is also revered for its simplicity and its gender equality. But amongst present-day Shetlanders the crofting women of the past are not pitied and neither is there any surprise at the physical and outdoor nature of their work. Rather, crofting women are celebrated and revered for their ability to do 'men's work'. They are represented as resourceful, skilful and unique, and the female crofter represents much that is admired about the resilience of Shetlanders in the past.

Since the beginning of the twentieth century crofting has declined as a significant economic activity in the islands in the sense of providing a living, and it has increasingly been subsumed by large-scale sheep farming. Hence crofting in Shetland has 'more salience as an idea than as an economic activity'.[22] The idea or meaning of the croft for Shetlanders has been retained as symbolising a 'way of life' that has largely been lost. More than this, crofting is talked about as encapsulating a certain type of gender relations based upon equality of the sexes, said to be characteristic of Shetland in general. But there

2 Women harrowing in Norwick, Unst, 1890s

is little about the female crofting experience that conforms to this romantic representation, mediated through film and popular literature.[23] As the nineteenth-century visitors correctly observed, croft work was hard, back-breaking work which yielded a subsistence living at best.

The small agricultural holdings tenanted by most rural Shetlanders in the nineteenth century consisted of a dwelling, a small area of arable or cultivable ground (which, while runrig was still practised, could be scattered and fragmented around the township), rights to pasture livestock on the scattald and rights to harvest peats from the hill. This form of farming rarely provided a livelihood, and needed to be supplemented by other activities. In Shetland the sea provided the additional income via the system of fishing-tenure. Hence, the croft was the prime means of subsistence, providing food for the household and goods for sale for cash. Under this system the able-bodied men of the croft were away from the land for long periods engaged in the haaf or deep-sea fishing in the summer months and the herring fishing from spring until late summer. Men not engaged in fishing for their landlords commonly found work in the merchant marine and on whaling vessels which took them away from home for months, if not years, at a stretch. In this context women were often left alone to manage the croft during the busiest times of year, the spring and summer. 'He [father] would go when seeds were sown', recalled Mrs Laurenson, born in 1890, 'and he would come back just when the harvest was in . . . and we did everything that was needed . . . Me and my mother, yes.'[24] A wife would rarely manage the croft, the household and child care responsibilities alone. She would be aided by other women who lived in the household: spinster sisters and sisters-in-law, aunts, mothers and older daughters. Jessie Sinclair remembered her aunt staying with the family when she was small. She explained: 'And that happened in a lot of houses – say your mother's sister was single – well my aunt married when she was 31 I think. But before that she lived with us – and that more or less brought up the little ones. I can remember runnin more to me aunt than me mother because she'd more time for us than me mother, because she was out in the fields all day long.'[25] Extra help around the house was a necessity in big families and on the larger crofts: 'They couldna leave da bairns in even ta go oot ta da milking . . . it wis a job, you ken, you could manage if you were maybe keepin one cow, but you couldna manage wi a lot.'[26] The work of all of these women was necessary to maintain a croft and the domestic concerns, and in the absence of a man his wife would take on the physical labour of croft work while another woman in the house would assume the domestic role. The extended and predominantly female Shetland household, encountered in the previous chapter, was functional in this context.

The active crofting year ran from the voar until the late summer hairst, and during this time the work was varied and continuous, although peaks of activity occurred with the sowing in April and May and the harvest in September. Men often tried to be at home for the sowing but, as Agnes Tulloch explained, 'As soon as the voar was finished, then it was the peats and the peats began aboot when the voar was finished according to the weather in the first weeks of May . . . so I guid wi my Dad tae cast the peats . . . but as soon as the peats were cut the men were off and then they were getting the boats underway . . . for the herring fishing . . .'[27] The men tended to return to the croft in August or September, when they could help with the harvest of corn. But most of the everyday work on the croft was undertaken by females of all ages. Starting in the spring they delled the ground for sowing and planting of seed and vegetables (potatoes, cabbage, kale and turnips). The sowing complete, women turned their attention to peat raising – cutting and turning the peat on the hill. Through the summer they hoed the vegetables, heaped the potatoes, spread manure or seaweed on the fields and rooed the sheep, and by the end of the crofting year they began to bring the peats down from the hill to be stacked to dry at the croft. At harvest time they would cut the hay and gather it into skroos, and potatoes would be lifted and stored along with turnips. In addition to the seasonal jobs, women would be continually working with the live-stock – cows, sheep and maybe hens – and they gathered firewood, winkles, whelks and shingle (for the hens) from the beach, made butter and cheese, salted meat and fish and were forever bringing peats down from the hill in kishies on their backs or carried by ponies. During the haddock fishing season in winter, women and children would be responsible for baiting the lines with hundreds of mussels and keeping the dredged-up mussels fresh on the shore by frequently dousing them with buckets of water. Sometimes the haddock boats would go out twice a day, 'An de wid leave dat lines ta da wife ta bait – dat wimmin hed haird times, I can assure you.'[28] By October the crofting year was over and families would hope that their harvest would see them through the winter.

The celebration of the female crofter as on a par with a man in terms of the nature of work undertaken is ubiquitous in all kinds of sources – written and oral. In 1899 a correspondent in *The Scotsman* wrote that:

The women are practically independent, and seem quite equal to their work, without putting on any airs about it. Those who maintain the perfect equality of the sexes should be glad to know that Shetland women were shown before the Crofters' Commission to be quite able to do the work of men, and they were much more conversant with practical workings of the crofts than the men were. They show quite good sense and discretion in discharging all their responsibilities, and seem in a fair way to return to the honourable state of the women of the Odal time, from whom they inherit their simple, industrious habits and wholesome contempt of luxury.[29]

The language of gender equality saturates narratives of the past, with many respondents emphasising the ability of women to do 'men's work'. 'There werena this, what do they call it ... what the women are ... equality nowadays ... equality was den a days too in a different wye. You were doin' men's work', commented one woman.[30] Nan Paton, born in 1918 and interviewed in 1985, was fulsome in talking about her widowed mother. Her father had been lost at sea when Nan was just four months old:

[Mother] used to go with the milk and she'd come home and she'd cut her peats and when it was time for cutting the hay she'd mow like any man cut the hay, she could bigg (build) haystacks, she could bigg peat stacks, corn stacks or anything, built dykes, you name it she could do it and she was a great woman with dogs, she could caa (drive) the whole hill, you know ... Yeah, well she could do anything and she was wanting to be the driving party for the scattald ... and she was the main one for driving the sheep and all this and if anybody needed her they just roared for her and she went. So she was not very big but by jove she could work.[31]

A discourse of gender equality has considerable purchase in modern Shetland. People repeatedly state that in the past men and women were equal – they both worked hard, they both contributed to the household, and women in particular worked the croft while the men were at sea. Implicit in this language is the assertion that there was gender equality in Shetland because women were economically active and autonomous (at least whilst the men were away) unlike elsewhere in Scotland, where, it is alleged, women were oppressed by their menfolk and were subordinate in the workplace. And yet implicit in the assertion of equality is a recognition that there was a sexual division of labour, or at least that there were tasks ascribed separately to men and to women even though they might be undertaken by either sex. In very general terms fishing was men's work whilst women toiled on the land, but on the croft there was a division of labour that was understood if not always practised. Women are thus celebrated for their skill in undertaking what is described as 'men's work'. Agnes Leask articulated this discourse on equality and difference:

> Oh yes, inside da hoose, dat wis aa da wimmin's wark. An actually da croftwark, dat wis mostly wimmin's wark: it wis da wimmin who kept da everyday wark o da croft goin. An dey milked da coo, an dey calfed da coos, an anythin sickly it wis wimmin at attendit too hit. Men wirna allood in da byre at da calvin, no no, you didna allow men ta see dat things happenin ... dey tocht it wid embarrass da men, dat wisna a men's job at aa, dat wis a totally female domain ... An da men actually did da heavy wark, peat cuttin an dat sort o thing – buildin da walls ... any drainin at wis done, an dat sort o thing. But da diggin da fields, da men, if dey were aboot, dey'd help, da fields were all turned ower wi a spade, an dey wid help wi dat; but if dere wis no men aboot, da wimmin jist simply got on wi it, demselves.[32]

Later on Agnes Leask remarked, 'It was deemed men's work but the wife would do it.'[33]

Women left on their own to run the croft were capable: they could turn their hand to most jobs with the exception of harvesting the corn with the scythe, which was deemed too heavy an implement for women to manage. Women could even sail and row a boat, commonly regarded as the most masculine of work: 'sail on a boat, was deemed men's work,' remarked Agnes Leask, 'but a big lot of the women could row a boat and sail a boat as good as any man.'[34] In the absence of roads women regularly rowed to transport peats home, to reach the nearest merchant with their hosiery, or in extremis, to catch fish in the voe. 'Women could row, you understand,' recalled Mary Ellen Odie:

> they could row and they could use heavy lines because they couldn't afford if the men was away and they saw a nice plank of wood that could be made into useful things, they learned to do the heavy [work] ... and they shopped using the boats. The North of Voe women at the regattas would outrow the Mid Yell women because they rowed every week across the voe and there were always women's rowing races at the regattas and that's when you would put a huge bet on a North Voe boat winning the rowing race.[35]

Sowing, too, was widely regarded as 'men's work'. 'If a man had been around they would've looked to him to sow the corn ... The sowing was surrounded by a bit of mythology too because the tide had to be right and the moon had to be right,' commented Mary Ellen Odie.

3   Two women's rowing crews at Lerwick regatta, 1890s

And even as late as 1920 the male sower was apparently treated with reverence if this rather idealised description is to be believed:

> When the seed box is filled and strapped firmly over his shoulders . . . the sower prepares for action. He discards his coat, rolls up his sleeves, and with head thrown back, he takes his handfuls of the golden grain and scatters the seed broad-cast, to right and left over the field. Just for one moment the women folk gaze after him, reverence and submission in their looks. For them, the sower appears to be invested with the power of some ancient deity whom they have appeased with sacrifice. He assumes god-like proportions.[36]

But it was only in the absence of men that women could demonstrate their multiple skills. Speaking of her great-great-grandmother Nelly Kitty, who was widowed when her husband drowned in the 1832 fishing disaster, Mary Ellen Odie mentioned

> the things that she did because there were no men left in the village to do physical work and they say not only physical work but the sort of difficult to judge kind of things like sowing the corn and the oats that was. Well she, the first year Nelly sowed the oats for the whole village you see, and she took the boat and went to the fishing to catch something to eat just like a man would . . .[37]

Similarly, Agnes Leask's aunt, a spinster who lived with her brother on a distant croft, 'did all the croft work, and of course, living out there, there was no road and all the goods she needed had to come by boat, and she'd think nothing of taking the boat hoisting the sail, sailing to Scalloway for a drum of paraffin . . .'[38]

Women, then, were capable of doing tasks labelled as 'men's work', they were fully involved in the production of goods as well as playing the major role in social reproduction. Yet they were certainly not rewarded equally for their labour. In this respect Shetland was no different from anywhere else; women were paid less than men.[39] In 1841 it was remarked in the parish of Sandsting and Aithsting that women's wages for farm work were 4d compared with 6d for men, and on Yell a whole day's work by a woman delling the soil was worth just half that done by a man.[40]

There were few tasks precisely designated as women's work. Superstition may have prevented men from being permitted to help with a calving cow – 'a man wasn't supposed to go near the byre' – but even knitting had an ambiguous status. 'There was things like that that men didn't do, and believe it or not men didn't knit,' commented Agnes Leask, but she then went on to say: 'but a lot of them did knit quietly, yeh oh yeh they did . . .'[41] And others recall men knitting at home: 'I had an old uncle there . . . he could knit, he could make this, guernseys an stockins and yer inside wear, he could a' that . . . if it was the wrang wool, he could caird it and spin it . . . You would hardly believe what they could do!'[42] When the MP for Shetland and Orkney, Mr Wason, was spotted knitting a Shetland stocking in the smoking room of the House of Commons, he appeared to be oblivious to the mockery of his colleagues: 'he smiled benevolently through his glasses and kept steadily on. "I heed not the laughter or the comments that are made upon my knitting" he said. "Only those who have tried it can realise what a soothing, calming effect upon reason and nerves this occupation produces."'[43] It is unlikely that the mass of Shetland menfolk would have shrugged off other men's derision in such a manner, and women would have laughed at the notion of knitting as an antidote to stress.

Crofting today is perceived more as a way of life than as a productive activity. Since the 1930s, with a few exceptions, crofting has transmuted into sheep farming, which is much less labour-intensive and which provides a secondary income at best. However, crofting has come to symbolise community co-operation and mutual support, tradition, a form of environmentally friendly agriculture, independence and self-sufficiency. Crofting in Shetland is much less romanticised than in the West Highlands and Islands, but it is important in contributing to the ways in which modern Shetlanders understand themselves and their past, and thus it is rare to hear criticism of the crofting way of life.[44] 'I mean even in my young days life was hard,' commented Agnes Leask:

> but people were happier . . . everybody was happier. There was none of this keeping up with the Joneses. And actually here when I was a child every place was habited, and families in them. There was as many people in one house then as there is a whole mile of road-way now. And if somebody got an illness or sickness or maybe a

bereavement in the family, everybody would go along and help them, do the work for them until they got back on their feet again. It was really communal working at its best. But now that's all going.[45]

Since the 1970s oil boom in Shetland, more meaning has been attached to the idea of crofting than to the activities associated with running a croft. In the 1970s and 1980s women's role on the croft has declined with the increasing use of tractors and other mechanical aids, although recent conservation reforms to promote environmentally sensitive farming have gone some way towards facilitating an accommodation of women into crofting once again.[46] But in Shetland crofting has never been a primary or sole form of economic activity, and women especially have always had to combine a number of tasks. Today women are most likely to undertake full- or part-time paid work in the service sector or in the health and education professions, merely helping their husbands with the crofting or treating it as a hobby.[47]

Knitting

Knitting was a life-line for Shetland households. It was a domestic industry that engaged up to two-thirds of all women at any one time – well above the official census figure of around 30 per cent, which most likely included only those women who stated that hand-knitting was their sole occupation.[48] All girls learned to knit at a young age and were producing simple items such as spencers or vests just as soon as they could master the needles. 'Oh we used to knit before you can walk sometimes,' remarked Mrs Laurenson.[49] Katherine Bairnson recalled that she was around six years old when she knitted her first spencers, for which she received 10d each in the years before the First World War.[50] Jeannie Hardie, who lived with her widowed mother and five siblings, recalled the tyranny of hand-knitting for women and young girls. She remembered her mother sitting up until the small hours to finish an item, 'And she wid pit up dis black cloth so dat da neeboors didna see dat she had ta git dees finished. Dat she wis late ta feenish dis hosiery.' When Jeannie herself was old enough to knit she recalled helping her mother. 'Oh whin I wis maybe eight or nine you see. And den later on doing jumpers . . . You see, sometimes I'd be sitting – I'd be a bit older den – and I forget I'd daydream and she wid say, "You're no knitting. Whit's wrong you're no knitting?"'[51] Hand-knitting, then, evokes vivid memories amongst women who regard it as a skilled activity largely unrecognised in the representations of Shetland's past.

Women's hand-knitting was an economic necessity in a place where there were few alternative earning opportunities. For most it was an important supplement to other types of female employment. Few made a living solely by hand-knitting although there were some elderly and infirm women who did rely upon this means of income generation. In the main, it was fitted around other activities on the croft – no woman would ever go out without her 'sock', a Shetland term for her knitting. 'You hed never ta lose a minute. Whin you sat you hed ta have your sock dere ta start on till him, every minute.'[52] Jeannie Hardie from Bressay quickly learned the marginal and insecure nature of hand-knitting. Jeannie, born in 1903, had left the island to work in service in Edinburgh but returned at the age of eighteen to run a croft. Knitting was a non-negotiable part of croft life for women:

> Oh yes, we hed ta hiv time fir knitting. Dir hed ta be a garment or something every week. You hed ta make a point o hivoin dat feenished, regardless o whit wis. So you hed ta hutty up and git up and work ootside . . . Weel ta start wi hit wis usually shawls and dey wid be aboot two an six and if you got hit oot, like if you selled dem in a shop at didna hiv groceries (and you wir needin groceries) den you hed ta leave thruspence ta every shilling. I always shoppped around till you knew exactly wher ta go . . . Da only thing wis, dere wir no steady market for da hosiery! You'd maybe go two weeks and everything wis fine and dey wid be buying dem, and den da next week you wid go and dey hed stopped buying day and dey wir needing something else! And you wid hiv ta ga home and start knitting something else; hit wis a bit precarious! Dere wis no security in hit.[53]

The only time when women could make a decent living from hand-knitting was during the Second World War. A new domestic market of servicemen based on Shetland looking for gifts to send their families and sweethearts, and a thriving demand for knitted goods from clothes suppliers on the mainland, meant that women like Ella Law, who recalled how her mother had said she 'never coulda keepit da hoose goin if hit wisna whit sho made', were never short of work:

> All through the war I was machining for dear life because you could get a good price: that was the only time we made any money. It didn't matter if it was awful good because they were that eager for it. I mind big firms like Marks and Spencer advertising in the Shetland Times for children's jumpers and pantaloons, and me machining it and sending it to London. All of a sudden the war ended and the bottom went out of the hosiery market. There was nothing else you could do.[54]

For the most part hosiery production was a necessary activity, literally to put food on the table, as Nan Paton, who lived with her widowed mother, recalled: 'I had to learn to knit so that we could . . . have a jumper every week to go to the shop to get groceries with.'[55] Indeed, the fact that female recipients of poor relief frequently admitted to earning a little through knitting supports the contention that knitting alone could not earn enough to support a person. A woman who knitted, though, was characterised by the parochial board as 'active' and 'industrious' and thus qualified to receive help, in contrast to those who reputedly did not lift a finger to help themselves. The sub-text visible in the parochial board minutes is that the ability or willingness to support oneself through hand-knitting was a sign of good moral character. It was likely assumed that all Shetland women could knit; hence if they did not they were feckless or lazy.

Unlike knitting elsewhere in the British Isles, knitting in Shetland was not merely a domestic industry for home consumption, nor was it organised in a cottage system. Rather, in these islands knitting was at the centre of a vast and complicated web of economic and cultural transactions governed by the system of barter-truck.[56] And these transactions had a profound effect on women's identity as producers as well as on their relationships with other women. The Shetland hosiery industry operated thus. A women wishing to knit items of clothing such as shawls, vests, socks or veils would require spun wool known as worsted. Raw wool, though, was not an easy commodity to obtain. Some knitters obtained wool from their own Shetland sheep. Those who had cash would buy wool or worsted from the Northern Isles – Yell and Unst – where it was more plentiful. Others received wool in payment for work. Catherine Petrie, who lived on the island of Fetlar, explained to the Truck Commission in 1872 that she sometimes bought wool from a Mrs Smith on the island, or received wool in exchange for work:

> Any kind of household work that they have to do. People employ others to do so much work, and give them wool for it.
> Q: Do you mean work on their farms or ground?
> Yes; and they will give them wool in return, because the wool in Fetlar is so scarce.[57]

The wool was rooed from the animal (Shetland sheep were never shorn) and then cleaned, sorted, carded and spun into worsted of various qualities. Country dwellers commonly carried out these processes within the extended family; indeed, carding parties became the focus for female sociability in the winter. But there were also specialist spinners who bought wool from crofters and sold their worsted to merchants. Those knitters who did not have easy access to wool or worsted – and this applied especially to Lerwick-based women – had to find means of purchasing their raw materials since no merchant would exchange wool for hosiery. Worsted could be purchased only with cash: 'they say it is a money article', explained Janet Irvine.[58] Elizabeth Robertson described to the Truck Commissioners the complicated means by which she acquired wool in Lerwick; a local dressmaker gave her wool or cash in exchange for the credit notes (known as lines) Elizabeth received from the merchant for her finished hosiery:

> She takes goods from me on lines which I get for my shawls and she gives me wool and cash to favour me, because she knows I have no other way of getting money ... When I sell a shawl to any hosiery merchant in the town, I get any sort of goods that are in the shop, except wool to knit with; but if I don't want the goods at the time, then the gentleman will give me a line to the amount

4 Women carding wool inside a crofthouse, with fish drying above the fire, c.1900

I have to get . . . If I go back to the shop with the line, or send anybody back with it, the merchant's servants will serve the party who brings it with the amount.

Q: They will give you full value for it? – Yes, to the full value of the lines.

Q: Then Miss Robertson takes these I O U's from you, and gives you worsted for them? – Yes.

Q: That worsted you knit into shawls, and these shawls you sell to the merchants, getting from them I O U's? – Yes.

Q: Are you any better off under this system than you were before? – Yes. She brings home the wools, and shows me the invoice for them, and I get the wools at what she pays for them. That is much cheaper than I can purchase them for in Lerwick.[59]

Wool, and worsted even more so, was like gold dust because it could be immediately converted into an item to sell. Joan Williamson recalled working on neighbouring crofts to help with raising the peats and sometimes receiving worsted in payment at a time when crofters were sending their wool away to be spun. 'We towt wi wir gotten just a quantity o money, git dis head o yarn, hit wis laek gittin gold. Du sees, dir wis nae, dir wis nae money dan ta pay anybody wi.'[60] Knitters who were employed by merchants received their worsted in advance of knitting particular items for that merchant, and the cost of the wool was deducted from the final sum offered for the finished item. In 1872 Barbara Johnston from the township of Sandwick explained to the Truck Commission how she knitted for Robert Linklater, a merchant in Lerwick. Linklater supplied the worsted, weighing it in advance of Barbara knitting her shawl, and he then weighed the finished item when she returned. He always refused to give her worsted in exchange for her finished goods, and she never had sufficient cash to purchase her own raw materials.[61] Already, then, before she even began to knit, a woman may have dealt with two or three others in a series of barter exchanges in order to secure her raw materials.

Once she had completed knitting a few items a hand-knitter would have to find someone to dress her hosiery. Dressing or finishing involved whitening with brimstone, washing, stretching and sometimes mending shawls, veils, underwear and other knitted goods to prepare them for sale. Hosiery dressing was carried out by specialists who worked independently either for the hand-knitter or for the merchant. Dressers and finishers required payment in cash, sorely stretching some knitters, who rarely had money to hand. 'Sometimes, when my daughters have knitted a shawl', remarked John Leask from Channerwick, 'and it is ready to go to the dresser, there may be no money in the house to pay for the dressing of it, and it has to be paid in money. I have known my daughters detained in that way for some days, until I went to a neighbour and borrowed a shilling to pay for the dressing of a shawl, or until I could sell something off the farm.'[62] Ann Arcus, one of Lerwick's foremost dressers, would advance credit to women who had no cash to pay her until the shawl was sold.[63] Some dressers also sold on the hosiery to merchants for a commission, acting as intermediaries between the producer and the merchant. Catherine Petrie from Fetlar had to travel to Lerwick to sell her shawls there as there were no merchants on Fetlar. She explained: 'When I come down I employ a person to dress the shawls, and then that person sells them for me in the shop, and I get back a note from her, stating the amount in goods that I am to get for them.'[64] This was a system that relied upon co-operation and trust amongst female hosiery workers.

At the core of Shetland's hand-knitting industry was the relationship between the knitter and the merchant. Shetland was dotted with country merchant stores, buying all manner of goods produced in the district and supplying items to the inhabitants. Lerwick stores, on the other hand, tended to specialise in hosiery and drapery and sometimes dry goods such as tea, leaving the supply of foodstuffs to grocers. A hand-knitter had two options if she wanted to find a buyer for her product. She could do business with a merchant, either independently or as an employee, albeit with no formal contract; or she could try to sell her hosiery to visitors, travelling salesmen or people who had contacts on the Scottish mainland. Those knitters who sold their goods independently of the local merchants were more likely to receive cash in payment and may have obtained a better price for their hosiery. Mary Hutchison, who lived in Lerwick, was an agent for a hosiery seller in Edinburgh, and because she paid for goods in cash she was never at a loss for women to knit for her: 'they are anxious to get money'.[65]

Selling to a merchant, on the other hand, was more reliable. One could almost always achieve a sale whatever the quality, character, size or colour of the items, but this involved the producer in a barter-truck relationship with the merchant. Merchants rarely paid cash for goods, a system that was a legacy of the early trading system in Shetland with the Hanseatic merchants and Dutch and German fishermen. Moreover, for much of the nineteenth century most fishermen were engaged to fish for their landlords on a barter-truck basis. Thus truck was commonplace and knitting merely slotted in to this system. By the mid-nineteenth century the barter system was regarded by knitters and justified by merchants as customary. When asked in 1872 why she did not ask for the whole payment for her hosiery in money, Margaret Ollason replied, 'I thought it was the custom of the place'.[66] Similarly Christina Williamson said that she knew she would not get money for her shawls 'because it is not the custom to give it.'[67] Thus, when a woman delivered her hosiery to a merchant she would be offered a non-negotiable price for her product and paid in goods or given credit in the form of a 'line' or IOU. Merchants dealt in a similar way with knitters employed by them and with those who were self-employed. The merchant fixed the price of an item of hosiery, taking into account whether the merchant had supplied the wool and the condition or quality of the item. Neither category of knitter was paid wholly in cash, although it was sometimes possible to receive a small cash payment of a shilling or so. In 1872 Catherine Winwick from Lerwick described the relationship she had with the merchant, Mr Linklater, for whom she knitted on a regular basis.

Q: Are you paid in money? – Some in money and some in goods.

Q: What is your system of dealing? When you go with anything you have knitted to Mr. Linklater's shop, do you put a price upon it? – No; he gives what he thinks right.

Q: He puts the price upon it? – Yes.

Q: Does he pay you that price usually in money? – Part in money and part in goods. He does not pay all in money . . .

Q: Do you get all the money you want? – I always get what money I ask for; but I never ask for all in money. I have asked for a few shillings in money, and I have always got it.

Q: Why did you not ask for the whole in money? – Because he was not in the habit of giving all money for his knitting.

Q: Do you mean that you knew if you had asked for it you would not have got it? – I don't think I would have got it all in money; I never asked him for it all, but I always got what I asked for. If I asked him for a few shillings of money, he always gave it to me.

Q: Is a settlement always made when you bring your work back? – Sometimes it is, and sometimes not. Perhaps sometimes I have something in his hands to get, and perhaps sometimes I am due him a little.

Q: Due him for what? – For anything. Perhaps he might give me something sometimes when I did not have it to get, if I asked him for it.

Q: Did you ever wish to buy your goods at any other place? – No; I could not buy my goods at any other place.[68]

For most of the nineteenth century Shetland was a cash-hungry society. Merchants, especially those in country districts, carried out most of their everyday trade using the barter system. Few customers had cash – any money received by a crofter would go to pay rent or buy necessities – and thus hosiery became a substitute currency for merchants who had to agree to take knitted items in order to sell their goods. In this respect, it has been argued, the merchants were of benefit to the producers in that the former continued to purchase hosiery even when they did not have a market for it. A woman could always find a purchaser. In Lerwick, where hosiery merchants stocked a limited range of goods in their stores, tea and drapery goods as well as credit notes substituted for cash as it was these items that knitters most frequently received in payment for their hosiery. Girls like Cathy Hodge learned early on how to dispose of their knitting:

> I wida been eleven or twal year auld. An I wis nivir selled hosiery in me life . . . but I guid ta Jimmy Smith, he wis wantin dis peerie haps . . . I tink dey wir just fower hanks o wirst in it . . . I gied doon wi did hap an he said whit wis I wantin fur it, and I said . . . weel, Mammy hed no idea whit I wid git fur da hap, you see, and he selled goods . . . An she said tak da wirt o it in tea, tinkin I wid maybe get a pound o tea – an I just cam hame wi a great parcel o tea.[69]

The consequence of this system of payment was that hand-knitters were forced to spend much time and energy turning the payment they received for their hosiery into items they needed or into cash since, as Andrina Murray commented, 'there is many a thing that can be done with money.'[70] In Lerwick especially, a family could not live on tea and drapery goods alone. Drapery goods in exchange for hosiery might keep a woman well dressed – there were numerous, often critical, reports of labouring women regaled in fancy and colourful clothing – but they would not feed her. Elizabeth Robertson explained the dilemma when questioned by the Truck Commissioners in 1872:

> Q: Does this system of not getting money, or being paid in goods, make you buy more dress or clothing than you would otherwise care for? – Yes; I would not need one half the clothes I get, if I could get money.
> Q: That is to say, you would prefer to take the money, and spend it upon food? – Yes.[71]

In order to procure foodstuffs, fuel for heating and cooking and cash to pay the rent, women had to exchange their credit or dry goods into things they needed to live. If a woman did manage to obtain a cash payment she knew the value would be less than that of a payment in goods, usually 3d in every shilling, and therefore many agreed to take payment in kind and endeavoured to exchange their goods for cash elsewhere. Others attempted to achieve a more favourable deal when refused what they regarded as a reasonable cash payment by a merchant. On being offered 1s 4d for a veil by Sinclair's store, the knitter requested she be paid the amount in cash. According to Isabella Sinclair this was refused, 'because the veil season was over; and also I did think that money and goods were the same thing. I said I would give her 1s 1d in money, and she asked if I would give her 1s 2d. I said "No"; I would only give her 1s 1d and she took that and went away.'[72] Knitters were always in a weak position. Merchants rarely needed the items they were buying (with the exception of fine shawls and fancier Fair Isle garments in the inter-war years), and many stockpiled hosiery for months at a time before they found a market in the south. So women's bargaining power was severely limited. When asked whether she could haggle over the price offered for her hosiery, Ida Manson said, 'Weel you could aye say hit, bit you'd git nae mair! I mean you could say whit you wanted! No I niver think dat I tried very aften, I joost took whit I got.'[73]

The dilemma experienced by these women is described by Mary Coutts from Scalloway, who had for many years knitted shawls and veils for Lerwick merchants. Mary lived with a sister, her elderly father and her aunt, and the two sisters were the prime means of support in the household. Despite asking for money, Mary rarely received more than a few pence from the merchant and was paid chiefly in tea and other dry goods from Mr Linklater's Lerwick store. A request for 1s when she needed to pay for boot repairs was refused. In order to obtain food such as meal, potatoes and other perishable goods, the sisters had to exchange tea with farmers. Their elderly aunt would travel long distances to the west side of Shetland to purchase these necessities, and on occasion she had even travelled as far as Papa Stour, an island lying off the west coast and some 24 miles from Lerwick. When asked if they had to barter goods for less than they were worth Mary replied: 'Sometimes, if there had been 2½ yards of cotton lying and a peck of meal came in, we would give it for the meal. The cotton would be worth 6d. a yard, or 15d.; and the meal would be worth 1s. I remember doing that about three years ago; but we frequently sold the goods for less than they had cost us in Lerwick.'[74] Elizabeth Robertson also explained to the Truck Commissioners that she received only soft goods, tea and sugar in exchange for her knitting, so that if she needed meal or bread she was obliged to sell the goods to her neighbours at a loss. 'Any neighbours that knew me would take from me some of the goods I had, and perhaps give them to a country friend of theirs, and get the money for them.'[75] Tea was a common form of currency in Shetland. It could be traded for all manner of goods or it could be sold on for cash. Criticism of women whose 'fondness for tea' was carried to excess, so that 'for the sake of it she knits at all opportunities' resulting in a husband suffering 'by his wife's intemperance, not in spirits but in tea', was misplaced.[76] Margaret Tulloch in Lerwick explained how she made money from selling and making tea for visiting men from the country. She also used it to pay wages: 'When people were working for me, then I had to give them a quarter of a pound of tea in order to pay them, because I did not have money to give them.'[77] Similarly, Catharine Borthwick, who was owed a few shillings by the merchant Mr Sinclair for a shawl, after she had taken the goods she required, also took a petticoat 'to give to a girl who had been working in our peats . . . the girl took it because she knew I could not get the money'.[78] Some knitters used hawkers or other intermediaries to exchange their goods for cash. Elizabeth Morrison from Lerwick vociferously denied to the Truck Commission in 1872 that she bought tea and cloth from knitters to sell on to third parties:

> Q: Did you get that cotton from a woman who had got it for her knitting? – I don't know in what way she may have got it, but I got it from a woman. Who she was I cannot say, because she picked me up in the street and gave it to me.
> Q: Did you get it sold for her? – I did. I don't remember who bought it; it was some country person.[79]

But it was clear that this was a strategy adopted in this cash-poor society.[80]

Other women traded in credit notes. It was possible to find people who would buy a credit note for cash if they wished to purchase items in the merchant's store. Elizabeth Robertson in Lerwick sold her credit notes to a dressmaker and to other acquaintances for money so that she could pay her rent and buy peat for the winter. She also passed them on to dealers in fish and bread, who were happy to exchange the notes in the merchant's store or even pass them to a third party for cash.[81] Elizabeth regularly traded her credit notes, received from the merchant Robert Sinclair, with a neighbour, who stated, 'often I buy from her lines for money, because she is a poor girl and needs money.'[82] The trade in credit notes was still prevalent after the introduction of the Truck Amendment Act in 1887, which made in-kind payments for hosiery illegal. Katie Inkster recalled how, before the First World War, merchants continued to refuse to pay cash for hosiery, so she found a solution:

So I fell in lucky, dey wir a Mrs Hunter at I used ta go upon . . . so she said tae me, she says I'll tell you, gie me yun lines, I'll go tae da shop, my boys is all away sailin an my lasses is no auld enough tae knit, I'll buy me groceries fir your lines an I'll gie you da money. So I got da money fae her. Mrs Clark shouldn't a been laek dat, you ken. She tought if she wis startin laek dat everyeen wid want da same. But Mam, my midder wis aye sending her jumpers too.[83]

Although it was denied that credit notes were traded more than once, it is clear that in the absence of cash Shetlanders would use anything to obtain money, and merchants were not fussy about who presented the lines in their shops.

The implication of women in this complex web of economic relationships centred upon hosiery production challenges the generalised image of women in the nineteenth century as increasingly divorced from the market. In Shetland, women of all social classes, from the poorest hand-knitters to the wives of merchants and independent ladies who dabbled in trading hosiery on the British mainland, were intimately and directly bound up with production, exchange relations and trade. It was said that hosiery had 'enabled the women of the islands to be more independent than women usually are.'[84] Shetland women rarely used intermediaries to trade on their behalf. Indeed, independent trading by women had long been a feature of Shetland society. Some of the earliest reports of Lerwick, dating from in the seventeenth century, comment upon the lively trade between women and the Dutch fishermen who came to the port to trade their fish from booths on the shore. According to one visitor in 1700, 'Stockings are also brought by the country people from all quarters to Lerwick and sold to these fishers.'[85] After a lull in trade and economic decline during the first half of the eighteenth century, the brisk trade in hosiery revived so that by 1774, 'the whole time the [Dutch] fleet lay the country people flocked to Lerwick with loads of coarse stockings, gloves, nightcaps, rugs . . . The country folk are very smart in their bargains with the Dutch; they are now paid in money for everything.'[86] Christopher Thomson, who arrived on a visiting whaling ship in 1820, remarked how 'The women were famous for knitting and were untiring in seeking to make exchanges for their merchandise for articles from England, particularly cotton handkerchiefs and Staffordshire pots.'[87] Thus women had a long history as autonomous traders, but by the nineteenth century they mostly traded with the Shetland merchants instead of visitors. At a young age they became accustomed to producing their own goods and selling them independently. 'I sold my first allover Fair Isle jumper when I was 13', recalled Jessie Sinclair. 'And I still remember, I got £3 for it, which I thought was a fortune, all my own work.'[88] They shopped around to get the best deal for their hosiery. And women travelled extensively to sell their goods. Those who lived outside Lerwick journeyed to the town to exchange their hosiery, either on foot or by boat when long distances were involved. Ruby Ewenson recalled walking ten miles to Lerwick from Whiteness to sell her hosiery.[89] The domestic production of hosiery therefore necessitated that women travel beyond the domestic sphere to trade, to haggle and to deal.

Unlike their sisters elsewhere in textile-producing parts of the country such as the Scottish Borders and the English Midlands, where hosiery had become standardised and was mass-produced in factories or regulated by a system of quality control, Shetland women retained their autonomy as independent producers.[90] They continued to knit by hand at home. Knitting machines did not make headway until the inter-war years, and knitting factories did not make an impact until after the Second World War, although some stages of the production process such as spinning and finishing were moved into factories by the 1940s. Knitting remained a cottage industry in Shetland, with workers contracted to produce at home using their own machinery. Thus Shetland women retained control over what items they produced and the quantity and quality of these items. There was no standardisation of production, to the regret of some merchants who were unable to supply their southern markets with large orders of identical stockings or spencers.

But the corollary of this autonomy was a requirement that women participated in the market at all stages of the production process. And this activity of making deals with spinners and finishers, negotiating with merchants, finding alternative purchasers and exchanging goods and credit notes for cash and everyday consumer items involved women in a wide range of social relationships characterised by reciprocity and, inevitably, tension. Hand-knitting defined women's position in Shetland, for it immediately placed them in a set of relationships determined by the market. The number and types of relationships were determined by the ubiquitous use of truck and barter-truck in these islands from the 1840s onwards.

Hosiery production and the truck system created a kind of shadow economy where goods and credit were semi-openly traded by women (with the connivance of the merchants). After 1887, when the Truck Amendment Act outlawed the practice, they may have become more surreptitious in their actions. Such a system, which relied on verbal agreement and trust, was open to exploitation and manipulation.

Perhaps it is not surprising that some women used the weaknesses in the system to their own advantage, to obtain much-needed cash or luxury goods which could rarely be purchased with hosiery. The case of Barbara Barnson, prosecuted for the theft of stockings in 1864, is typical. Barbara visited a store in Scalloway and asked to view some stockings for a local widow, Mrs Russell. It was not uncommon for store owners to allow goods to be taken from the shop in anticipation of a sale to a third party. Barbara took away seventeen pairs and later returned for more. 'I fancied Mrs Russell had an order from the south when the girl came for the second lot as she then stated that Mrs Russell would take 100 pairs if she could get them', stated the store owner. But Barbara Barnson used the stockings to buy some jewellery from a hawker, who told the sheriff: 'The girl asked if I would take stockings for the balance and I said that I would prefer any money but would take stockings if she could not give me cash.'[91] Hosiery was almost as good as cash in Shetland; there was always someone who would deal in knitted goods. Stealing items to sell for cash was relatively common, possibly on account of the ubiquitous trade in goods for hosiery, which ensured that few would suspect they were purchasing stolen goods from a woman. In 1877 Mary Ratter from Lerwick obtained four pairs of stockings from Anderson's hosiery store in the town, saying that she was to show them to the wife of a grocer with a view to purchase. However, Mary gave them to a cousin, who 'could not give me money for them so I got other stockings and gave them back to Anderson.' She also obtained a muff from another store in the name of her employer. 'I had been working for her and she had been kind to me so I thought I could ask it in her name.'[92] Mary Ratter was working the system to her advantage to obtain cash.

Did the barter-truck system encourage theft, or the illegal trade in goods? It certainly acquainted women with the market; they were familiar with the substitution of goods for money; they habitually traded items, and they used the credit notes from merchant stores as a form of currency. So when Charlotte Robertson owed several months' rent to her landlady Grace Robertson in Burns Lane, Lerwick, Grace suggested that Charlotte speak to her employer Robert Sinclair, who was a merchant in the town, presumably intimating that he might advance her, Charlotte, or even Grace, certain goods that she could sell for cash or exchange. Grace commented that she 'had books with various hosiers in Lerwick and can do as well with goods as with money payments.' Taking her landlady's advice, Charlotte obtained lengths of cloth from the store that she passed to Grace Robertson, who, in turn, made it up into articles of clothing and exchanged these for hosiery from girls who knitted for her. However, Charlotte had stolen the goods from her employer using an intermediary who would go to the store and ask for the items to carry home on approval. It appeared that Grace was implicated in the scam, carrying on a 'traffic in soft goods and Shetland shawls and hosiery', but the system of barter and credit vouchers created a scenario within which it was relatively simple and tempting to operate an illegal trading operation.[93]

In present-day Shetland, hand-knitting constitutes one of the myths about Shetland women. It is remembered fondly for the skill women possessed in the past and the sociability the work engendered. Today, few women still produce genuine hand-knitted items for the market, and those who do, especially those knitting Fair Isle patterns, are able to sell their products overseas for very high prices. Lerwick still has many stores selling Shetland knitted products, most of which have been produced on hand-knitting machines, and Shetland hosiery is one of the key identifiers for the distinctive Shetland way of life. Yet Shetland hosiery is, somewhat akin to peat, another 'material referent' in Shetland society. It is a product which is a sign of the mythic Shetland past and of the mythic Shetland woman. Unlike peat, though, hand-knitting evokes little sentimentality from women, for they are conscious of its alternative symbolism – of exploitation of women's labour and skills by merchants.

Gutting

The female crofter and knitter has an iconic and symbolic status in Shetland, but the female herring gutter is a more ambiguous character who features more rarely in representations of the past. Yet, between the 1880s and 1914, Shetland was transformed by the herring industry, and jobs in fish processing – gutting, curing, salting and packing – employed women in large numbers, albeit on a seasonal basis.

Herring fishing had been prosecuted in Shetland since the early nineteenth century, and the islands were dotted with small curing stations which preserved the fish using the so-called 'Scotch cure': a method of salting and barrelling the fish for export. On the island of Bressay, where there was one large curing station, around thirty women and children were employed there in 1841.[94] In the 1870s and 1880s a huge expansion of the herring fishery took place in Shetland; the number of local boats increased, and boats and curers already active further south moved north to benefit from the early summer herring off the coast of Shetland. By 1885 Shetland was the most important Scottish station for herring landings. More than 900 boats were fishing off Shetland, employing upwards of 5,000 men. There were 123 curing stations located from Baltasound on Unst in the far north to Grutness in South Mainland, employing approximately 3,800 coopers, curers, gutters and packers, the majority female.[95] By 1900 open boats and sail boats were being replaced by steam drifters, which had a much greater catch capacity. By 1905, the peak year for herring landings, more than 9,000 in total (taking into account the possible double if not triple counting of women as they moved from one station to another throughout the season) were employed on the curing stations, with around half located at Baltasound.[96] With the exception of Lerwick and Bressay, the curing stations were seasonal, operating from May until early September.

The curing stations provided an important source of employment for Shetland women, especially young women before they married and those who were born in Lerwick who had few alternatives. Yet the majority of women employed here were not from the islands at all. In 1905 just 195 out of 2,865 women employed in the curing stations on Unst were Shetlanders. The majority hailed from the Moray Firth and east coast ports (1,710) and from the west Highlands and Islands (948).[97] The women were employed in crews of three – one packer and two gutters – for the season of between twelve and sixteen weeks. They lived together in huts at the gutting yards or they took lodgings nearby. Many women started at the curing stations as teenagers and some continued into old age, travelling with the herring down the east coast of Britain as far as Lowestoft each season. More commonly, gutting was an occupation undertaken for a few seasons before a woman married and had children although it was known for widows to return to the gutting to provide an income. It was one of the few ways for a woman to bring cash into the household. Gutters were hired by a curer and usually paid arles – a one-off fee of engagement – and thereafter they were paid piece rates. Agnes Tulloch, who worked at gutting from the age of seventeen at Levenwick before she moved to Lerwick, earned 8d for every barrel and 3d an hour, more than she earned as an assistant teacher.[98] In the summer of 1882 at J. Mitchell, fishcurers of Lerwick, Margaret Cowie and her crew earned £2 1s 4d in a very good week, but their weekly wage fluctuated markedly depending upon the catch and averaged around £1 10s a week.[99] Before 1914, an average weekly wage of 25s was considered reasonable.[100] It was certainly more than could be earned in most other labouring jobs. However, much of the weekly wage went towards lodgings and groceries. What was known as barrel money – the money paid at the end of the season – was taken home.

The work of the herring gutter was hard, dirty and smelly in conditions few outsiders could stomach, at least not the correspondent of an American newspaper, whose description of Lerwick gutters combined disgust with voyeurism:

> The scene was a fish wharf in Lerwick . . . The background was a fishy panorama of red-sailed drifters, screaming sea-gulls, yellow barrels – and fish. The air was fishy. The mud underfoot was composed of blood, salt and fish scales. The herring were everywhere, shimmering in slithering, silvery heaps on the decks of the drifters, coming out of the drifters' holds, being rushed on hand trucks to the gutting troughs to have their throats cut by two rows of blood-stained, scale-spattered, slim-waisted girls. Gutting is a discomforting performance.[101]

The women stood in the yard at long troughs called farlins into which the herring were tipped and roused in salt. They would take a herring, slit its throat with a knife, take out the gut and throw the fish in the barrel. The women wore ordinary working clothes, 'jist any old remnants at you could git', later protected by long oilskin aprons, which soon became

5   Women gutting at the farlins, Gremista, Lerwick, 1890s

wet and filthy. Agnes Tulloch recalled how her father had coated her oilskins with a mixture of black paint and the whites of seagulls' eggs to give them a glossy finish.[102] Their hands were protected with nothing more than pieces of cloth known as cloots to prevent them from slicing into their fingers with the knife and to avoid getting the salt into the cuts. But it was ineffective, as Agnes Halcrow described in graphic terms:

> When you wrought wi da herring, you gutted, then you tied up every finger, in da morning afore you göd oot, roond dem up wi a bit o curtain or somethin, and den tie dem up, and tie den wi your teeth when you couldna use your hands . . . it fairly saved your hands, But sometimes, du kens, da saat would geng in under, and den you'd git saaty holes. Only cure for dat wis ta put dem in a barrel o pickle in da morning. Dat kinda cleaned oot da holes, and oh you had abse on your hands sometimes. It wis just like a peerie cut or scratches, painful, and your hands wir just roasting at night . . . And den you du sees dat saat wis dat sharp it got up under da clouts, da clouts you wir rowed in, and hit made holes, saaty holes. And dere were aa yellow and green mould, dat was da cure, put your hands in a barrell o pickle.[103]

Alongside the occupational hazard of 'salty holes' in the hands was rheumatism from standing for hours outside in the wind and the wet, and back pain from bending over the farlins. Moreover, sanitary conditions were primitive. In 1905 inspectors visiting the gutting stations at Baltasound and Lerwick remarked upon the inadequate sanitary structures placed on the 'sea edge of the yard . . . overhanging the beach' and 'where coopers and others are always working, and fishermen are constantly coming and going': conditions which could only outrage the 'shy sensitive feelings' of the Highland women based there.[104] In Lerwick the one three-seated privy available to the 247 women was occupied by a man when the inspectors called.[105]

The tempo of the work was dependent upon the weight and timing of the catch, so that sometimes crews of women worked all day and into the night, which, of course, was possible in midsummer in Shetland. Prosecutions under the 1901 Factory Acts are evidence of women working much longer than the twelve hours stipulated in the legislation. For instance, in 1914 one fishcurer's firm in Lerwick was charged with having worked a female crew from 4 o'clock in the morning until 7 o'clock in the evening rolling empty barrels from a vessel to the yard.[106]

Working at the herring stations was unlike any other form of work available to women in Shetland. Unlike croft work and knitting, which could so often be solitary, it entailed working in teams amongst many others of their sex. In many cases the women lived away from home.

They mixed with women from other parts of Scotland and further afield and developed a cameraderie that helped them to overcome the privations of their accommodation. They had a lot of fun together; 'we enjoyed wirselves tae the core', recalled Agnes Tulloch.[107] And they were paid in cash. In these aspects, then, this kind of work may have offered women a greater degree of freedom alongside their menfolk, who also operated as relatively free agents in contrast with the fishing-tenure system that had bound so many. Here, as elsewhere along the Scottish east coast, it was precisely these aspects of their employment that prompted unflattering descriptions and concerns for the women's morality. 'The Shetland girls who go to the fishing are, as a class, modest and well behaved. Intemperance is unknown amongst them, and they have a sturdy sense of self respect, and are quite able to keep their own place', remarked the Lady Correspondent of the *Dundee Advertiser* in 1898. 'But, notwithstanding, it is inevitable that a country girl who goes year after year to bothy life for months at a time should have her moral standards lowered and the bloom taken off her modesty.'[108] In contrast to the so-called fishwives, who were frequently depicted as ignorant, rough women who drank and used uncouth language and whose morals were questionable on account of their association with rough men, the gutters were heaped with praise. Unst women employed at the Baltasound stations were said to 'keep to themselves' as they worked in the company of 'foul mouthed' Fraserburgh gypsies and coopers.[109] As in the case of factory workers at the time, their sex was often questioned, for they resembled strange creatures dressed in their odd clothes and spattered with fish entrails.[110] In Shetland, however, local observers and visitors alike went out of their way to distinguish the Shetland gutters from the east-coast workers. In 1902 a correspondent of the *Shetland Times*, responding to concerns regarding the sanitary arrangements at the stations, reminded readers to 'keep in mind that a large percentage of our native workers are girls from the country, of a modest, retiring disposition, who would rather endure much hardship than resort to the unchaste and unladylike ways practised by imported workers.'[111] And even the lady inspectors' report for 1905 singled out the Shetland workers for their 'high standard of conduct, their reticence and dignity'.[112]

In spite of these paeans to the Shetland herring gutter she does not possess the same status in representations of Shetland life in the past as the crofter or the hand-knitter. Somehow, the image of the gutters does not fit the myth system of the fishing-crofting economy. Certainly, the gutters were a temporary feature of Shetland life, but perhaps more significant is the fact that herring gutting was not regarded as intrinsically 'Shetland'. Having alerted readers to the 'scaly mermaids' at the gutting huts, one writer for the *Ladies' Field* magazine in 1907 continued: 'But you will probably prefer to study the Shetland women and girls in that magical twilight . . . when they gather around the public fountain to fill their pitchers.'[113] At the largest stations the majority of gutters hailed from outside the islands, and the nature of the work bore little relation to any experience of work hitherto, with the exception of straw plaiting much earlier in the century. Herring gutters have not, therefore, been appropriated as representatives of a Shetland way of life. Perhaps the sense that these women were challenging traditional Shetland norms – they were working for men, living away from home and doing a job that was quite separate from the domestic economy, engaging in a transient occupation and earning cash wages – has been difficult to square with the dominant crofting narrative which allows women a prominent place in a constrained and traditional space, the croft. Nevertheless, oral testimonies of working at the stations resonate with the same sense of self and of pride in one's work that we encounter in other female employment sectors on the islands. Oral respondents recall in tremendous detail the processes involved in gutting, salting and packing the various types of herring, the conditions at the stations and their herring 'career', whether this was confined to Shetland or extended down the east coast to East Anglia. So while herring gutters as a group do not conform to the ideal type of Shetland womanhood, the gutters themselves express the same kinds of sentiments about female identity as women in other occupations.

Conclusions

The three sectors discussed in this chapter cover the majority of the work experiences of Shetland women. Whilst some worked in other jobs (retailing for instance), the numbers were small. An understanding of women's work patterns and experiences is central to any analysis of women's lives in Shetland and the gender relations contingent upon this. Shetland women were autonomous, independent workers whose day-to-day productive experiences implicated them in all sorts of social and economic relationships outside the home. In contrast with the dominant historical narrative of European women's work in northern industrialising countries, which tells of women withdrawing from agricultural labour at this time, and of the power of the discourses on femininity and domesticity which defined women first and foremost as reproducers whether or not they undertook paid work outside the home,

Shetland women had little choice but to sustain their place in the world of production. In such a marginal economy and in the absence of so many men of prime working age, women became key economic actors throughout the year.

One of the consequences of this situation was that work was central to women's identity throughout their lives from around eight to ten years of age until infirmity or death. This is obvious in the nineteenth-century sources where we hear women's voices, such as in the evidence to the 1872 Truck Commission. It also permeates women's more recent oral testimonies. Women who tell stories of their mothers and grandmothers, as well as relating the details of their own work experiences, do not question the interest shown in their working lives; indeed they regard productive work as central to the identities of Shetland women in the past. Similar patterns in women's oral testimony have emerged elsewhere and have ensured that we are beginning to rethink the assumption that home and family were central to women's self-identity. One of the products of this strong sense of self amongst Shetland women is the appropriation of the image of the economically productive, autonomous woman as a symbol or marker of Shetland identity. The espousal of a system of gender equality within the fishing-crofting household is contrasted with what is sometimes portrayed as a Scottish and even British subordination of women in the home and the workplace. Thus the working woman in Shetland casts a ray of benevolent light on the islands as a whole.

Women's words are the expression of women's consciousness. Whether they speak to us from the pages of evidence presented to a government commission or whether we hear them in an oral history interview, they are the articulation of subjective experiences which are rooted in the material and cultural conditions of their lives. Women's words from Shetland speak to us of economic autonomy in a culture where the discourses of separate spheres and of domesticity had little purchase. In the chapters that follow, the impact of women's identity as workers will be explored in respect of the development of a female economic and moral culture in the islands and in terms of women's access to power.

Notes

1 L. A. Tilly and J. W. Scott, *Women, Work and Family* (London, Routledge, 1987).
2 These models conceal a complex story. See D. Simonton, *A History of European Women's Work, 1700 to the Present* (London, Routledge, 1998); Abrams, *The Making*

of Modern Woman, chapter 8; K. Honeyman, *Women, Gender and Industrialisation in England, 1700–1870* (Basingstoke, Macmillan, 2000). On women's rural labour in England see K. Sayer, *Women of the Fields: Representations of Rural Women in the Nineteenth Century* (Manchester, Manchester University Press, 1996); Verdon, *Rural Women Workers*.

3 Figures calculated from 1861 census return for Shetland. The total of females employed was calculated excluding those described as 'wives', 'widows', 'children and relatives' and 'scholars' as well as paupers, lunatics, prisoners and vagrants.

4 Census, 1901: Shetland.

5 Census, 1911.

6 On the continuities of women's work in Europe from the medieval era to the nineteenth century see J. Bennett, 'History that stands still: women's work in the European past', *Feminist Studies* 14 (1988), pp. 269–83.

7 See Verdon, *Rural Women Workers*, p. 197.

8 On the decline of women's active participation in the formal agricultural economy see Verdon, *Rural Women Workers*, pp. 164–5 and Bourke, *Husbandry to Housewifery*.

9 See D. Smith, *Shetland Life and Trade*, esp. chapter 2.

10 Fenton, *The Northern Isles*, pp. 270–1.

11 SA, SC 12/6/1811/43: Breach of contract, Thomas Ogilvy merchant in Lerwick for John Isbister, straw plait manufacturer in London v Catherine Peterson, servant.

12 SA, D 1/135: *The Scotsman*, 22 Aug. 1903.

13 *New Statistical Account*, vol. XV (1845), p. 4.

14 Fenton, *The Northern Isles*, pp. 64–6.

15 R. L. Johnson, *A Shetland Country Merchant: A Biography of James Williamson of Mid Yell: 1800–1872* (Scalloway, Shetland Publishing Company, 1979), pp. 55–9.

16 See Macdonald, *Reimagining Culture*, pp. 119–25.

17 J. Hunter, *The Making of the Crofting Community* (Edinburgh, John Donald, 1976).

18 Cohen, *Whalsay*, p. 21.

19 SA, D 1/134: *Northern Ensign*, 25 April 1861.

20 SA, D 1/134: *Chambers' Journal*, 7 April 1883.

21 SA, D 1/134: *Ladies' Journal*, 3 Oct. 1891.

22 Cohen, *Whalsay*, p. 100.

23 See *The Rugged Island*, directed by Jenny Brown; *The Work They Say is Mine*, directed by Rosie Gibson (made for Channel 4 television, 1986); J. C. Spence, *Inga's Story* (Lerwick, Shetland Publishing Company, 1988).

24 SA, 3/2/102: Mrs K. Laurenson.

25 SA, 3/1/179: Jessie Sinclair.

26 SA, 3/1/124/3: Katie Inkster.

27 SA, 3/1/103: Agnes Tulloch.

28 H. R. in I. Mitchell, *Ahint da Deeks* (Lerwick, Shetland Amenity Trust, 1987), p. 9.

29 *The Scotsman*, 27 Dec. 1899.

30 Respondent RR quoted in Jack, 'Shetland women and crofting'.

31 SA, 3/1/237: Nan Paton.

32 SA, 3/1/162/2: Agnes Leask.

33 Interview with Agnes Leask.

34 Interview with Agnes Leask.
35 Interview with Mary Ellen Odie.
36 *Shetland News*, 3 April 1920.
37 Interview with Mary Ellen Odie.
38 Interview with Agnes Leask.
39 A comparable situation has been described for rural Iceland in the eighteenth century. See M. Johnson, 'Domestic work in rural Iceland: an historical overview', in N. Long (ed.), *Family and Work in Rural Societies: Perspectives on Non-Wage Labour* (London, Tavistock, 1984), pp. 160–74, here p. 163.
40 *New Statistical Account*, vol. XV (1845), p. 127 and p. 180.
41 Interview with Agnes Leask.
42 SA, 3/2/103/2: Magnus and Helen Anderson.
43 *Irish News*, 24 Feb. 1902.
44 On the romanticisation of crofting and allusion to tradition see Macdonald, *Reimagining Culture*, pp. 101–11. See also Cohen, *Whalsay*, pp. 98–110.
45 Interview with Agnes Leask.
46 Jack, 'Women and crofting in Shetland', pp. 238–59.
47 Jack, 'Women and crofting in Shetland', pp. 117–41.
48 Fryer, *Knitting by the Fireside*, p. 25.
49 SA, 3/2/102: Mrs K. Laurenson.
50 SA, 3/2/109/2: Katherine Bairnson.
51 SA, 3/2/10/1: Jeannie Hardie.
52 SA, 3/2/19/2: Joan Williamson.
53 SA, 3/2/10/1: Jeannie Hardie.
54 SA, 3/75/1: Ella Law.
55 SA, 3/1/237: Nan Paton.
56 See Fryer, *Knitting by the Fireside* for a more detailed description of the various processes and elements of hosiery production, pp. 24–37.
57 British Parliamentary Papers, C (1st series) 555 I: *Commission to Inquire into the Truck System, Second Report (Shetland), 1872*, Evidence (hereafter Truck 1872), lines 1,429–30.
58 Truck 1872, line 117.
59 Truck 1872, line 247.
60 SA, 3/2/19/2: Joan Williamson.
61 Truck 1872, lines 444–9.
62 Truck 1872, line 1,374.
63 Truck 1872, line 1,762.
64 Truck 1872, line 1,435.
65 Truck 1872, line 1,581.
66 Truck 1872, lines 1,907–8.
67 Truck 1872, line 163.
68 Truck 1872, lines 9–20.
69 Cathy Hodge in I. Mitchell, A. Johnson and I. Coghill, *Living Memory: A Photographic and Oral History of Lerwick, Gulberwick and Sound* (Lerwick, Shetland Amenity Trust, 1986), p. 12.
70 Truck 1872, line 318.

71 Truck 1872, lines 284–5.
72 Truck 1872, lines 3,252–3.
73 SA, 3/1/20: Ida Manson.
74 Truck 1872, line 11,605.
75 Truck 1872, lines 236–44.
76 E. Standen, *A Paper on the Shetland Islands* (orig. 1845; Lingfield, Mill Print, 2000), p. 21.
77 Truck 1872, line 1,501.
78 Truck 1872, lines 1,645–7.
79 Truck 1872, lines 15,669–70.
80 Truck 1872, lines 15,637 ff.
81 Truck 1872, lines 257–300.
82 SA, SC 12/6/1871/63: Theft and reset, Charlotte Robertson, 24 Nov. 1871.
83 SA, 3/1/124/1–2: Katie Inkster.
84 SA, D 1/134: 'The Shetland hosiery trade', unattributed, c.1890.
85 Brand quoted in Fryer, *Knitting by the Fireside*, p. 7.
86 Low quoted in Fryer, *Knitting by the Fireside*, p. 8.
87 Christopher Thomson (1820) quoted in Flinn, *Travellers in a Bygone Shetland*, p. 77.
88 SA, 3/1/179: Jessie Sinclair.
89 SA, 3/1/130/1: Ruby Ewenson.
90 Fryer, *Knitting by the Fireside*, p. 37. See also S. O. Rose, *Limited Livelihoods: Gender and Class in Nineteenth Century England* (London, Routledge, 1992) on the hosiery industry in England.
91 SA, AD 22/2/8/22: Precognition – Barbara Barnson, theft, 1 March 1864.
92 SA, SC 12/6/1877/14: Complaint – theft, falsehood and wilful imposition, 1 March 1877.
93 SA, SC 12/6/1871/63: Theft and reset, 24 Nov. 1871; AD 22/2/12/18: Precognition of Charlotte Robertson, 12 Aug. 1871.
94 *New Statistical Account*, vol. XV (1845), p. 16.
95 J. R. Coull, 'The boom in the herring fishery in the Shetland Islands, 1880–1914', *Northern Scotland* 8 (1988), pp. 25–37, here p. 28.
96 Coull, 'The boom in the herring fishery', p. 31.
97 SA, 2/216/9: Factories and workshops: annual report for 1905 (material on Lerwick and Baltasound gutting stations).
98 SA, 3/1/103: Agnes Tulloch.
99 SA, D 1/228/11: Ledger with accounts of 'women's work', etc., 1880–82.
100 S. Telford, *'In a World a Wir Ane': A Shetland Herring Girl's Story* (Lerwick, Shetland Times Ltd, 1998), p. 5.
101 SA, D 1/135: *Chicago Daily News*, Oct. 1927.
102 SA, 3/1/103/2: Agnes Tulloch.
103 SA, 3/1/154: Agnes Halcrow.
104 SA, 2/216/9: Factories and workshops, 1905.
105 SA, 2/216/9: Factories and workshops, 1905.
106 *Shetland Times*, 14 July 1914.
107 SA, 3/1/103: Agnes Tulloch.
108 SA, D 1/135: *Dundee Advertiser*, 9 Sept. 1898.

109 SA, D 1/135: *Newcastle Daily Journal*, 4 Aug. 1897.
110 Nadel-Klein, *Fishing for Heritage*, pp. 83–4.
111 *Shetland Times*, 4 April 1902.
112 SA, 2/216/9: Factories and workshops, 1905.
113 SA, D 1/135: *Ladies' Field*, 21 Sept. 1907.

5

Culture

The thing that was unusual was that the women were in among
things. That was the unusual thing. They bwirna supposed to be.
(Shetland Archive, 3/1/123: John Gear)

T HE EXTENSIVE NATURE of everyday intercourse between women
in Shetland spawned complex sets of relationships. Women's
prominence and independence in the world of work, their
residential groupings and their mutual reliance on one another in the
context of a high male absence and death rate resulted in a high degree of
female solidarity governed by codes of behaviour relevant to women's
culture. Shetland men were mobile, coming and going between land
and sea, but women's day-to-day lives were conducted within a tighter
framework of responsibilities and expectations in the township and
in Lerwick which, in turn, were influenced by demographic circumstances, economic conditions and cultural assumptions. For much of
the nineteenth century Shetland was a matrifocal or woman-centred
society where women possessed much autonomy, where they had some
economic independence and where their labour was valued.[1] Women's
economic authority gave them a considerable degree of decision-
making power.[2] And this meant that women possessed their own
behavioural codes to govern their relationships.

Female culture in Shetland was characterised by a combination of
solidarity, reciprocity and self-preservation. Solidarity and reciprocity
were essential for survival in a harsh economic environment, and
self-preservation was inevitable when resources – men, raw materials,
foodstuffs, cash – were hard to come by. A woman was, potentially,
always in a vulnerable position at every stage of the life cycle. Whether
she was young and single, middle-aged and married or elderly and
widowed, she spent much time with members of her own sex at work

and at leisure and she depended upon them for economic and emotional support. Yet at times she could be isolated, even marginalised by her sisters if she stepped across the boundaries of acceptable behaviour or if she became a liability. Women's culture is what happens amongst women of all generations in their day-to-day dealings with one another. In the realms of the home, the workplace, the street and the hill, women established codes of behaviour which governed everyday intercourse. Reputation was the foundation for all other transactions and activities which were played out around understandings of solidarity, trust and vulnerability and were cemented through female sociability and women's belief in traditional lore or superstition.

Shetland women established their reputation in two ways: through their engagement in the economy and as moral actors. The Shetland islands are distinctive within the western European culture of women for privileging the economic over the moral. Women were so vital to the economy of the islands that they were vital to each other's personal and family economy. Women relied on each other to an extraordinary extent. This made judgement of each other, of their reputation, primarily (although not exclusively) an economic judgement. Moral or sexual reputation was arguably secondary. A woman's economic reputation was hard-won, and a woman's sense of self, her identity, was driven by that economic imperative to an extent that historians have rarely acknowledged in other cultures. The driving force of both the Shetland economy and its society was the culture of the female economy.

Collectivity

In his anthropological study of the Shetland island of Whalsay in the 1970s, Anthony Cohen describes how the community's sense of collective self was expressed through a number of activities undertaken by men. The mutual reliance of the fishing crew, the self-recruiting 'clique' that was the football team, the parties known as sprees with a core membership of male drinkers, and work on the croft all contributed to the creation and maintenance of a set of boundaries – between the island community and the outside world and within the community itself – shaped by male association.[3] Similarly, Reginald Byron and Paul Thompson, writing in the 1980s, construct a typology of Shetland society which is focused upon male solidarities around fishing and the distinctive characteristics of the Shetland male at home.[4] Thompson argues that Shetland men helped with the children and the domestic tasks and exhibited a gentleness within the family in contrast with the more oppressive Calvinist attitudes to be found in other island communities.[5] Both Cohen and Thompson represent Shetland in terms of its relationship with the sea and as a masculine place. The male bonding of Cohen's community and the gentle fishermen described by Thompson serves to delineate the markers of a fishing community. Thompson is alert to the important role played by women in fishing communities. However, by focusing upon the activity of fishing and thus underplaying the more mixed economy of Shetland, he interprets women's role solely in terms of their relationship with the fishing and within the family and thus fails to see how female culture might have had an autonomous character.[6] Jane Nadel-Klein, in her study of Scottish east-coast fishing communities, also represents women as primarily defined by those communities. Although she recognises that the stereotype of the fishwife is a mythical creation, she fails to investigate the more complex and exterior cultural world of women in such communities.[7]

Anthony Cohen's study of Whalsay introduced symbolic anthropology to the study of European marginal communities. He can be criticised for giving little attention to Whalsay women. However, his typology may be applied to women's culture in Shetland in the nineteenth and early twentieth centuries. Certain activities undertaken by women, and often only women, may provide an insight into this female world of solidarity, reciprocity and self-preservation. Cohen describes fairly well-defined and discrete male bonding opportunities in work and leisure, but for the historian of Shetland women it is more difficult to identify concrete organisations or communal activities through which we can observe women's construction of a cultural community. With the exception of herring gutters and, for a short period at the start of the nineteenth century, straw plaiters, women did not work in teams. Collective working on the croft was spasmodic and seasonal depending upon the nature of the tasks to be carried out. Most hosiery production was undertaken at home, although memories of carding and spinning parties persist. Women's relationships with one another were governed primarily by domestic concerns. By this I mean ensuring family survival through reproduction and production. But there were occasions of female collective working and mutual reliance, and, as we have seen, women maintained complex relationships with other women centred upon hosiery production, crofting and everyday relations characterised by the exchange of goods and services. With the exception of the gutters, fishing as a work activity was not at the heart of Shetland female culture as it was for many men, and yet fishing and men's reliance on the sea were what facilitated and even necessitated this distinctive female world.

Solidarity

Historians and anthropologists have often characterised maritime
societies by their strong sense of solidarity and mutual obligation.
Fishing required collaborative teams, that is men who were shareholders
in a fishing boat or, in the case of Shetland, were contracted to a
merchant to fish for him for the season.[8] Cohen, in his study of Whalsay,
exemplifies this approach. He describes the fishing crew as 'the
community-at-sea' and the structures and values of the community as
embedded in the fishery.[9] Gender relations, in his view, are determined
by the vicissitudes of the fishery. The roles of women bend according
to the requirements of the fishing industry; they shift from complementary workers in the nineteenth-century subsistence economy to
unpaid housekeepers in the 1960s and 1970s and finally to part-time
workers in the late twentieth century with the expansion of the fish-
processing industry.[10] There is little sense in Cohen's study of Whalsay
of an autonomous culture amongst women or even any acknowledgement of female autonomy. The solidarity of the male crews is seen to
transmit to the community even when they are away for long periods: 'a
daily flow of news between the boats and the island . . . enables the ties
of family, friendship and community to bridge the physical distance
and to sustain a sense of physical distinctiveness.'[11]

However, as Byron explains in the case of Sweden, the organisation
and work rhythms of fishing crews do not always determine the culture
of the land-based community. In Sweden the absence of men at sea for
weeks, months and sometimes years at a time left the management
of the household and croft and day-to-day social intercourse to women.
Because income from the fishery was not sufficient to support a family, women were obliged to engage in production. In Byron's words,
'making ends meet required that women ally themselves with others to
enlarge the pool of labour available to them.'[12] Owing to the inherent
instability of the fishery from one season to another, households had
to use their resources in flexible ways, the result being a 'consociation
of elementary families'. Each household lived as an independent
unit under one roof but engaged in production, consumption and
distribution with others.[13] Similarly, as Brettell argues for a Portuguese
community where large-scale male migration left women to tend the
farms, the pooling of resources amongst neighbouring households
in order to carry out labour-intensive work at certain points during
the year was an appropriate strategy which helped to cement bonds of
neighbourship.[14]

It has been observed for maritime households in the North Sea region (which includes Sweden and Norway as well as Shetland), where fishing and crofting were not viable alternatives but necessary adjuncts, that women's roles were so pluralistic that they had to rely on other women in order to maintain a functioning household.[15] Visitors to Shetland expressed surprise at the ubiquity of 'servant girls' on poor crofts: 'It was surprising to me that they could get them; and secondly that they could support them', commented the Revd Catton, who visited in 1838.[16] But here, where the demographic imbalance was so marked, there were always females available for domestic tasks, and households required extra hands. 'Dey wir always wan or two, possible, maiden aunts an old folk at mair or less browt up da bairns', recalled Nina Charleson from Yell.[17] Indeed, a woman who did not have extra help around the house would have struggled to manage her productive and reproductive roles. Hosiery production, croft work and domestic and childcare chores were not compatible, especially in the busy summer months. 'Dey wida needed till a been wirkin braaly anxious at it an probably maybe been anidder woman ida hoose fur I couldna see a hoose wi wan wife ida hoose doin dat, alang wi aa da rest o her wark', commented Joan Williamson.[18] Mrs Laurenson, who lived in Delting and whose father was away for long periods at the fishing, remembered how her widowed grandmother lived with her parents along with her mother's unmarried sister, who was 'a great baker and a splendid housewife . . . you would say the very core of the house. She baked the best cakes. Knitted all the hearthrugs and kept the house clean and always had a fire on, everything was happy when Aunty Meg was there.'[19] Netta Inkster had two great aunts on Yell who never married: 'There was just a lot o women that never married but who would more or less stay at home and work around the croft and do the work and probably look after elderly parents and all things like that.'[20]

One of the consequences of the demographic imbalance, combined with the ubiquity of fishing-tenure and the narrow range of alternative employment options for women, was the vulnerable position of older unmarried women and widows. It was extremely difficult for an elderly or infirm person to survive alone despite the existence of a sense of community obligation to these women. Mary Ellen Odie recalled how those who had nobody to fish for them were provided for:

> I can distinctly remember hearing the men at the beach when they came ashore with the fish em . . . just to give everybody their share plus somebody who didn't have somebody to fish for them. And I can

remember the Schollay lasses [three single sisters] they were called lasses because they were elderly, the Schollay lasses, I can hear my grandfather shouting that out, Schollay lasses, so I can see too that they parted the fish em they were usually in the baskets that they got the fishies . . . but I can mind seeing the Schollay lasses' fish with a different kind of container and then we had to deliver them. So they did that and that was how many people survived, there but for the grace, that had been a provision for a long time. That's how women survived really because they had to do it, that was their insurance too. They wouldn't want to get old and not be able to [go to] the fishing.[21]

Ruby Ewenson from Weisdale on the Shetland mainland also recalled a story told her by her grandmother:

I'll tell you aboot an old person dat wis here in Weisdale, but I don't know her name and I couldn't tell you where she belonged to, that was a true story for my old grandma knew her when she was young. She said she had nothing . . . she went round all the places. Some gae her a few tatties and some wid gie her bread and some wid gie her a coarn o mael you ken. Some wid maybe gie her an egg.[22]

Of course many of these older women were incorporated into the homes of their sons and daughters or formed households with unmarried kin, often sisters or daughters. Some appeared to manage well, like the eighty-one-year-old widow Marble Jamieson, who lived at the quaintly named 'seaside cottage and shop' on North Yell with her unmarried daughter Margaret, aged fifty-four, who was employed as a retail grocer.[23]

Female-dominated households usually had to adopt a variety of strategies to manage the domestic chores and the croft work and to generate income in the form of goods or cash. It is sometimes difficult for the historian to recreate the character of everyday, mundane transactions which enabled women to get by. Some historians of working-class urban communities have utilised police and court records but these are likely to present a picture characterised by strife and competition for resources, whereas autobiographical and oral narratives more often evoke a spirit of solidarity and reciprocity amongst households in the past.[24] A similar dichotomy can be drawn in Shetland. The records of sheriff court cases are full of verbal and physical strife amongst women in the context of the competition for resources such as peat, wool, potatoes and even shellfish, as in the case of the widow Isabella Halcrow and her daughter Mary Moncrieff, who were accused of breach of the peace and assault whilst allegedly violently dispossessing Margaret Irvine and her young son of the shellfish they had been gathering on the beach at Houlland, Trondra.[25] But oral memory narratives paint a rosier picture of community mutual reliance. When asked whether there was much evidence of women 'getting together and helping one another' on the croft, Agnes Leask evoked a romantic image of female solidarity as an element of an idealised past:

> Oh yes, yes, oh yes, dat wis very much da way it wis done in dose days – an if you saw a neighbour wis getting behind, well you'd finish your own work, and you'd all, jist da whole family, wid go in block ta da neighbour . . . An heavy jobs, lik buildin da haystack an things lik dat, you'd build mebbe say dat folks' haystack wan day, an den dey'd all come over an build for my folk da next day . . . But unfortunately dat deys hev passed.[26]

Communal working was a reality and a necessity at a time when croft work was unmechanised. Women were regularly seen in groups of three or more delling. Tommy Goudie remembered his grandmother and three grand aunts 'dellin da yard, fower o dem side by side'.[27] Another task commonly undertaken by groups of women was peat raising and flitting, that is bringing the peats down from the hill. Women worked at the peat bank, filling the kishies which would be carried down by ponies or on their own backs. Much of the work at the peat bank was carried out on a community basis, each household being helped to bring in its own fuel and each family being obliged to send a girl to each peat-raising. Jeannie Hardie from Bressay recalled spending her summer holidays at the peats, 'go up ta da hill curing and wirking da peats and den ta barrow dem doon.'[28] As late as the 1960s, peat casting was still carried out on a collective basis. In Netta Inkster's family on Yell in 1969 the peat cutting began in April and was not complete until 28 May. Through May and June neighbours made frequent trips to the peat bank to raise the peats. On 24 June they began to bring the peats down to the roadside in wheelbarrows, and by 17 July the baskets of peats were being moved from the road to the barns and shelters next to the houses.[29]

But community reciprocity had its limits. Most women worked because they needed the money rather than out of a sense of community obligation, and they undertook croft work for payment. Agnes Halcrow recalled her mother doing anything she could to make a living:

> Yes, yes. I'll tell dee, my midder wis maybe ootside da school wi a kishie on her back, at four o'clock waitin for wis tae come oot. An den sho had a bit o bread in da kishie, an den we'd walk fae dere until da North Hill, an wi da paets – fur maybe eight or nine o'clock. An den we'd walk home again. An whan it wasnae da peat hill, it was da taetie

rig you hed ta go tae: an hoe an haep him . . . an den me an me middere wid go ta Outnabrake, an gadder corn an stook, an wark wi neeps an anything we could do – an hit wis dat little money at you got, you needed ta geng. Dere were a lok o' dem [women with babies] hit wis just a trend o livin denedays, du sees, you jist hed ta try ta do something if you could.[30]

When Agnes herself left school she worked at the herring stations in the week and went to the peat hill at the weekend for 2d an hour. A rather different picture of female work relationships emerges from this evidence. By hiring themselves out as labourers for cash wages women engaged in a different set of relationships from those governed by reciprocal obligation and mutual aid.

Although not deriving from Shetland, the autobiography of Christian Watt, born in 1833 into a fishing family on the Moray Firth coast of the Scottish mainland, provides an insight into the changes that affected her community and her family as a result of the shift from white fish to herring fishing. The herring fishing, which reached a peak along the east coast of the British Isles in the 1880s, was run as an industry. It required thousands of shore workers to gut, salt and pack the fish in a number of ports from Shetland in the far north to Lowestoft in the south. For Watt, although this new industry offered women the opportunity to earn money wages, it was also uncertain and exploitative for, as she explained, 'you could not barter herring for dairy produce the same way as you could do with white fish . . . times were now geared to put all the profit into the curer's pocket . . . In truth we had been robbed of our independence.'[31] In Shetland it is likely that a similar situation applied, although here the desire for cash payment may have outweighed the uncertainty of working for a fickle employer. In Shetland two images emerge from the oral testimony of former herring gutters. On the one hand women recall the hard work, the poor pay, the uncertainty of the work and the recognition that they were positioned in a quite different working relationship from what they had been used to. The women were taken on in teams of three and paid arles at the start of the season, which, as Barbara Williamson remarked, 'sorta binded you ta da employer'. Thereafter they were paid per barrel and their earnings were dependent upon the tonnage of fish landed. 'We just got whit barrels we could gut, you know . . . An sometimes, you know, dey wirna a great lot o herring . . . Sometimes we'd be idle oh, a day sometimes.'[32] On the other hand, almost without exception, women recall the camaraderie that existed amongst the herring girls. It was common for women from the same township to travel to the nearest herring station – be it at

Baltasound on Unst, Lerwick, Bressay, Sandwick or Levenwick. Agnes Halcrow from Scalloway worked in a team with her two sisters in Lerwick; the three of them worked during the week, stayed in primitive huts at the quayside provided by the employers, and went home for the weekend.[33] But such was the demand for gutters that women travelled from all over the islands to the stations and from further afield, mostly from the east-coast fishing towns and the Western Isles. 'Dere were a fine jolly crood', recalled Agnes Halcrow, 'Eens cam fae sooth at mixed wi Shetland wimmin . . . Got on like a hoose on fire.'[34]

The female solidarity and camaraderie of the herring station was of a different nature to that in the township. The latter was borne of a need to co-operate to achieve the necessary tasks and to make ends meet, whereas at the herring station the teams of gutters lived and worked continuously together for wages. At the end of the season the team would disperse, whereas in the township households had a continuous existence separate from work. This meant that the solidarity of the township was a complex phenomenon whereby networks of reciprocity centred upon work were influenced by multiple factors beyond the economic.

Trust

Historians of nineteenth- and twentieth-century urban working-class communities have argued strongly that female culture was characterised by reciprocity. When economic and material resources were stretched, women pooled their skills, their limited goods and their time, they lent items in the expectation of return, they did a favour in the knowledge that their goodwill would be reciprocated.[35] Minding a child and lending a twist of tea or a piece of coal for the fire were acts not merely of kindness but of good neighbourliness and community preservation. However, these actions were predicated upon certain shared assumptions and areas of communal agreement and trust. In Lerwick and in the countryside, Shetland women operated similar reciprocal systems interlaced with the complex trading and work relationships that characterised their everyday lives. Failure to adhere to the unspoken rules of fair exchange or a breach of trust was destabilising in such a fragile community. Reputation – for fair dealing, for good work and for a respectable demeanour – was a central element of reciprocal trust.

In the crowded lanes of Lerwick, where scores of women sought to work in a variety of domestic trades, with hosiery production, sewing and laundry work chief amongst them, access to and use of limited communal land was an important advantage. Drying-greens and bleach-fields were essential resources for those who made their living servicing others. So in June 1864, when five women residing near a well-used bleach-field at North Hillhead reported stolen a number of linen and clothing items they had placed there on trust, there was understandable concern. Clementina Paton, who had lost a petticoat, a bedgown and a shift, having placed them on the field at six o'clock one evening and expecting them still to be there the following morning, stated that she had 'no particular reason to suspect anybody of having stolen the [items] but I have heard that Janet Robertson, residing in Quendale Lane, a person of suspicious character, has been seen in the neighbourhood of the park on the night in question and had been seen washing a petticoat which she had not previously had possession.'[36] Subsequently it was discovered that another local resident had purchased a shift and a petticoat from Janet Robertson, who had claimed the clothes were her own and that she was selling them 'from necessity'; 'she was in great need and forced to do it'. What does this common everyday case of theft – and thefts from bleach-fields were fairly common – tell us about women's culture in Lerwick? It tells us that the use of open bleach-fields was governed by trust, and that strangers who were not part of the reciprocal network were likely to be placed under suspicion. The police officer made short work of tracing Janet Robertson's complicated exchanges of the stolen goods in the Lerwick stores accustomed to dealing in second-hand clothing.

In the kind of female economy operating in nineteenth-century Lerwick, women were seeking to make a bare living from servicing other women's domestic needs. The close living conditions and the informal employment arrangements meant that the opportunities for theft were legion. Margaret Paton had been the washerwoman for the fairly well-to-do Sinclair family in Lerwick for some years when in 1865 she was accused of stealing a variety of items, from various pieces of bedlinen to children's clothing, pocket handkerchiefs and a bolt of cloth, many of which were clearly labelled as belonging to the Sinclairs.[37] Margaret Paton, the wife of a tinsmith, made numerous excuses when accused, but it was clear that she had taken advantage of her privileged long-term relationship with the Sinclairs, of the trust which they placed in her and of the proximity of her dwelling to the Sinclairs' garden. Margaret Mann, another Lerwick washerwoman, was equally promiscuous in her choice of property to steal from a client, which included four nightcaps, a pair of man's drawers, two aprons, a bed gown and numerous other clothing items.[38] These women took advantage of the relationships of trust upon which Lerwick women working in an informal economy depended.

In the culture of barter-truck promulgated by the hosiery merchants in Lerwick, we can see something of the wheeling and dealing carried out by women practised in the art of trade. The informal, even casual, system operated by merchants relied upon their own and their assistants' knowledge or trust of their customers. Not all merchants kept passbooks for their knitters. The complex system, described in Chapter 4, permitted many abuses, and it also provided a ready-made network for those who wished to exploit it. Thus, when Catherine Laing and Mary Duncan audaciously stole a large cut of beef from a back close off Commercial Street in Lerwick, they knew who to approach to sell it on. Firstly they went to a baker's wife, Margaret Calder, who was accustomed to buying fish and meat from one of the women and offered her a piece of meat. Margaret Calder balked at the price of 2$\frac{1}{2}$d per pound and bartered with the girls, who offered her the whole if she paid them 17d, which she did.[39]

In such a marginal economy as this, an economy of 'limited good', where the interests of the individual can often be advanced only by damaging the interests of one's neighbour, possession of a good reputation or good name becomes vital.[40] Amongst women in Shetland reputation assumed two guises: economic and moral. Moral reputation was based upon female chastity and respectability, and we shall pursue this in more detail in Chapter 6. Economic reputation incorporated issues of credit-worthiness and honesty in financial dealings and in the trade of goods and services. In Shetland, where so much of the economy was based upon barter, and where women were centrally implicated in the exchange of goods on a daily basis, one's reputation for probity was a valuable asset. So when Marion Bearnson from Dunrossness called Janet Aitken a 'theif [sic] in the presence of several reputable witnesses and immediately thereafter adding that she was H[...] Smith's theif that she the petitioner rooed a ewe of his and stole the wool', Janet Aitken was rightly concerned for her character as an honest woman because 'she will still be believed to be a theif until the contrary is proven.'[41] Wool, as we have seen, was a valuable commodity to women; it had to be purchased with cash, which few possessed. The theft of wool was common amongst women (along with the theft of other essential items such as peat and potatoes), but for women in the hosiery trades, who were dependent upon a whole series of exchange relationships with suppliers and sellers, their reputation as honest dealers was not to be risked, hence Janet Aitken's attempt to restate her good name by suing for defamation in the sheriff court.

Vulnerability

Shetland women like to remember a past characterised by self-help, neighbourly reciprocity and community solidarity. This collective memory of the crofting community serves to bolster a myth of the past which acts as a framework for the construction of individual memory. The crofting past carries such weight of meaning and symbolism for Shetland identity that individual experience that does not fit neatly with this collective construction of the past may be suppressed.[42] Even memories of hardship are often balanced by comparisons with what the respondent regards as easy conditions for folk today. Agnes Halcrow, who was born in 1901, described in detail the privations of her child-hood, the physical labour undertaken by her mother and her experience working at the gutting stations and on farms. The work was extremely hard and poorly paid but Agnes explained, 'you jist hed ta try ta do something if you could . . . You did onything ta hae a living – get twartree shillings. Denadays. But noo dere no caring . . . We aa wrought tigidder an pat it in ta da family.'[43]

Testimonies like this draw our attention to the very real hardship experienced by Shetlanders. There were limits to the extent to which kin and neighbours could extend support to the most vulnerable members of the community. The marginal conditions for survival within which most working women struggled meant that the resources at any woman's disposal were finite. Women's applications for poor relief are testament to the limited means of particularly elderly spinsters and widows and of their neighbours and kin. Sixty-two year-old Agnes Leask, for instance, applied to the Lerwick parochial board for relief in 1868. She had formerly been employed as a farm labourer but now that she was unable to get employment – probably because of her age – her resources were limited to a few potatoes 'planted in bits of ground received from her neighbours for work in spring' and some peats on the hill.[44] All-female households were especially vulnerable when relying solely upon a small croft and income from hosiery. The produce from the croft was never sufficient to see a family through twelve months, even in a good year, leaving what Mary Ellen Odie described as the 'hungry gap', a time when the destitute had to find food wherever they could. Mary Ellen's widowed great-grandmother had to resort to catching starlings for food, 'And they cooked limpets and whelks and all that.'[45] A woman who could be 'useful' to her family or neighbours could engage in reciprocal exchange of services or goods, but there were many whose 'usefulness' was limited on account of their age and their feeble state of health. Rheumatism and arthritis affecting the hands particularly afflicted women who had been used to earning a pittance from their knitting.

Those women who made their income from knitting were the most likely to become paupers, reliant on poor relief. Such was the fate of the seventy-year-old widow Margaret Laurenson from Cunningsburgh. We are privy to her plight because in 1891 she went to the Lerwick sheriff court in an attempt to force her son Adam to support her at a rate of 4s a week. Margaret had been widowed some fourteen years previously. Her husband had been the tenant of a croft called 'The Wilmin' rented from the landlord Bruce of Sumburgh, but upon her husband's death the stock was sold and the proceeds divided between herself, her son and the creditors, and conflicts had arisen between them over access rights.[46] Margaret had struggled on as a crofter with her two unmarried daughters, Helen aged thirty-seven and Joan aged thirty-two, until she was served with an eviction notice by the landlord. The circumstances in which these three women were living were described by Helen:

> [my mother] is not able for outdoor work or for indoor work owing to her infirmities . . . One cow is promised to a neighbour who advanced money for the rent . . . My mother could not subsist without help from me and my sister. I have been very ill for four years with chronic bronchitis . . . My sister Joan does most of the work on the croft. We have had to hire help for ploughing, cutting grass and peats and cutting and building the corn and hay and carting the peats. I have not worked at curing stations for five years. Sometimes I am too ill to knit and when I could knit I have to help my sister. I have not earned above two pounds a year recently. We have a pauper lunatic as boarder, 73 years old, for whom we get 5 shillings a week. He is of no assistance to us and we have no profit after paying for his keep. Last Martinmas rent is not paid and we are due a little for meal and groceries. We were able to sell nothing last year. The year before we sold a foal for seven pounds . . . We have had to buy meal and oilcake. Last year I paid twenty two shillings for cartage. What we all make together is not sufficient to support us. It would take almost all we have to pay our debts.[47]

Margaret's son Adam was a fisherman-crofter, married with six children. He had a part share in two fishing boats but his wife suffered from chronic bronchitis and thus was unable to work. Adam could not go to sea for any length of time as he would have to pay for hired help on the croft. His croft was close to the sea and therefore not very productive. In the previous year his potatoes were inedible and he had to buy in all his flour. The sheriff in the case ruled that despite Margaret Laurenson's desperate position Adam Laurenson was not able to support his mother. This was not the end of the story, however. Despite being threatened with eviction and failing in her attempt to get her son to support her, Margaret managed to come to an agreement with the landlord, and she and her daughters continued to reside at 'The Wilmin' with the help of paltry contributions from the poor fund. Margaret Laurenson died in 1897 aged eighty-three, but her fighting spirit was clearly inherited by her daughters, who continued to battle with the landlord and the inspector of the poor. The sisters were determined to stay on the croft and avoid admission to the poor house. In 1898 after a visit from the poor inspector he reported: '[Helen] lives with her sister in a littleworth house. She is unable to provide for herself and she demands to be provided for by the Parish. Has been offered the Poorhouse but emphatically refuses it'. In 1903 there was another attempt to evict the sisters from the croft, but again they managed to stay put. In 1907 Helen was finally admitted to the poor roll, which meant that she received a regular weekly payment, and it seems the sisters struggled on like this until they died, Joan in 1916 and Helen in 1923.

The Laurenson case is unusual only for the degree of visceral antagonism demonstrated by the parties in dispute. Support from kin was not always forthcoming. Unmarried women rarely had children to whom they could turn. Widows with adult children could not always rely upon filial attachment to see them through their old age, as Margaret Laurenson discovered. And even those fortunate to receive some help from family were still expected to help themselves. Typical was the case of fifty-six-year-old Robina Goudie, whose husband had died some twenty years previously and who received only occasional financial contributions from her three sons, all of whom were living in South Shields. When she applied for poor relief in 1868 she had in the previous ten weeks received 5s from one son and 10s from another. Her application was refused on the grounds that she was 'certified capable of doing such work as persons of her age may be expected to do'.[48] Eighty-three-year-old Ann Tulloch's predicament was worse. Since the death of her husband, Ann had shared her home with her daughter and son-in-law. 'But instead of receiving any kindness or consideration from them she says they shamefully ill treat her – threaten to kick her and order her out of the house.' Such was her distress that she was forced to take refuge with a nephew. In October 1895 Ann Tulloch applied for poor relief to the Dunrossness parochial board and was refused. Three further applications were also refused, all on the grounds that her daughter had the means to provide for her, despite Ann's assertion that she was forced to 'crawl about among the neighbours and get a mouthful here and there to keep her from actual starvation'.[49]

Cases of destitution like these were not unusual and go some way towards dispelling the myth of a society in which mutual aid, especially amongst kin, was unselfish and unconditional. When economic conditions are marginal, self-interest or self-preservation wins out over reciprocal support. Every individual of working age had to be useful. 'Usefulness' was a category used by poor relief officers but it also had a resonance in the day-to-day lives of poor families. In 1862, Barbara Brock, aged sixty, was residing with her son-in-law in Lerwick 'in whose family she is useful', and Innes Henderson too, a forty-six-year-old spinster, was said to be 'useful about her brother's family and earns share of food'.[50] As long as she could earn a little through her knitting or could mind younger children a dependent female could be accommodated. An elderly woman (or man, although few aged dependants were male) who outlived her usefulness to her family became a liability. This was the plight of the sick and disabled such as Jane Leslie, a seventy-five-year-old widow from Scatness, debilitated from bronchitis and rheumatism, whose son-in-law, with whom she resided, refused to support her saying that he 'had enough to do to support his own family'.[51] Unfortunately, in cases such as this, relief was generally refused, highlighting a tension between the assumptions made by the parochial board regarding the obligations of family and kin to support their members in need and the reality of life on the edge.

An alternative reading of these cases would ascribe a different motive to the refusal of kin to come to the aid of elderly dependants. Parochial boards were always on the look-out for those who tried to defraud the system. One ploy said to be adopted by single women was to remove themselves deliberately from their place of residence with relatives, claim they had been thrown out, and then, with no independent means of support, claim relief. It was claimed that Christina Jamieson from Levenwick had done just this when, in 1868, having lived with the family of her brother-in-law for twenty years, 'she had chosen to remove to a small hut, and as soon as she had done so, she applied to the Inspector for relief'. 'This was often the case', argued the Dunrossness poor inspector, 'with many of the single women who try to get a house for themselves, and then they try and get on the Poor Roll'.[52] But such were the constraints on the relief system that only those in desperate need and of good character were granted support.

The elderly and infirm were undoubtedly the most vulnerable in this society, but unmarried, deserted or widowed women with young children could test community support to its limits and still fall by the wayside. An unmarried mother who could not support herself and her child would apply for poor relief (before 1845 to the Church of Scotland kirk session, and after that date to the parochial board). Invariably, she would be pressed to name the father of the child in order that he could be pursued in the courts for child support or aliment. The records of 227 aliment cases heard in the Lerwick sheriff court between 1800 and 1890 probably represent the tip of the iceberg in terms of the true numbers of unmarried mothers with children to support. Only when the father refused financial support or was in no position to pay would a woman be eligible to apply for poor relief, and even then her fate was decided by the subjective judgement of the inspector of the poor. In urban parts of Scotland unmarried mothers risked being separated from their children under a law of 1884, on the grounds that freeing a mother from the responsibility of a child would enable her to find work. In Shetland this policy was not implemented but the plight of the single mother was just as trying, especially as parochial boards were not inclined to take into consideration the near impossibility of combining adequate paid work with the care of young children.

This was the plight of Christina Inkster, or Kirstie Caddel as she is more widely known, whose case has already attracted the considerable attention of historians and popular writers.[53] Kirstie Caddel was found dead in Lerwick in January 1855. She had died of destitution, cold, hunger and sickness. The events leading to her death were in one sense commonplace amongst women in Shetland at that time. She was born and brought up at Sullom, Northmavine, and followed 'the common avocation of a Zetland girl'.[54] At the age of twenty-five she married a local man and, with their first son, set up home on a small croft. Two years later the family decided to move to Lerwick, probably owing to the severe poverty they experienced in the hungry 1830s. They took a rented room and, while Kirstie spun and knitted, her husband went to the herring fishing. In September 1840 Kirstie was widowed when her husband died along with the crew of thirty boats in the fishing disaster of that year. Kirstie, now expecting her second child, found cheaper lodgings and tried to make a living making hosiery. At this point her fortunes plummeted. Her younger child died of smallpox, she repeatedly moved lodgings, she began a relationship and had another child with a man called Jarm Caddel whom she never married, and from 1841, having been refused poor relief in Lerwick because she was judged to have had a 'settlement' in the parish of Northmavine, she became dependent upon the kindness of strangers and what she could scrape together by her own exertions, which included the theft of clothing and bedding from the drying-greens of the town.[55] During her month's imprisonment for this crime her children were boarded out with a local woman.

Upon her release from gaol she was in a worse position than before. She became pregnant once more, and the father of the child died before it was born. When she applied for poor relief in 1846 she received a number of interim payments before the Lerwick parochial board decided she was able to support herself. Out of desperation Kirstie took the board to the sheriff court to appeal against its harsh decision. The hearing exposed the claims of the poor inspector as untruths – that she was a beggar and that she had refused to take work when offered it – in the light of the testimony provided by the denizens of Lerwick who had, in small ways, offered help when she and her children were destitute. Kirstie had never asked for charity, but numerous landlords had not pursued her for unpaid rent, neighbours had allowed the children to warm themselves by the fire, others had stored her few items of furniture or given her clothes for the children. In Kirstie's defence it was stated that:

> want of employment partly and inability in part to accept it, and at the same time care for her children have now reduced her to a state of perfect destitution. She has lately lain with her infants on the public roads and streets of the town and is only able to provide a shelter for them at present over night from the commiseration of private individuals. She has no prospect before her unless relieved either for herself or her children but death from want and exposure.[56]

Kirstie won her case and was placed on the poor roll. However, in the years that followed she was forced to engage in an increasingly bitter struggle with the new inspector of poor, who was seemingly determined to remove her from the roll. In the summer of 1854, when Kirstie and her daughter were sick, the family was evicted and thereafter lived in Church Lane on the street, begging for food and shelter. When neighbours grew tired of the family squatting at their stairhead, Kirstie found refuge in the Lerwick town house, and it was there that she died on 20 January 1855. The meagre support her neighbours were able to provide was not enough to save her.

Kirstie Caddel's story can tell us much about the plight of the destitute in Lerwick in the mid-nineteenth century, but the use of her case in popular discourses on Shetland life in the past may also be revealing. On the one hand she may be regarded as a victim of the punitive system of poor relief and of one man's unsympathetic and even vindictive attitude. On the other hand her story is testament to the strong sense of responsibility amongst Lerwegians for this desperate woman and her children. Yet her ultimate fate indicates the limits of community support in a society where the majority of labouring people were themselves struggling to survive. Kirstie Caddel stands as an icon of Shetland womanhood in many respects. Her experiences of widowhood, single motherhood, poverty, migration to Lerwick and the difficulties of combining paid work with child care were common in Shetland, and her story illustrates women's vulnerability in a fishing-crofting economy.

Kirstie Caddel's was not an isolated case. Her plight and her tenacity in seeking to improve her position through the courts were mirrored across Shetland. Women were not averse to defending their interests, in court if necessary. In 1847 Grizzle Duncan took the Delting parochial board to the sheriff court to plead her case for adequate relief. She was thirty-two years old, had three children under the age of five and was recently widowed. Her husband had rented a small farm but the produce from this had hardly been adequate to support the family.

> His protracted sickness had increased their difficulties so that upon his decease the few cattle and other trifling effects of which he was nominally possessed were scarcely adequate to discharge his sickbed and funeral expenses, arrears of land rent and other small debts contracted during his illness. Nothing was left for the applicant and her three children but a small parcel of corn, their bed clothes and a few household utensils of very trifling value. Having thus no cattle, and being totally unable otherways to retain possession of her husband's farm, the applicant was compelled on his decease to resign it of the landlord and cast herself and her children for a time upon the benevolence of her friends and the public. [57]

The family was living temporarily with Grizzle's sister but had been asked to move on. The youngest child required constant care and thus Grizzle was unable to find employment. Friends and neighbours were unable to provide shelter to the family 'owing to the inconvenience of affording the necessary accommodation in their small crowded huts, and the apprehension no doubt of entailing a farther burden upon means of subsistence too scanty to guard against destitution in their own families.'[58]

In a situation of scarce resources there was inevitably competition for those resources. Fuel (peat and wood), staple foodstuffs (potatoes, turnips, meal), raw materials (wool), shelter, cash and of course men were all in short supply for most of the nineteenth century. Women's access to all of these resources was limited. The commonest response was for women to adopt flexible strategies. They formed complex, multi-generational, often female-dominated households; they engaged in complicated exchange relationships to gain essential domestic items; they took advantage of cash-earning opportunities and they supported one another when they were able. But as the cases of Margaret Laurenson, Kirstie Caddel and Grizzle Duncan illustrate, the culture of the female economy had its limitations.

Sociability

So far the culture of Shetland women has been defined largely in terms of work experience. Such is the power of the discourse of the working woman in Shetland, that research agendas and women's own memory frames tend to be dominated by the language and experience of work. Women's social world is much harder to discern. Historians and anthropologists have found it easier to identify sociability within communities of men, in part because male work patterns have tended to be collective (the fishing crew is a good example) and because men have tended to spend their leisure time together in public. In Shetland, for instance, two totemic occasions for amusement – the spree and the festival of Up-helly-aa – are male-dominated events shaped by work and kin allegiance.[59] In contrast, until recently female employment has not been associated with collective ritual, either within or outside the workplace.[60] Moreover, nineteenth-century discourses on woman's ideal role situated her within the home, in opposition to public forms of amusement which were deemed a threat to family life. Thus female sociability has often been located by historians in spheres in which women might acceptably gather in groups: at wells, at communal wash houses, in church, at family life-cycle events. Implicit in this literature is an acceptance that women's sociability differs from that of men's in that it is centred upon family, kin and neighbourhood, that women do not identify leisure and amusement as discrete experiences in their lives separate from work and that women's choices are governed by notions of respectable behaviour.

In Shetland women's numeric preponderance, their role in the public world of work, their tendency to cluster in female-dominated house-holds and their emotional needs at times of tragedy all combined to create a context in which there were numerous opportunities for sociability. Indeed, we should not underestimate the degree to which women's culture was centred upon female-dominated occasions for collective conviviality. In the rural townships, in the absence of centres of amusement, women regularly gathered in one another's houses in the evenings for carding and knitting parties. 'Denadays, in mony ways, you hed ya make your enjoyment among yourselves', explained Harriet Robertson from Burra Isle; 'dere wis far more friendliness among da people dan dere is noo . . . If he wis a moderate night we took wir knittin ta ony hooses we wanted an opened da door an dey wid a said "lass, cum du in, foo ir you aa keepin? An foo is sic an een dat wisna weel?" '[61] Carding and knitting parties were almost certainly important occasions for mutual female support as well as the exchange of information. In fact, although a woman would always take a piece of knitting with her it is hard to escape the conclusion that the activity was an excuse for sociability rather than its *raison d'être*. 'We gied out at nights an we'd tak wir sock [knitting] wi wis dan wid maybe knit for a start', remembered Elizabeth Malcolmson. 'You never gied ooy at night withoot your sock, you just aye took your sock wi you whin you gied' – a practice that survived late into the twentieth century.[62] Carding parties provided an environment for the development of friendships amongst women, which could be as important as kinship ties and even on a par with marriage relationships, as these were often intermittent if a husband spent long periods at the fishing, or short-lived in the event of his death at sea.[63] However, carding and knitting evenings could also mutate into mixed parties for women and men: 'We wid caird fir da wool wis all done, generally maybe aboot half past ten, maybe eleven o'clock . . . and den dey wid come an dey wid sit doon and have dis tea and dan when dat was all cleared up then they made ready and cleared da floor. Dan da boys wid come . . . dey wid come fir da dance you see . . . And dey wid dance maybe fir three o'clock.'[64] 'It was sex and knitting and some spinning,' recalled Mary Ellen Odie. 'The boys came and they all stayed the night in this house.' In her mother's words, 'We worked as hard as we could and then we played as hard as we could.'[65]

In the rural townships organised amusements and diversions were relatively rare, which may explain the apparent eagerness amongst women to attend religious events. During the course of the nineteenth century Shetland was visited by numerous preachers and missionaries intent on evangelising amongst the needy of these benighted islands. By the end of the century there were Methodist, Baptist, United Presbyterian and Congregationalist churches, mostly in Lerwick but also scattered throughout the rural areas.[66] Moreover, the congregations were predominantly female. This is perhaps not surprising in a place where men were often away, but feminine piety was a feature of nineteenth-century cultural life in western Europe generally. The women's eagerness for religion was noted by John Lewis, a Methodist missionary from Lancashire who visited Shetland in 1823. On 1 July he recorded in his diary: 'Preached in the island of Brasa from Peter 3:9 the house full of women most of them hugely affected and wept abundantly whilst I showed the long sufferings of God towards them. May the impressions be lasting. All the women were without bonnets or hats healthy and pleasant looking the men were all in the Fishery.'[67] And the missionary Adam Clarke remarked upon a similar experience on Yell in 1828. His service, held in an unfinished chapel, attracted many women who 'had walked a distance of 4, 6, 8 and even 12 miles' in their bare feet in addition to two boat loads of women who had travelled by sea.[68]

It is fair to suppose that dissenting church missionaries and preachers during the early part of the century may have exerted greater appeal to women than the Church of Scotland and Free Church. One practical explanation for the popularity of services taken by itinerant preachers was the relative scarcity of churches in the rural parts of the islands. John Lewis estimated that he preached to five or six hundred people out of doors at Hoswick in May of 1824.[69] And when the Quaker Sarah Squire visited in 1835 she encountered a similar enthusiasm for her meetings. The meeting in Lerwick 'was crowded to excess, very many could not get in, and my mind continuing to feel an engagement to have another meeting, and with more particularly another class of people, a meeting was held this morning at 11 o'clock, which was well attended.'[70]

Another interpretation is that these travelling preachers were treated as itinerant entertainers. This certainly appears to have been the case in Sandwick in 1879, when the appearance of an American Mormon provided light relief at a time when, according to the *Shetland Times*, 'the sameness in this district is such that we are afraid our readers at a distance will be getting tired of our repetition'.

> The gentleman spoke in the open air upon a lawn called the 'swine-green', where the people tether their swine when they wish to give them the air. The men had just left for the fishing the same evening so that with the exception of two or three his audience were women who did not appear to appreciate his remarks, so much so that he did not hold another meeting, but went on in the direction for Dunrossness . . . we rather think our Shetland lasses will prefer the

rocky shores of their fatherland to the Salt Lake of America, and that he can save himself the trouble of making known to them his views of 'Mormonism.'[71]

One explanation of the popularity amongst women of visiting evangelical preachers, particularly in the early part of the century, was the contrast they posed with the moral and disciplinary stance adopted by ministers of the Church of Scotland and the Free Church (after 1843). It seems likely that some women were alienated by the harsh attitudes towards sexual offences displayed by these churches and their lay members through the kirk sessions, particularly when it was the women who took the full brunt of their moral punishment. Another reason was the disapprobation heaped upon women who consumed alcohol at a time when male culture amongst the labouring classes was, to a significant degree, lubricated by alcohol. Drink was widely available in the rural areas as well as at the herring stations and more especially in Lerwick, and some groups of women were singled out for their unrespectable habits. In 1809 it was the straw plaiters who were described by Arthur Edmonston as 'a number of girls unrestrained by the example, and removed from the protecting care of their parents' who soon assume 'habits of vice and extravagance'.[72] Herring gutters, similar to the straw plaiters in terms of their assumed independence and their receipt of cash wages, were tarred with a similar brush, with one temperance reformer alleging they had three glasses of whisky a day.[73] Respectable women did not drink. 'Da wimin niver drank, you sees. Dey tocht hit wis affil', commented Harriet Robertson.[74] 'If a woman was on the booze that was very peculiar, do knows. And tane tae, aabody widda kent aboot her.'[75] To be a woman who drank in public was to forfeit one's reputation as a trustworthy and respectable member of the community.

But it would be wrong to locate female sociability primarily in the churches, notwithstanding the interest aroused by travelling preachers. Religion certainly offered a physical space for women to gather together, and from the 1840s in Lerwick it also provided a springboard for numerous organisations concerned with temperance and moral recreation, such as the Women's Guild, the Girls' Friendly Society and, after the First World War, the Band of Hope. But the 'popular puritanism' of evangelical culture expressed in respectable recreation was not a substitute for more hedonistic or individualistic recreational activities which might have offered women a pleasurable and less judgemental space for sociability. In fact any girl who 'made a mistake' was excluded from the respectable organisations. 'They were supposed to be there to unite the women and to try to lift them up if they were down', remarked Katherine Bairnson, 'but it seemed to me to be the wrong thing if a girl had made a mistake to ban her from being a member.'[76]

Female-only sociability had its limits. Though carding parties and other social gatherings offered women an important source of female companionship, young women especially sought out occasions where they might meet potential husbands. Some met at country dances, but weddings, which often involved the whole neighbourhood, offered another opportunity for matchmaking, as John Gear explained:

> The weddings, there wir nae country halls in those days you see and the weddings came in here [Lerwick] an wir held in da Rechabite or in da Masonic. Well if that wedding was comin in, that country weddings was goin to have a mass of lasses and a very few chaps you see. And it was quite a regular thing for the Lerwick boys tae geng tae the wedding. Wirna invited or anything, just gied tae da wedding, you see . . . And were always welcomed . . . you were just there for the dance and for that you were welcomed and the girls were very glad to see you because that meant they were goin to get a better evening too, you see.[77]

Superstition

Finally we should consider the place of superstition and belief in the culture of women in Shetland. From readings of the folklore literature one might expect the realm of superstition and folklore belief to be a central element of female culture in the islands. Implicit in the writings of Shetland's most well known folklorists, such as Jessie Saxby and the Revd Biot Edmonston, is the assumption that folk belief (and especially belief in the fairies or trows) was a feminine phenomenon.[78] Moreover, evidence from oral history narratives and written archival sources ascribes both belief in the supernatural and the practice of alternative healing and cures to women. Those who were known as traditional healers were invariably wise-women, and their customers too were predominantly female, largely because wise-women tended to specialise in female complaints. Yet we should take care not to draw easy conclusions from this evidence for, as historians of folk beliefs and of oral narratives have suggested, stories about trows, about cures and spells or bewitchments, are often metaphors for something else. Telling a story or a traditional narrative is not in itself evidence of belief in the details and events narrated. Thus the stories about trows recorded by Edmonston and Saxby may tell us little about people's actual belief in trows and their powers and more about popular understandings of man's relationship with the environment or about popular moralities. Certainly, although late nineteenth-century Shetland intellectuals were keen to preserve knowledge of traditional folk belief which they feared was disappearing, other forms of evidence suggest a much more pragmatic approach to superstition and folk belief.

It is often assumed that women were closer to the spirit world than men. Women's reproductive role, their experience as pregnant women and as mothers, made them particularly vulnerable and thus placed them closer to the world of the spirits – of fairies and changelings.[79] A woman who had just given birth had to be protected in the event of the trows stealing away her baby; new-born babies that did not thrive were described as 'trow-stricken bairns'.[80] In a time before the medicalisation of pregnancy and childbirth, women sought to understand and take some control over their bodies by carrying out certain superstitious practices, by wearing amulets or good-luck charms and by allowing themselves to be protected from harm by a community of women which would include wise-women or healers. Women were also responsible for the health and well-being of family members (and valuable animals too), and this may explain why they were slow to abandon 'irrational' beliefs in charms, amulets, fairies, witches and spells and the use of folk remedies. In the absence of a medical service the use of traditional cures and the use of charms could be a rational response to uncertainty and vulnerability. As late as 1896 one commentator was sufficiently confident to suggest that 'perhaps there are even now, aged women who combine the preservation of this kind of knowledge with practices of witchcraft.'[81]

In Shetland there is little doubt that superstition or folk belief was still a significant feature within women's culture, maybe as late as the 1890s. The oral testimony of Mary Manson discussed in Chapter 2 suggests not only that seeking a cure from a wise-woman was an acceptable practice amongst the female community in the 1880s, but that the memory of this recourse to popular healers like Unst's Merran Winwick was still sufficiently respected in the 1980s for Mary Manson to tell the tale of her mother's journey to fetch a cure without need for explanation. Indeed, her narrative begins with a reference to the practice widely known as 'cast of the heart':

> This cousin of theirs took ill and . . . and they had a thing, I mind
> . . . ran their hearts does do mind?
> R.J. Casted a da heart.

> Yis, yis, casted the heart, and all this, I don't know what it was buit it
> was some sieve set on their head and boiling lead poured in till it,
> and if it set in if it formed, if it cam a form o' a heart then they had
> tea wear this around their neck and drink the liquid at cam aff o'
> dis for many days after that . . .[82]

Mary Manson's interviewer clearly had knowledge of the practice of casting the heart. Indeed this particular folk cure is widely dispersed in the literature. It is referred to by Samuel Hibbert in his *Description of the Shetland Islands* of 1822 thus:

> The charmers, who still exercise their profession, find stolen goods,
> and cure diseases. One practice familiar in former times is still known.
> It has been long a popular belief, that when any person is emaciated
> with sickness, his heart worn away; this is attributed to the agency of
> trows. The patient then seeks out a cunning woman, who, with several
> mystic economies, melts some lead, and allows it to drop through an
> open sieve into cold water. If an image, bearing some faint resemblance
> to the heart, is, after a certain number of trials, produced, it is an
> indication that the charm has been successful; but if no such figure
> appears, it is a sign that the decay of this organ is irremediable.[83]

And Hibbert refers us both to a 1644 account of witchcraft in which the practice is alluded to, and to a novel by the Lerwick author Miss Catherine Campbell in which she details the ceremony by which the wasting of the heart was cured. Casting the heart was also described by the minister of Sandsting in the *New Statistical Account* of 1841 and finally by Jessie Saxby in her *Shetland Traditional Lore* published in 1932.[84]

It is impossible for the historian to unravel these threads in order to separate out the intellectual from the popular. Modern scholars may be misled into assuming that intellectual representation mirrored popular belief. In the nineteenth century some educated observers almost made it their business to expose what they regarded as the misguided practices and beliefs of the common people, and it is in this spirit that we should read the minister of Sandsting's comments on the superstitions of his parishioners in 1841 when he remarked that:

> superstitious observances are not confined to the men only, their wives
> also share in them, and even carry them to a greater extent. These are
> practised chiefly, in attempting to cure diseases in man and beast,
> or in taking away the 'profits' of their neighbour's cows; that is, in
> appropriating, by certain charms, to their own dairy, the milk and
> butter which should have replenished that of their neighbour.[85]

Modern Shetlanders still retain the knowledge of superstitious or folkloric practices, partly from stories and customs passed down through families and partly as a result of the conscious telling and retelling of Shetland's heritage. But there is a degree of ambivalence expressed when someone is asked to speak about such things. Agnes Leask, when asked about superstitions and cures, spoke with great authority of the beliefs associated with fishing, crops and the weather but referred to them in the past tense: 'Speaking aboot beliefs, da folk believed a lok in kinda cures. I suppose kinda superstitious cures . . . folk wis far mair superstitious den as dey are noo.'[86] With reference to the numerous superstitions associated with fishing she commented: 'Oh, dey were some o da aulder men at wis very, very superstitious.' Agnes admitted that as a child she had absorbed knowledge about certain superstitious beliefs and cures. The story of the sick calf which could not be cured by conventional means but which responded when the young Agnes applied the Venck or cat to the animal is told not as evidence of the efficacy of folk belief in the curative properties of cats, but as an illustration of how past superstition can now be explained using rational argument. 'Actually, I mean looking back, anybody'd believe in . . . could've believed it was the cat, well it was the cat that cured it because the cat put its claws in the calf and made the calf [make] that extra effort.'[87] Harriet Robertson, interviewed in 1986, could describe in some detail the various folk medicines and superstitious practices common in Burra, but Harriet herself maintained a sceptical attitude. 'I heard somebody saying aboot dis trowie-folk dat dey heard dem playin – da trowie folk playin! [laughs].'[88] Jessie Sinclair was keen to distance herself and her family members from superstitious beliefs:

> I don't think any o dem would like ta admit dat dey were superstitious. I don't think they took hairs from the coos tails ta take da luck from somebody else and that sort o ting – that was done I believe. This is said ta be tru – this happened in Trondra: it wis 2 old ladies that lived together, and when dey sold a coo dey pulled a few hairs from the cow's tail before dey gave her over to da new owner, ta keep da luck. Our people never did anything like dat. But I don't think that any fisherman could say that he was without superstition. Certain people dey didna want ta meet when dey were set out on dere way ta da boat – dat sort o ting. And of course turn the boat the wrong way was a terrible thing ta do – you must turn the boat with the sun. Course nearly everybody does that just naturally. [89]

On the subject of trows she was even more categorical: 'mother had a lot of stories that she had been told when she was a child – of course it was all trows . . . I don't believe in trows.' Shetlanders appear to have reached a situation of amused tolerance for superstitious practices. When asked by an interviewer, 'And what about meeting a woman on the way to the boat?' (a well-known sailors' superstition), Magnus and Helen Anderson replied: 'Oh yes, yes. A woman – or a Minister. Try to keep clear o' em! . . . No, no, we paid no attention to that at all.'[90]

Folklore and superstition are part and parcel of the memory of Shetland popular culture of the past, and one element of this is the knowledge that female culture tolerated superstitious and healing practices. But, notwithstanding the presence of wise-women like Merran Winwick – 'a wife at could cure everything' – and the stories that have survived about her healing skills, by the nineteenth century narratives about trows and folklore customs appear to have operated more as cultural survivals. Folk healing and traditional lore did not define women's culture in Shetland. They were a part of everyday life, practised as a defence against hardship and malevolence, invoked in times of trouble.

Conclusions

This chapter has argued that women's culture in Shetland actually had only a marginal connection to the islands' dominant economic activity – fishing. Women's interests stood apart from men's. There was a stand-alone female culture in which women created networks founded upon their work and sociability. It was their economic autonomy that empowered a cultural autonomy. The result was that Shetland women's culture was fiercely located outside the home and outside the orbit of the domestic values that prevailed elsewhere in most of Britain and Europe.

The discourse of the crofting past through which present-day Shetlanders are apt to formulate their memories, tell their stories and interpret their history produces a somewhat rose-tinted picture of women's reciprocity. Certainly, in marginal economic conditions, co-operation was a more sensible survival strategy than conflict, but competition for resources meant that the basis of co-operation and mutual aid was conformity to a set of rules, rules established by the community of women. According to Byron and Chalmers, the women of the fishing communities of east Fife experienced a conflict between the 'ideal and the practical, what women wanted and what they had to settle for'.[91] In nineteenth-century Shetland self-preservation was a means of resolving the tension between the desire to be mistress of one's own household and the continuous struggle to gain access to the resources that would permit this.

Since the Second World War economic changes in Shetland have impacted upon women's relationships with one another. The rise of a wage-earning economy and the decline of crofting and hosiery production, alongside changes in residential patterns and welfare support, have reduced the need for a culture of mutuality amongst women. Moreover, since the 1970s, when many communities expanded with the arrival and settlement of workers and their families from the mainland of Britain, female reciprocity and sociability have become a divided experience, operating amongst newcomers and indigenous Shetlanders but rarely between them. For instance, in a study carried out in Dunrossness in 1979 examining the impact of industrial development (oil and the airport at Sumburgh) on social cohesiveness, it was found that Shetland women continued to adhere to a belief in fundamental distinctions between men and women, and that they met on a regular basis to talk and knit in each other's homes. Incomers, on the other hand, many of whom were partners of young professionals, experienced social isolation. In their former lives they had been used to socialising outside the home, and the morning shopping trip had been regarded as a social event, 'an opportunity to meet socially with people other than one's neighbours on neutral ground.'[92] In Shetland, these women felt 'cut off from the social world around them', either because the opportunities for mixing simply did not exist or because they did not feel welcomed into existing female networks. For instance, it was remarked that in the Scottish Women's Rural Institute there were 'closed circles of Shetlander women and closed circles of incomer women who seldom mix with one another.'[93]

Shetland in the twenty-first century is no longer a matrifocal society. The substantial economic and demographic shifts over the course of the twentieth century, and more especially after the 1960s and 1970s, have effected a transformation in women's roles which is still ongoing. Women still play a major role in the island economy at all levels – in 2001 58 per cent of women aged sixteen to seventy-four were in paid employment, significantly higher than the Scottish average of 49 per cent, although a higher percentage of Shetland women were in part-time work.[94] However, the distribution of female employment across the various sectors has altered dramatically. In 2001 just over 3 per cent of working females were employed in agriculture and fishing, whereas health, social work and education accounted for 36 per cent.[95] The diverse nature of their work roles, the ascendancy of the wage-based household and the decline of the croft and of the fishing industry have meant that there is less impetus for gender-specific activities and behavioural codes and less need for the values of co-operation, reciprocity and trust.[96] In a vital way it is the disappearance of those old nineteenth- and twentieth-century structures of economy, demography and culture surrounding Shetland women that raises the representation of them to new heights of importance. It is the context of change that gives a greater potency to present-day discourses on mutuality and reciprocity in Shetland women's culture.

Notes

1 Brettell, *Men who Migrate*, p. 265. This term has also been applied to Galicia and Malta; see J. Boissevain, 'Towards a social anthropology of the Mediterranean', *Current Anthropology* 20 (1979), pp. 81–93.

2 See Cole, *Women of the Praia*, pp. 43–4 for the application of this argument to the maritime households of northern Portugal.

3 Cohen, *Whalsay*. For a similar emphasis on male collective working and sociability see R. Byron, *Sea Change: A Shetland Society, 1970–79* (St John's, Newfoundland, Institute of Social and Economic Research, 1986).

4 P. Thompson, T. Wailey and T. Lummis, *Living the Fishing* (London, Routledge & Kegan Paul, 1983), pp. 336–42; Byron, *Sea Change*.

5 Thompson draws an explicit contrast with the Isle of Lewis. See Thompson, *Living the Fishing*, pp. 336–48.

6 Thompson, 'Women in the fishing'.

7 Nadel-Klein, *Fishing for Heritage*, pp. 51–92.

8 See Byron, 'The maritime household in northern Europe'.

9 Cohen, *Whalsay*, p. 145.

10 Cohen, *Whalsay*, pp. 173–5.

11 Cohen, *Whalsay*, p. 175.

12 Byron, 'The maritime household in northern Europe', p. 282.

13 Byron, 'The maritime household in northern Europe', p. 284.

14 Brettell, *Men who Migrate*, pp. 157–63.

15 Byron, 'The maritime household in northern Europe', p. 279.

16 Revd James Catton, *The History and Description of the Shetland Islands* (1838) in Kendall, *With Naught but Kin*, p. 68.

17 SA, 3/1/37/1: Nina Charleson.

18 SA, 3/2/19/2: Joan Williamson.

19 SA, 3/2/102: Mrs K. Laurenson.

20 Interview with Netta Inkster, 9 April 2001.

21 Interview with Mary Ellen Odie.

22 SA, 3/1/130/1: Ruby Ewenson.

23 Census, 1881: North Yell.

24 E. Ross, 'Fierce questions and taunts: married life in working-class London, 1870–1914', *Feminist Studies* 8 (1982), pp. 575–602; E. Ross, 'Survival networks: women's neighbourhood sharing in London before World War One', *History Workshop* 15 (1983), pp. 4–27; E. Roberts, *A Woman's Place: An Oral History of Working-Class Women 1890–1940* (Oxford, Blackwell, 1984).

25 SA, SC 12/6/1868/60: Complaint, breach of the peace and assault, 2 Oct. 1868.

26 SA, 3/1/162/1: Agnes Leask.

27 Tommy Goudie in I. Mitchell et al., *Living Memory*, p. 7.

28 SA, 3/2/10/1: Jeannie Hardie.

29 Interview with Netta Inkster, 19 March 2002; Mary Manson's diary, 1969 (unpublished), courtesy of Mrs Netta Inkster.

30 SA, 3/1/154: Agnes Halcrow.

31 D. Fraser, *The Christian Watt Papers* (Edinburgh, Paul Harris, 1983), p. 70.

32 SA, 3/1/99: Barbara Williamson.

33 SA, 3/1/154: Agnes Halcrow.

34 SA, 3/1/154: Agnes Halcrow.

35 See Ross, 'Survival networks'; Roberts, *A Women's Place*.

36 SA, AD 22/2/8/7: Janet Robertson, theft, 10 June 1864.

37 SA, AD 22/2/8/65: Margaret Tait or Paton, theft, 21 Oct. 1865.

38 SA, SC 12/6/1881/31: Margaret Mann, theft of clothing, 4 July 1881.

39 SA, AD 22/2/1/23: Precognition, Mary Duncan and Catherine Laing, theft, Feb. 1853.

40 G. M. Foster, 'Peasant society and the image of limited good', *American Anthropologist*, new series, 67:2 (1965), pp. 293–315.

41 SA, SC 12/6/1803/43: Petition anent defamation, 16 Nov. 1803.

42 On the ways in which personal accounts draw upon collective memory see A. Thomson, 'Anzac memories: putting popular memory theory into practice in Australia', *Oral History Journal* 18 (1990), pp. 25–31.

43 SA, 3/1/154: Agnes Halcrow.

44 SA, CO 6/7/32: Record of applications for parochial relief, Lerwick, 1857–69, 4 Sept. 1868. This Agnes Leask is not to be confused with the oral history respondent of the same name.

45 Interview with Mary Ellen Odie.

46 For more detail on the history of this case see G. Johnston, 'Widow Laurenson of Da Wilmin', *The New Shetlander* 221 (Hairst 2002), pp. 55–8 and G. Johnston, 'An inspector calls: poor relief in Cunningsburgh before and after the First World War', *The New Shetlander* 227 (Voar 2004), pp. 16–22.

47 SA, SC 12/6/1891/45: Laurenson, aliment, 1891.

48 SA, CO 6/7/32: Record of applications for parochial relief, parish of Lerwick, 1857–69, 8 June 1868.

49 SA, CO 6/5/14: Record of applications for parochial relief, parish of Dunrossness, 1892–1906, 4 Oct. 1896.

50 SA, CO 6/7/23: General register of poor belonging to the parish of Lerwick, 1865–77, 31 Dec. 1862 and 5 July 1862.

51 SA, CO 6/5/14: Record of applications for parochial relief, parish of Dunrossness, 1892–1906, 24 Jan. 1905.

52 SA, CO 6/5/30: Minutes of Dunrossness, Sandwick and Cunningsburgh parochial board, 1845–71, 11 Sept. 1868.

53 B. Smith, 'Kirstie Caddel's Christmas: "national prosperity" and mid-Victorian Shetland', in J. J. Graham and J. Tait (eds), *Shetland Folk Book*, vol. VIII (Lerwick, 1988), pp. 1–13. Kirstie's story has also been rendered into a popular tale in Sheenagh Pugh, *Kirstie's Witnesses* (Lerwick, Shetland Times Ltd, 1988).

54 SA, SC 12/6/1846/74: Application for parochial relief, 20 March 1846.

55 SA, SC 12/6/1846/190: Petition, theft of clothing, 10 Oct. 1846.

56 SA, SC 12/6/1846/74: Application for parochial relief, 20 March 1846.

57 SA, SC 12/6/1847/140: Application for parochial relief, 6 Dec. 1847.

58 SA, SC 12/6/1847/140: Application for parochial relief, 6 Dec. 1847.

59 Cohen, *Whalsay*; Brown, *Up-helly-aa*.

60 Recent studies of female workplace culture include K. Canning, *Languages of Labor and Gender: Female Factory Work in Germany, 1850–1914* (Ithaca, NY, Cornell University Press, 1996); Gordon, *Woman and the Labour Movement in Scotland*.

61 SA, 3/1/178: Harriet Robertson.

62 Elizabeth Malcomson in Mitchell et al., *Living Memory*, p. 22; Cohen, *Whalsay*, p. 86.

63 On the interpretation of female friendship see R. Kennedy, 'Women's friendships on Crete: a psychological perspective', in J. Dubisch (ed.), *Gender and Power in Rural Greece* (Princeton, NJ, Princeton University Press, 1986), pp. 121–38.

64 SA, 3/1/130/1: Ruby Ewenson, b. 1896.

65 Interview with Mary Ellen Odie.

66 See Brown, *Up-helly-aa*, p. 130.

67 SA, John Lewis (Methodist missionary), diary (uncatalogued).

68 A. Clarke (1828) in Flinn (ed.), *Travellers in a Bygone Shetland*, p. 149.

69 SA, John Lewis, diary.

70 SA, D 1/83: Journal of Sarah Squire.

71 *Shetland Times*, 7 Aug. 1879.

72 A. Edmonston, *A View of the Present State of the Zetland Isles*, 2 vols (Edinburgh, James Ballantyne & Co., 1809) quoted in Kendall, *With Naught but Kin*, p. 105.

73 Dunlop (1834) quoted in Brown, *Up-helly-aa*, p. 107.

74 SA, 3/1/178: Harriet Robertson.

75 SA, 3/1/123/1: John Gear.

76 SA, 3/2/109/2: Katherine Bairnson.

77 SA, 3/1/123/1: John Gear.

78 B. Edmonston and J. M. E. Saxby, *The Home of a Naturalist* (London, Nesbit, 1888); Saxby, *Shetland Traditional Lore*.

79 See D. Purkiss, *Troublesome Things: A History of Fairies and Fairy Stories* (London, Penguin, 2000), pp. 52–63. See also L. Henderson and E. J. Cowan, *Scottish Fairy Belief* (East Linton, Tuckwell Press, 2001).

80 Edmonston and Saxby (1888) quoted in Black, *County Folklore*, vol. III: *Orkney and Shetland Islands*, p. 31.

81 Blind, 'Shetland folklore', p. 165.

82 SA, 3/1/77/2: Mary Manson.

83 Hibbert, *A Description of the Shetland Islands*, p. 585.

84 *New Statistical Account*, vol. xv (1845), pp. 144–5; Saxby, *Shetland Traditional Lore*, pp. 175–6.

85 *New Statistical Account*, vol. xv (1845), p. 142.

86 SA, 3/1/162/1: Agnes Leask.

87 Interview with Agnes Leask.

88 SA, 3/1/178: Harriet Robertson.

89 SA, 3/1/179: Jessie Sinclair.

90 SA, 3/2/103/2: Magnus and Helen Anderson.

91 Byron and Chalmers, 'The fisherwomen of Fife', pp. 109–10.

92 Byron and McFarlane, *Social Change in Dunrossness*, p. 94.

93 Byron and McFarlane, *Social Change in Dunrossness*, p. 85. A similar division was noted in the community of 'Carnan' on Skye in the keep-fit group. See Macdonald, *Reimagining Culture*, p. 194.

94 Scottish census results 2001 online, www.scrol.gov.uk: Table KS09c, Economic activity – females (consulted 25 March 2004).

95 Scottish census results 2001 online, www.scrol.gov.uk: Table KS11c, Industry of employment – females (consulted 25 March 2004).

96 Similar developments have been noted in other fishing communities. See Johnson, 'Domestic work in rural Iceland', p. 171 and S. Cole, 'The sexual division of labour and social change in a Portuguese fishery', in Nadel-Klein and Davis (eds), *To Work and To Weep*, pp. 169–89, here pp. 184–5.

6

Sexualities

[Shetland women] are modest virgins, and virtuous wives: for adultery is not known among them. Among the common sort fornication sometimes happens; but their constancy is such, that they are sure to marry one among another. (Capt. Thomas Preston, 12 May 1744, quoted in Thomas Gifford, *An Historical Description of the Zetland Islands*, p. 104)

I N THE NINETEENTH CENTURY, official conceptions of moral order were largely equated with female sexuality. A moral society was one in which women's bodies were controlled through an ideological system that defined women primarily as wives and mothers, thereby placing restrictions on female sexual expression and fertility. By this measure Shetland was the most moral place in Scotland. The islands had the lowest illegitimacy rate in the country in the nineteenth century. In 1861, compared with the Scottish average of 9.2 illegitimate births for every 100 births, the figure in Shetland was 4.3, and it remained low throughout the century. These figures are all the more remarkable when one remembers the population imbalance. In other communities displaying a marked surplus of females the proportion of illegitimate births tends to be high.[1] So if so few Shetland women were having children out of wedlock, it seems that the ideological and disciplinary forces of the church and the state must have been effective and broadly accepted by the populace. Hence a low illegitimacy rate was taken as a sign that the ideology that defined women as fitted for the domestic realm, ideally contained within the family, had been successfully implanted in the popular belief system, and that the disciplinary authorities effectively contained and quashed deviant sexual behaviour.

In this chapter I argue that the negligible figures for children born outside wedlock are a poor guide to understanding the moral order in nineteenth-century Shetland, and are practically useless if we wish to gain an insight into how men and especially women understood and negotiated sexuality and the broader moral universe. When we shift our focus from quantitative representations of moral and sexual activity to women's own interpretations and representations of their experiences, we can begin to construct an image of a Shetland in which female sexuality was intimately related to women's material circumstances rather than determined by a set of external rules. And we can build a more complex picture of a place where gender relations were being played out within a constantly shifting ideological and economic framework.

Moralities

Nineteenth-century perceptions of the moral state of Shetland were quite varied, suggesting to us that there was no unitary or homogeneous sense of moral rules or boundaries here. To some, this was a place where the normal codes pertaining to acceptable sexual activity did not apply. Strangers experienced difficulty in navigating their way through a moral maze. According to Alexander Trotter, a Glasgow medical student who alighted at Lerwick from a whaling ship in 1856:

> There were a great many people apparently respectable enough walking about. But for my part I would not give much for their respectability, especially the female part of them. Indeed, to tell the truth in Lerwick it is said to be impossible to tell what woman is decent and what one is respectable. Possibly one third are bad: a thing which I should say cannot be said of any other place.[2]

Perhaps Trotter was surprised by the town – a busy, bustling, cosmopolitan place – and thus had difficulty in understanding the codes and rules of behaviour. Certainly Lerwick probably bore more comparison with metropolitan Glasgow than other Scottish provincial towns in the Highlands and Islands, and it was certainly very different from the more rural parts of Shetland. Since the seventeenth century Lerwick had been a frontier town, hosting smugglers, sailors, seamen and merchants from the countries bordering the North Atlantic. In the eighteenth century Lerwick had a reputation for heavy drinking and loose morals, as a town over which the civil authorities had little control.[3] Dutch, German, Norwegian, English and Scots seafarers passed through the small town, particularly in the summer months, swelling the winter population of around 2,500 by up to 5,000 extra inhabitants,

6 Women at Albert wharf, Lerwick, c.1880

most of them men. Lerwick was a port, a trading centre, a point of embarkation for journeys south, a welcome harbour, an employment centre and leisure hot-spot. It also had a garrison. Lerwick, then, was unlike anywhere else in Shetland or, for that matter, anywhere else in Scotland. It had a reputation for high jinks, for irreligion and for alcohol-fuelled reverie. In winter, the long dark days were alleviated by guising, skekkling and street festivities accompanied by fire-arms and flaming tar barrels.[4] In summer the town was full of seamen and, by the 1880s, workers associated with the herring industry – fishermen, coopers, curers and female gutters and packers, all of whom relished their time off. Lerwick was consequently a magnet for Shetlanders, men and women, from all over the islands. They went there to sell their wares – hosiery and products from the croft. They travelled to Lerwick to bid goodbye to loved ones and to meet long-departed sons and fathers. And they went there for work and for amusement. An American clergyman visitor to Lerwick in 1888 observed groups of sailors and young girls chatting and flirting.

Many of these girls come to Lerwick from the interior of the islands to secure a husband, and are ready to work for their board for the privilege of associating with the seamen who visit this port. This will not appear so strange when we explain that in consequence of the loss of so many of the young men at sea there are about three females for every male in these islands. We could never think of making our home in the Shetland Isles, for there is scarcely a house without its old maid and many of them are so browned and wrinkled with the smoke from their peat fires that they resemble the mummies we saw in the Museums of London ... On leaving the south of Scotland a prudent lady who was acquainted in Shetland advised us to publish every-where that we were unmarriageable or we would never get away from the islands without assuming domestic responsibilities – 'whether ye will or no.' These superfluous women should be imported and sent west amongst the lonely but gallant cowboys.[5]

The Revd Ridlon's observations appeared in the *Shetland News*, and Shetlanders lost little time in ridiculing his remarks and defending their womenfolk from the deprecatory comments of an outsider. His views were deemed insulting to Shetland women, whose respectability and moral standing were not in doubt amongst the indigenous population. After all, the rate of illegitimate births was negligible and Shetlanders were proud of their moral islands. 'What a picture!' exclaimed a Cunningsburgh reader:

it is erroneous in the extreme – a very ungracious attack on the manners of our country girls, and even on their morals ... It is a well-known fact that our Shetland country girls are a very modest class ... The mildest inference that anyone can draw from such statements is that our native girls are represented to be a class of systematic husband hunters ... I think it is the duty of those who are better informed to uphold the rights of our women, and denounce anything that is detrimental to their honour. The hardy daughters of Shetland are a respectable class.[6]

Lerwick was not representative of Shetland in moral terms. The 'culture of sexual licence' in Lerwick was alleged to have been the worst in Scotland while, at the same time, rural areas were described by contem-poraries as models of moral discipline and self-control, epitomised by women's chastity and respectability. But Shetlanders themselves, or at least those sufficiently educated to correspond with the newspapers, those who had embraced the evangelical culture of temperance and improving recreation, were loath to associate themselves publicly with the forward behaviour to be seen on the streets of the town. For them, it was the morality of rural Shetland and its women that was deemed a better image to portray to outsiders.

There appear to be two quite contrasting views expressed here: the outsiders' view of Shetland women as sexually promiscuous husband-hunters and the Shetlanders' more romantic representation of their women as respectable and chaste. Both opinions, though, are informed by nineteenth-century discourses on ideal womanhood and domesticity which were becoming increasingly widespread and diffuse through the course of the century. In Shetland, as elsewhere in the British Isles, Europe and North America, the language of piety, purity and self-control assigned to ideal womanhood by ministers, novelists, writers of instructional literature and teachers was pervasive, maturing into a composite stereotype of the ideal woman who was modest, good-tempered and industrious in the domestic sphere and in appropriate public works. Her opposite was an equally unlikely character, the loose or lewd woman, the unruly, undisciplined woman, the immodest, voluble gossip and the woman who worked outside the home for wages.

Visitors to Shetland from the Scottish mainland and overseas were surprised to see women active in the public sphere and found their assertive manner somewhat discomforting. They equated women's substantial and visible presence in the streets of Lerwick as a sign of their sexual promiscuity, and they contrasted these working-class women with 'women above the common rank' who 'seldom appear out of doors, unless at church'.[7] Women in Shetland had a prominent public presence, and it was difficult for the church or civil authorities to control their behaviour. Women worked in the fields, they travelled to and from Lerwick alone, they moved about freely and without hindrance. They were not expected to be confined within the domestic sphere. Women commonly walked out alone or together for work and for fun. The streets of Lerwick were often described as thronging with men and women looking for amusement. But not everyone regarded this as harmless fun. Indeed, a minor moral panic accompanied the emergence of the new industries of tobacco and straw plaiting at the beginning of the nineteenth century because they attracted young, single women to the town. According to Arthur Edmonston writing in 1809:

> The assemblage in a small place of a number of girls unrestrained by the example and removed from the protecting care of their parents, and suddenly acquiring comparative wealth, soon lays the habits of vice and extravagance. As they come from every different parish, they carry back with them, on their return, more or less of the sentiments and manners which they have acquired, and thus gradually weaken

respect for decorum, and undermine in others, the principles of virtue and morality.[8]

The fears surrounding these working women are reminiscent of identical concerns focused upon the mill girls on the British mainland. In 1811 it was said that 'the girls and young women belonging to the straw manufactories in this town not only make it common practice to patrol the streets when they come out of these factories, but also, to behave themselves in a very unbecoming manner; by going together in large companies, linked arm and arm together.'[9] To some men, these women's presence in public and their feisty attitude gave them licence to be roughly used. The aforesaid straw plaiters were set upon and assaulted by a number of young men who had been parading the streets 'making considerable noise and bustle'. Margaret Sinclair and Janet Edwardson were chased along the street by the gang of men 'roaring, scoffing and hallooing at them'.[10] Almost a century later in 1905, herring gutters – particularly those from the east coast of Scotland – had a similar reputation, and were seen as fair game for the attentions of men. Annie McLennan from Cromarty, employed by a Bressay fishcurer, was out walking across the fields after work with two friends when they spied three Dutchmen. The men followed the women, and one seized hold of Annie McLennan by the wrist, pulled up her clothes and touched her inappropriately so that she was 'of the opinion that he wished to ravish me'.[11] But the straw plaiters and herring gutters were not, on the whole, appropriated by Shetlanders as suitable models of Shetland womanhood.

Educated Shetlanders, particularly those who engaged in literary debate in the newspaper columns or who, like Jessie Saxby, had been acculturated to the norms of Victorian idealised domestic womanhood which were pervasive in the middle-class realm she inhabited in Edinburgh, used the language of separate spheres to champion the good name of Shetland womenfolk.[12] They stressed their respectability, their good manners, their patience and their morality. Resistance to temptation was regarded as a 'greater sign of moral courage and of good morality'.[13]

Historians have been no less guilty of interpreting behaviour in terms of the dominant discourses on moral issues which have been largely formulated within patriarchal institutions. The ideology of separate spheres, which equated gender roles with activities in the public and private spheres, had at its heart the representation of woman as a sexual being whose body had to be controlled or disciplined, whose nature determined her social role. In Scotland especially, woman has been represented by historians as a victim of the ways in which the civil authorities of church and state constructed her, first and foremost, as a sexual being. The kirk session in particular, with its God-given duty to impose discipline on its wayward or unruly parishioners, was obsessed with sexual sin. Fornication and adultery cases were the bread-and-butter of the kirk session system across Scotland.[14] It is commonly argued that women in Scotland were victims of an all-encompassing and oppressive moral system imposed by the Protestant church and bolstered and eventually continued by the state. The kirk session, the parochial and school boards and the sheriff courts are seen as the means by which those with power – men – oppressed those without – women – by defining them as reproducers rather than producers. From the witch-craft accusations in the sixteenth century to the nineteenth-century campaigns against prostitutes and wayward girls, the patriarchal institutions of social control subordinated women. Some have argued that this disciplinary system was an effective means of social control, imposing a strict and unbending moral system on individuals and communities. Moreover, focusing upon the kirk session, Leneman and Mitchison argue that 'it seems that most people of both sexes accepted the systems of control under which they lived, and actively co-operated with that of the Church.'[15] The alternative viewpoint – that there was greater dissent towards these institutions and their ideological systems than has hitherto been acknowledged – is only just beginning to be heard.[16]

In Mediterranean Europe a similar model has been widely applied by historians and anthropologists. Here, it was argued, the gendered code of honour and shame subordinated women and made them become passive victims of their sexuality. According to this interpretation, men were preoccupied with honour which could be assured only through the control of the sexual behaviour of their womenfolk. This control was achieved through 'the domestication of women's sexuality and fertility – through the social construction of women as wives and mothers – and through the conflation of women with shame (and men with honour). For their part, women exhibited respect for male honour through their deference to the moral code of shame exhibited by their virginity and chastity.'[17] Here, as in the Scottish historiography, the concept of social control has been utilised to describe how an ideological system operated in a face-to-face community. Woman's behaviour was regulated and constrained by a system which placed the responsibility for family honour on her shoulders. The parallels between southern European societies and Presbyterian Scotland are clear.

More recently, however, feminist historians and anthropologists of southern Europe have challenged this model of understanding women's lives on the grounds that it fails to represent women in their own terms, and thus it is 'incomplete and demeaning'.[18] Starting from a feminist standpoint means taking women's experience as the central reality, rather than institutional ideologies or functions, and it urges us to reassess our assumptions about the interplay between ideologies and experience.[19] So as Cole has shown in the case of northern Portugal, the honour–shame code promulgated by the church and the state, which emphasised women's role as reproducers and their bodies as the site of control, came into conflict with women's self-perception and experience. In the fishing village of Vila Chã on Portugal's northern coast, women saw themselves primarily as productive workers and household managers. Thus, the honour–shame gender system which rested upon the control of female sexuality should not be utilised as the prime explanatory framework by which to understand gender relations in this society because women themselves did not experience their lives solely through their sexual identity. As Cole states, 'local gender systems do not merely mirror the hegemonic constructions of church and state'. Gender works at the level of the household and the community, and women and men negotiate their identities and their social relations in the context of local conditions.[20] We can see this in nineteenth-century Scotland too, where significant variations in illegitimacy rates – from a high of 16 per cent in the north-east to around 6 per cent in the north-western counties – indicates major local differences in perceptions of acceptable sexual behaviour amongst the labouring classes and differing material responses to the unwed mother and her child.[21] Dominant or hegemonic discourses should, of course, be recognised and their influence acknowledged, but we should not read experience from institutional pronouncements and actions.

Historians of Scottish women have begun to identify ways in which women challenged the dominant discourses on womanhood and resisted attempts to define them purely in terms of their sexuality.[22] This approach, stressing resistance over passivity, seeing women as agents rather than victims, is welcome, but it does not alter the overall picture of social and moral control by patriarchal institutions because there is no attempt to redefine the terms of reference. Historians have largely mirrored the ways in which contemporaries constructed woman – in terms of her sexuality rather than her economic role or any other identity construct – rather than taking women's self-representation as the starting point. Shetland offers an opportunity to shift the paradigm.

We know that Shetland women had a strong self-image as workers, and that they regarded themselves as equal and valued participants in the household and wider economy. They did not identify themselves as oppressed women who were judged only by their sexuality and fertility. The very fact that women formed the majority of inhabitants for all of the century was a practical determinant of this identity since so many women did not marry or become mothers and many became independent – if marginal – producers. Of course we should not underestimate or deny the presence and influence of the moral codes propagated or supported by the church and the state, and neither should we forget that most women probably aspired to marriage and motherhood even if they did not attain that status. At the same time we should not assume that the ideals that drove women's decision-making were determined by the way they were constructed as sexual beings rather than economic actors. In short, both women's experience and their identity should be combined in the analysis, and from that position we can then analyse how they engaged and negotiated with competing discourses that clashed with their self-perception.

How do we begin to represent women as they themselves would wish to be seen, given that the sources are, in the main, produced by institutions that adhered to a set of ideals at variance with women's own lives? In Shetland, as elsewhere, there were numerous opportunities for women to exhibit or 'perform' their sense of self, and the historian is granted a privileged insight into the self-perception of these working women at moments when their lives were subjected to official scrutiny, by the legal system, the kirk session or the parochial board.[23] On these occasions we can hear the mediated voices of ordinary women as they spoke about their everyday lives and routines. The circumstances that brought women into the public arena were often relatively mundane: they were accused of fornication or pre-marital pregnancy by the kirk session; they were pursuing absent fathers of their illegitimate children for aliment or maintenance in the sheriff court; and they were petitioning the parochial board for financial support. On other occasions, though, women found themselves at the centre of extraordinary events as defendants, complainants or witnesses in cases of child murder and concealment of pregnancy, in situations of assault, rape and domestic violence and in breach of promise cases. In the church and civil courts we can see women engaging and negotiating with the discourses on womanhood prevalent within the church and legal hierarchies and representing themselves as individuals with power in their own right.

The ubiquity and thoroughness of the institutions of church and state which regulated moral behaviours should not blind us to the fact that there was no unitary or static moral order in nineteenth-century Shetland. The kirk session minute books and sheriff court precognitions and processes may give the impression of an efficient disciplinary system, but we should not confuse the efficiency of record keeping with the effectiveness of the system. Throughout the period people engaged with a number of moral discourses, some of them competing or in conflict and all of them shifting, in the rapidly changing Shetland society. Shetland was not an isolated or inward-looking place. In fact it was more open to outside influences than many Scottish communities on account of its maritime identity and its mobile and transient population. So, in addition to inhabiting the moral universe propagated by the parish churches of the established Church of Scotland (each with its own kirk session and board of heritors), Shetlanders became accustomed to absorbing the messages of dissenting preachers and missionaries. Many of the clergy were born outside Shetland, and the dissenters were dominated by English Methodists and evangelical Presbyterians from the Scottish mainland. Those who presided over the island's legal institutions were not native Shetlanders either. Sheriff Rampini, for instance, the most well-known of Lerwick's sheriffs between 1878 and 1885, was a Glaswegian Italian. And the majority of schoolteachers were from outside the islands. So Shetland's institutions were being constantly re-staffed by men and women from the rest of the British Isles. In addition, Shetland had its own newspapers which published material from across the United Kingdom and further afield, and people consumed a range of reading matter, from magazines to popular literature, which communicated a range of discourses on moral issues.

For most of the century traditional or customary practices governing relations between the sexes existed side by side with, and not always in conflict with, new models of behaviour increasingly drawn from bourgeois evangelical culture. Shetland is a place where one can observe the interplay between these two worlds. The discourse of domesticity and female piety which, in the rest of Britain, had been acculturated at all levels of society by the early nineteenth century took longer to reach Shetland. Thus, at least until the 1850s, the early modern discourse on womanhood, which emphasised control of an unruly female sexuality and the potential dangers posed by the single woman, still informed the actions of the kirk session, and this came into conflict with the legal system, which had taken on board the new view of womanhood as virtuous and maternal. In these islands, then, in the nineteenth century we can move back and forth across the threshold between the pre-modern and modern world view. And Shetland women did this themselves by negotiating with alternative meanings. Instead of using the disciplinary structures of church and state to structure our understanding of the moral order in Shetland, it is more useful to use the structures – the kirk session, the sheriff court – and their procedures as a microscope, to inform our understanding of how men and women sought to govern relations between the sexes.

Meanings

When the novelist and exiled Unst resident Jessie Saxby precipitated a debate within Shetland in 1894 on the subject of customary courtship practices she, perhaps unwittingly, demonstrated how wide was the gap between popular notions of acceptable behaviour between courting couples in Shetland and the moral boundaries of nineteenth-century bourgeois society elsewhere. Saxby intervened in the case of the twenty-eight-year-old Robina Georgeson, who had gone to court to sue Arthur Walterson for £100 damages, accusing him of breach of promise to marry. Breach of promise cases were fairly rare in Shetland – just fifteen cases can be identified in the Lerwick sheriff court records between 1828 and 1890. But this one was singular for the claims made by both parties and for the public reaction to a particular assertion by Robina's counsel and one of her witnesses: that it was customary in Shetland for a courting couple to sleep together before the marriage.[24] Public opinion was outraged that the honour of Shetland women was being impugned in a public court by reference to the apparent regularity of this practice. 'Why are Shetland men silent when the morality of their countrywomen is impugned by Scots?' enquired Saxby in a letter to the *Shetland Times*. 'I care nothing at all for "conventional respectability", and despise the morality which leans on Kirk and Law for its support:' she continued, 'but I assert that a purer and more lasting love has its home in Shetland than in any other part of "religious" Scotland.'[25]

Saxby's outrage was directed at the employer and the lawyer of the female complainant. Robina's lawyer had allegedly stated in open court that 'the "morals" of Melby are the morals of all Shetland.'[26] Robina Georgeson had admitted in court that she had slept with Arthur Walterson whilst she was working as a servant at Melby House. She explained that he had visited her two or three times a week and 'Walterson slept with me when he came to see me . . . If he had not been courting me with a view to marriage I would not have allowed him to do so.'[27] However, she continued, 'There were no familiarities between us when defender and I slept together. That is just the recognised manner of courting in Shetland and nothing wrong is done.' She also claimed that Walterson visited her at her mother's house, and there too he 'stayed all night with me.' And when he first asked her to marry him 'we were in bed together at the time'. Moreover, Robina's employer Robert Scott was aware that the couple were sleeping together: 'It is a usual custom in the country for young people courting to sleep together. I would not have allowed defender to come as he did if I had not thought that he would marry Pursuer.' However, he continued, 'Under certain circumstances considering the climate and the want of facilities for [social] intercourse the so-called Shetland courtship may mean nothing more than lad and lass making acquaintance. It does not of necessity mean courtship with a view to marriage.' For his part, Arthur Walterson was unrepentant. He had been away from Shetland at the Greenland fishing since the age of seventeen. He had started to meet Robina Georgeson in 1890 when she was twenty-eight years old and he was twenty-one. However, he vehemently denied promising to marry her and claimed that the courtship custom, cited by Robina's lawyer to win the case for his client, was of no significance. Walterson claimed he had just visited Robina 'for a lark', that he had slept with her but never promised to marry her. Furthermore, he claimed that the romantic language he used in his correspondence with her during his three-year absence at sea – 'your loving sweetheart' – just meant that he was 'corresponding with her as a friend'. 'I never heard that there was any harm in lads and lasses sleeping together. It doesn't mean that they have any intention of marrying . . . It is not understood to mean that young people mean marriage when they behave in the manner described as Shetland courtship.' Walterson appeared to be on safe ground. Speaking for his defence, the seventy-five-year-old retired sea-pilot George Slater stated in court:

> I am well acquainted with Shetland customs, no one better . . . To 'court' in Shetland means just to keep company & many a lad may 'court' a girl simply as being a friend without thinking of marriage. It may mean a great deal or a very little. Every young woman likes to have a young man, but she is not worth a button unless she has more than one. I would not have cared to marry a wife that had no more sweethearts than me. It has been the custom for hundreds of years for young men to visit young women at night without any harm being done. It is an old Norwegian or Danish custom. It is often done just for a lark. I never heard of any presumption rising there from that the

young people taking part in it were engaged to be married – not even if it went on for some months. It was mostly frolic and diversion . . . it was not very respectable for a young man to sleep with a young woman. Some mothers would have allowed it but a good mother would not allow it. No man going to be married to a respectable girl would do it. Many a man coming home wants to hear the news and goes to sleep with a girl friend and gets the news from her.[28]

A number of other witnesses confirmed Slater's view, that the custom of sleeping together was not an indication of engagement or promise of marriage. Indeed, according to sixty-four-year-old Ann Sinclair, the couple 'might be both good people, and no harm in it. Even in such circumstances they might correspond and he might call her "sweetheart", & yet no marriage be in prospect.'[29]

Jessie Saxby's intervention in this case revealed her background as the daughter of a Shetland doctor as well as her immersion in the morality of Edinburgh bourgeois society, where she had lived for twenty years since leaving her native island of Unst. She had misunderstood the meaning of the complex, unwritten and ambiguous behavioural codes by which members of the Shetland crofting and fishing community conducted their courtships. Indeed, her mistake was to assume that there were fixed courtship rituals or modes of behaviour which governed all relationships. Her assertion that 'a purer and more lasting love has its home in Shetland than in any other part of "religious" Scotland' and her belief that 'no such "customs" . . . were the customs of our young people when I was a Shetlander in Shetland' revealed a cultural viewpoint somewhat divorced from everyday life in her native land. Other correspondents to the newspaper debate on this topic were similarly keen to uphold the reputation of Shetland for its morality. According to one contributor the custom – in the context of the low illegitimacy rate in the islands – was really a sign of 'moral courage and good morality in being able to resist temptation when you are face to face with it'.[30]

The Melby case was not unusual, and it raises a number of points regarding the interpretation of sexual morality. First, it is clear that the court's decision had to rest on the ambiguity of interpretation of the meaning of 'courting'. To court was to go out with, but did this mean that a man and woman were going out with each other to the exclusion of others, or could it mean that each had multiple courtship partners? Other cases certainly suggest the latter. In another case Arthur Tait, who maintained a lengthy correspondence with Robina Morrison while he was at sea, suggested in one of his letters that Shetland women were not monogamous in this regard. 'It is the way now with the young women: they are got that many on hand that they don't know what one to take', although he was careful to tell Robina, 'but mind I am not thinking you are doing that'.[31] In the Melby case the defending man and his witness put forward the notion that it was customary for both sexes to have multiple courting partners. Robina, on the other hand, clearly implied that to her courtship was exclusive with a view to marriage.

Second, the meaning of the act of 'sleeping' together is ambiguous. It is claimed as a custom from Norway or Denmark, which suggests that its origins were old and traditional but unprovable. It is also described by both the defendant and his primary witness, George Slater, as 'a lark' – both men using the same word, which may suggest some collusion or preparation by the defending solicitor. Indeed, this latter interpretation is made more likely by Slater's use of the phrase 'frolic and diversion'. We can hear here the intervention of a lawyer intoning the voice of laddishness that was heard so often in Shetland court cases involving young men and their pranks. Indeed, the suggestion that sleeping beside a woman in the act of courtship was some kind of prankish gesture of fun tends to associate for the court the activities of young men in courtship with their other rituals (at Yuletide and Up-helly-aa for instance). Yet Slater seems to contradict himself. He alludes to the discourse of respectability and solitary courtship to which the complainant (and Saxby) was appealing. He intones the concept of 'respectability', that word of power and self-control in Victorian society. Slater is slipping in and out of a traditional Shetland idea of a loose courtship and towards a tighter concept that would have resonated with observers like Jessie Saxby.

There is little doubt that courtship customs in Shetland, as elsewhere in the British Isles and Europe, did incorporate couples 'sleeping' with one another – sometimes described as 'bundling' – before marriage. Whether or not this meant sexual intercourse is hard to interpret. In 1871, twenty years before Saxby's interventions, Robert Cowie, who came to know the islands well in his medical role, had expressed his surprise at the apparent superior nature of Shetlanders' morality 'when we remember there are fully twice as many women as men in the country, and even more so in view of certain strange customs which prevail'. The customs to which he was referring were 'barn bundlings', which commonly took place after country weddings.

> The festivities over for the night, the dancers, instead of returning to their homes, adjourn to the barn of their host's cottage, which serves

as a dormitory, the members of each sex being alternately ranged along the floor on a huge couch of straw ... The people enter quite innocently into these 'barn bundlings' as they are termed, and both statistics and the testimony of respectable persons who have taken part in them, prove that nothing immoral occurs. But 'barn bundlings' and all other relics of a barbarous age, are fast disappearing before the advance of truth.[32]

Shetlanders were keen to defend their reputation for strict moral probity and resistance to temptation. 'You know in other parts of the country except for Shetland, if a girl and a boy go to bed together it's for one purpose and one purpose only. But here in Shetland a girl and boy would go to bed together as if they might go for a walk', remarked one commentator on Shetland morals.[33]

Yet, as the kirk session records testify, not all sleep-overs remained so innocent. As one witness in the Georgeson case had remarked, the long winter nights, the inclement climate and the lack of facilities for social intercourse meant that young men and women regularly visited one another at home. Isabella Halcrow testified in 1823 that James Davidson, whom she was suing for damages for breach of promise to marry after she had become pregnant,

> formed a very strong and evident attachment to her and visited her repeatedly ... both night and day at the house in which she was a servant (according to the practice in the country of persons in their rank, when in courtship) and that his said visits both before and subsequent to its being discovered that she had become with child to him were understood and considered as on the terms of marriage.[34]

Women always endeavoured to show that they had succumbed to the entreaties of their sweetheart only on the promise of marriage, indicating that they were well aware of the ambiguity of the moral system. Courtship rituals were accepted as long as the woman emerged unscathed. Margaret Sinclair claimed that the seaman Anthony Jameson, the father of her illegitimate daughter, was 'regularly in the habit of coming to my house ... at night he came at the late supper time, 10, 11, 12 o'clock sometimes – sometimes he remained all night ... he and I went to bed after the others had gone to bed ... he remained until about sunrise in the morning. I have seen the sunrise with him and I would sunder he promised to marry me.[35] Witnesses in this case were more ambivalent about the nature of their relationship, however. Agnes Jamieson remarked that 'people supposed by all appearance that he was courting her, I saw them some few times out together walking, I saw them in company in her own house . . . his arm was round her shoulder'. Yet she added, 'it is very common in the country in Shetland for a lad to put his arm round the neck of a lass.'[36]

The moral universe was changing in Shetland by the 1860s. People were no longer sure of the significance of certain actions in the absence of a disciplinary body which, with the tacit consent of its parishioners, made black-and-white decisions about moral actions and thereby established firm boundaries for acceptable and unacceptable behaviour. By this date the kirk session's role in disciplining sexual morality was weakening. This is not to say that kirk morality and discipline had determined people's behaviour before this time, but it had established a set of rules which allowed for little ambiguity. One had either committed adultery or fornication or not, and even those women who attempted to circumvent the system, for instance by refusing to co-operate with the session's procedure, rarely succeeded. For instance, when Jean Fraser was called to appear before the Walls and Sandness kirk session in 1793 on account of her illegitimate pregnancy, she refused to name the father of her child and claimed that 'an act of violence had been committed against her in the fields by a person to her unknown.' Jean was not believed and she was 'seriously enjoined to retract her declaration and adhere to truth'. A month later Jean persisted in her story 'and seemed hardened in her iniquity'. Her punishment was to appear in public for her rebuke five times, once more than usual, 'on account of her dishonest declaration repeatedly and to be a means to induce others, if unhappily led to commit a crime of a similar nature to be more candid and ingenuous in future'.[37] Until the early decades of the nineteenth century the kirk session had been concerned with admissions of guilt and expressions of remorse. It was not interested in the complexity of human relationships or with uncertainty, doubt or ambiguity. But with the demise of church discipline in the third and fourth quarters of the nineteenth century, the moral universe, as we read it through the civil courts, became more complex.

The interpretation of courtship rituals nicely illustrates how there could be many competing meanings drawn from observation of the relationships between couples. The signs of courtship were frequently interpreted as ambiguous. In 1888 Arthur Tait was confronted in court with the series of letters he had written to Robina Morrison, in which he addressed her as 'dear love' and expressed the hope that she would 'keep as true as me'. Defending himself against the case for breach of promise brought against him for £50 damages, he demurred: 'The letters were written by me just as a boyish adventure. Sailors must have sweethearts.' He continued: 'I never professed to love her, or sit with my hand around her waist, kissing her and calling her my dear love. If I came across [to] her in that free and easy way I did not mean anything by it except just a boyish flirtation.'[38] 'Courtship', according to Tait's lawyer, 'was a very elastic term.'[39] But Robina and her father clearly interpreted Arthur Tait's letters, actions and gifts – he gave her a locket and chain when she travelled to Lerwick to see him off to sea in 1875 – quite differently. She said she understood that when Tait corresponded with her on his first voyage 'he was making love to her.' Sheriff MacKenzie agreed with Robina's interpretation. But even he admitted that the signs in this case were open to interpretation:

> The whole tenor of the defender's correspondence, however, is such as to leave no doubt in the mind of anyone perusing it that the defender entertained or professed to entertain feelings of love and affection towards the pursuer, and looked upon her and himself as affianced lovers . . . It is proverbially difficult to measure the sincerity of an amorous profession, or to appraise the language of love, but I think I do not err in holding that the letters in question are practically speaking a continuous promise of marriage. Mere language of admiration or of loving sentiment would not necessarily bear this construction, but there is something more here. There are references to his future and to hers, to money matters and so forth, which show that his passion had become consolidated into a practical intention.[40]

But other signs were similarly open to interpretation, with various consequences. James Hunter and Thomas Smith, both in their late teens, had regularly visited the house of Barbara and Mary Banks, who were in their twenties. As Barbara explained, 'they would sit at the fireside while my sister and I knitted our hosiery. James Hunter would sometimes put his hand around my waist and sometimes on my neck. Thomas Smith would do the same with my sister. There was no harm in this as my sister and mother were always present on these occasions. I would just say let me be or such like.'[41] The lads started to accompany the women to the barn to help them thresh corn, and on one night both assaulted Barbara Banks. 'The lads thrashed for some time and I sat knitting my gloves . . . They then put out the light, took hold of me and threw me down and James Hunter got on top of me. He lifted my petticoats and unbuttoned his trousers and had connection with me.' Barbara made no complaint about the rape; indeed she mentioned it to no-one, and the men continued to frequent the house as if nothing had happened. Barbara pursued the rape accusation against the men only because she became pregnant and presumably hoped for some financial support.

Did the men and the women in this case read the signs differently? Did the sisters interpret the visits and expressions of affection from the two men as no more than friendly companionship, and did Hunter and Smith assume that because their expressions of affection towards the women had not been rebuffed they could take things further?

Unlike kirk session hearings, when a woman would merely have to admit to a sexual crime to receive absolution, in the civil courts women had to provide detailed evidence in order to make a solid case for their claim of damages. In breach of promise or child maintenance cases, the discourse of sentiment was usefully employed by women and their legal representatives in order to achieve economic security. Shetland women, as we saw in Chapter 3, were less likely to find a marriage partner than women almost anywhere else in the British Isles. The proportion of women who never married was high. They knew that spinsterhood would be fraught with insecurity and that life as an unmarried mother would be extremely hard. They had been brought up to be productive, to think of themselves as workers, but were canny enough to know that marriage offered them the best chance of economic autonomy within their own household. The alternative was eking out a living producing hosiery or working as a labourer or servant in someone else's household. This was the fate of Robina Morrison whilst she waited for Arthur Tait to return home, and most likely she remained living in her father's household after the case was resolved. Thus women interpreted the actions and sentiments of their sweethearts as the prelude to marriage, an unwritten contract. In the event of the man reneging on his promise, the woman believed that she had entered into a contract which had been broken and therefore she demanded financial recompense to permit her to live the life she had envisaged. And these women knew that their chance of marriage had passed. Many of those who brought breach of promise cases were already into their late twenties and some were older. A woman's economic interests were paramount, and she used the courts in an attempt to achieve some degree of economic security.

In January 1870, thirty-eight-year-old Margaret Abernethy brought a case against Robert Mann in Lerwick sheriff court for breach of promise to marry. The pair were both from the township of Culswick and had started courting when they were both in their twenties, although Robert was seven years younger than Margaret. In 1860 Robert, like many of his contemporaries, left Shetland to go to sea. Margaret claimed that he had promised to marry her on his return, and she produced in court a series of letters from her fiancé which appeared to support her case. In 1861 Robert wrote to her from Liverpool: 'I hope that you will not get married until I come home I cannot set on no time yet . . . but I never intend to break my word and what I say I shall do if God spares my life and health and I hope my dear that you will never forget me for my heart is in you though I be far from you and I hope that you will prove kind and true.'[42] The letters kept coming – from all over the world. By 1864 Robert was in Australia but still hoping that Margaret was waiting for him. 'I am glad to see you are well and not married yet for they are all getting married at home now', wrote Robert from Melbourne. 'I hope that you will not get married until I come home. I hear that you have been at some weddings, perhaps you have got another sweetheart but I hope not, I hope that you will keep me in mind for I will not forget you.' Once again Robert told Margaret that he could not say when he would be home but hoped 'it will not be long now.' He signed off, 'your wellwisher, lover and sweetheart till death.' This correspondence between the couple continued until 1868, when Robert wrote from New Zealand: 'My dear I am made up my mind to come home. I am done working here . . . it might take 3 months or it might take 6 months.' Robert did eventually return to Shetland, but when he did he swiftly married another woman. This was the final straw for Margaret, who by the time when the case came to court in 1870 was thirty-eight-years-old and unlikely to find another man to marry. Her case was partially successful; the parties agreed that Robert would pay Margaret £5 and another £5 in eighteen months' time and would bear the costs of the court process. Both Margaret and Robert stayed in the same parish but their fortunes thereafter diverged. While Robert married, had three children and pursued a living as a fisherman, Margaret resided in the extended household of her widowed sister, and was employed as a knitter of hosiery.[43]

Margaret Abernethy had waited for Robert Mann for eight years on the understanding that she had a firm promise of marriage. The letters she had received from him she had interpreted as declarations of intent. Mann, like many of his contemporaries, wrote to his 'sweetheart' using a sentimental style of language which mimicked that found in popular literature. Sailors purchased attractive notepaper headed with sentimental poems on which they penned their brief lines home. George MacKay from Lerwick went to sea in 1876, and during his travels around the world he wrote to Joan Anderson, leading her to believe that when he did return home they would be married. Joan received a letter every three or four months containing George's expressions of love and his hope that soon the couple would be together. 'Dear Joan I am always dreaming about you my dreams by night and my thoughts by day,' he wrote from Port Chalmers, New Zealand, in November 1877. And then in a postscript he commented, 'I suppose all the young men will be getting married this winter surely our time will come yet.'[44] In the summer of 1878 he was in Glasgow, unable or unwilling to return home whilst there was work to be had, but still 'living in hope of you that you will be my wife some day.' During the next two years George MacKay travelled between Glasgow, New Zealand and Quebec, continually promising Joan that he would soon be home, teasing her with his expressions of love and desire: 'look out for me about the first of April if the steamer comes in the night I will climb over the wall and come and kiss you while you're sleeping so look out'. When he did eventually return to Shetland in 1879, after Joan had waited three years in expectation of marriage, he refused to marry her, citing her inappropriate behaviour in public as justification for not fulfilling his promise. But Joan, now aged twenty-six and still living with her widowed mother in Lerwick, was determined to make George MacKay satisfy his side of the 'contract'. In February 1880, just short of a year after he had returned from sea, she lodged a petition for £100 damages as recompense for her expectation of marriage and the associated economic security. The sheriff ruled in favour of Joan but assessed the damages at £25, and Joan remained living in her mother's household in the Lerwick widows' asylum.[45] Not all men were so fickle, however. Hugh Williamson, a sailor from Hillswick, restores our faith in the constancy of love on the evidence of his last will and testament. Hugh died in the South Seas in 1858. His last thoughts were of his sweetheart Ann at home in Shetland. 'I was to have married Ann if I had com home with my life and health. There is a small bit of gold in one of the pocket books along with the ring I wor and brest pin . . . [I] recollect the earning of it has cost my life.'[46] The nugget of gold was valued at one pound.

The traditional discursive world which offered little scope for negotiation was, by the second half of the century, co-existing with a new set of moral codes dressed up in the language of sentiment and respectability. For women this was double-edged. In court cases where they were the complainants, they were able to appeal to notions of romantic courtship and respectable or honourable behaviour, language that was understood by lawyers and sheriffs with bourgeois sensibilities. Women, and their legal representatives, consciously appealed to the modern construct of ideal womanhood. When Robina Russell's expectations of marriage were thwarted by Thomas Williamson in 1871 she did all in her power to gain the sympathy of the court and to tar the reputation of the man who had cheated her.

After the marriage between her and the defender was broken off she became impatient at home, her health became affected and she lost her spirits . . . ever since Defender's marriage . . . the Pursuer has been wandering about from place to place, her heart broken, her peace of mind destroyed and the home of her childhood – formerly to her the dearest spot on earth – now rendered through former associations and the perfidy of her unscrupulous lover one of the bitterest . . . Trusting to his honour she gave up to the Pursuer what was as valuable as her life – her love. That once pledged she could never recall even though her love had been misplaced and the poor girl is now pining and in all probability will pine away under the burden of a broken heart.[47]

Robina Russell was a merchant's daughter and therefore perhaps more likely than her lower-class counterparts to deploy this kind of language. But most Shetland women who appeared in court led lives somewhat far removed from the language of ideal womanhood and femininity, and yet they too were beginning to be judged against a set of ideals which bore little relation to their own experience. Men increasingly invoked the language of reputation and respectability in court in order to throw doubt on a woman's claim to damages. Arthur Tait had accused Robina Morrison of 'behaving very rudely for a lady'. William Hunter, appearing on behalf of his friend, recounted how at winter dances 'her conversation in private and her behaviour in company was rude and boisterous. She was in the habit of using rough language . . . she began to take liquor more freely than before', although Hunter admitted that he had never actually heard her swearing and she never drank to excess.[48] And according to Morrison's aunt, Robina 'did not conduct herself quietly. She was rather boisterous.'[49] Women, then, could use the language of ideal femininity to their advantage, but it could also be used against them; and in Shetland, where women had traditionally led a public and productive life, women were vulnerable to slurs based on their alleged unfeminine behaviour.

Uncertainties

There was one set of women who found themselves trapped between the ideology of the pre-modern moral world and the more confusing sexual morality of the modern. Women who concealed their pregnancies and murdered their children were few and far between in nineteenth-century Shetland. In Scotland as a whole hundreds of women were investigated or indicted for this crime between the 1660s and the 1920s.

But in Shetland there were just forty cases of alleged child murder or concealment of pregnancy for the period between 1699 and 1920, and only seventeen women were tried in the sheriff court. But these cases, more than any others, exemplify the changing nature of the moral order as the pre-modern disciplinary system presided over by the kirk session gave way to a more modern form of censure controlled by the state's legal system and the medical profession. Extraordinary cases can often reveal a great deal about the ordinary or everyday world. The treatment of women who were suspected of committing infanticide illustrates the shift from the era of moral certainty, when the church taught and policed strict behavioural norms in the realm of sexual mores, to an era of moral uncertainty and ambiguity.

In the early modern era the infanticidal woman stood adjacent to the witch as the archetypal demonic force in contemporary discourse. During the seventeenth and eighteenth centuries, the murdering mother was regarded as an unnatural monster, one who denied her maternal sentiment, the perpetrator of a premeditated homicide.[50] Across Europe, including Scotland, where the 1690 Act Anent Child Murder treated infanticide as a capital crime, the prevalence of the death sentence for convicted women reflected this harsh attitude. By the nineteenth century the infanticidal mother was more likely to be considered sympathetically, as a victim of circumstance rather than the perpetrator of an evil act. In Scotland the statute of 1809, which interpreted the deliberate concealment of pregnancy and failure to call for assistance at the birth as culpable homicide warranting no more than two years in prison, signalled a sea-change in the way the legal system dealt with suspected women. In Shetland, the shift in legal attitudes had unforeseen consequences because this was a place where pre-modern beliefs and practices arguably survived longer than anywhere else in Britain. Thus, the 'modern' attitude towards the infanticidal mother on the part of the legal system existed in a tension with community discipline – the measures adopted both by the church courts and by lay members of the community.

The overwhelming majority of women accused of the crime of concealment or child murder were pregnant with an illegitimate child. Illegitimacy was not uncommon here, although far from pervasive. 'Although from their modes of life, the freest intercourse prevails, yet in the country parishes, deviations from chastity are by no means frequent', observed Arthur Edmonston in 1809.[51] It is possible that such women were victims of expectations based on courtship patterns which were no longer stable or commonly agreed. As the previous section has demonstrated, courtship customs, including sleeping together in the same bed, were under negotiation. Women still anticipated that pre-marital sex was consented to upon the promise of marriage, and a pregnancy would hasten that end, whereas it is clear that some of the men involved felt no such responsibility to their lovers.[52] For example, in 1859 when Jemima Nicolson told her lover that she was pregnant she recalled, 'he always tried to reason me out of it . . . that it was a mere whim with me fancying that I was with child and that I said it merely with the view of getting him to marry me.'[53]

Historical explanations of infanticide tend to focus on the twin factors of economic marginality and the culture of shame surrounding illegitimacy. Fear of ostracism and the dishonour an illegitimate child would confer on a woman was certainly a factor in some European societies, more especially in Catholic regions.[54] But here in Shetland, community censure was part and parcel of the system by which sexuality was regulated, and illegitimate children were generally incorporated into the community. This is not to say that unmarried pregnant women who were summoned to appear before the elders of the kirk session were not humiliated and shamed by the experience, and of course absolution was granted only if a woman provided the name of the father of her illegitimate child. If paternity was established the father would be pressured to admit his moral and financial responsibility and thereby relieve the session poor fund of another demand on its income. Once a woman had been rebuked for her immoral conduct she would be absolved and her child could be baptised. Those unmarried mothers who conformed to this process may have been in an economically and socially more advantageous position than those who refused to co-operate. Shetland women did not hesitate to use the sheriff court to claim aliment for the support of their children, and records show that many who did so continued to live within the community.[55] For instance, in 1868 Margaret Fraser petitioned the sheriff court for £2 lying-in expenses and £1 quarterly aliment from Laurence Tulloch for her son born some months earlier. By 1881, according to the census, Margaret was still living in the family home headed by her farmer father, she was working as an agricultural labourer, and her thirteen-year-old son was identified as a scholar.[56]

Moreover, there was often no shortage of people willing to take in an illegitimate child. As the wife of Malcolm Malcolmson magnanimously said, when confronted with the news that her husband was the father of Marion Henrysdaughter's dead child, 'she would have provided for the child as if it had been her own.'[57] Similarly, in 1859

Magnus Manson testified that he had come to an agreement with his servant Mary Gilbertson, who was pregnant with his child. Manson's wife Isabella was to attend Mary during her confinement and thereafter the child was to be given up to Manson and his wife on the payment of £1. 'I could not have taken more care of it had it been my own', declared Isabella Manson following the unfortunate death of the child of a bronchial infection.[58]

Notwithstanding these circumstances, a very small number of women committed infanticide in Shetland for reasons we cannot know. What we do know, however, is that such women were neither deviant nor dangerous, but merely women who were desperately trying to conform to an idealised model of womanhood which their illegitimate pregnancy threatened to undermine. The narratives constructed by the women themselves support this. Every woman who denied her pregnancy or the death of her infant did so as a result of unique individual circumstances, and the historian cannot reach far beyond the surviving legal texts in order to explain motivation. However, the infanticide narrative rehearsed in court does provide an insight into the interplay between sexual morality and gender relations in Shetland communities over the course of the century.

In 1794 twenty-three-year-old Marion Henrysdaughter from Dunrossness appeared in the Lerwick sheriff court charged with child murder. There had been rumours about the neighbourhood that she was with child, but she had vehemently denied the reports. According to one witness she had answered one enquirer that 'she never knew a man in her life as she should answer to God'.[59] Marion's father had also heard the rumours. 'He heard several people in his neighbourhood say that his daughter . . . was with child but that as she constantly denied it and he the declarent never suspected her of any intrigue or courtship he believed the report to be false and that her complaints proceeded from obstruction which his daughter affirmed to be the case.' Marion gave birth to the child alone when the other family members were away cutting corn. She kept the body of the child in bed with her all day, and the following day she took it to a skeo, a small hut for drying fish, dug a hole, buried the child's body and covered it with a flat stone. Some days later rumours were spreading that milk was running down Marion's breasts and that the neighbours had been disturbed in the night by her cries. On hearing these reports Robert Ollason, an elder in the Dunrossness kirk session, 'considered it his duty to make further enquiry'. Ollason, accompanied by three more elders, one of whom was Marion's uncle, called at the house of Marion Henrysdaughter and 'desired [her] to show her breasts'. Marion refused to do so, and her mother defended her saying, 'God judge me if either man or woman shall have satisfaction.' The following day, under orders from the parish minister, Ollason and two elders returned to the house. Marion reportedly 'showed her breasts but of which the milk flowed plentifully, and upon enquiry declared that the said Malcolm Malcolmson was the father of the child, but she would not tell what she had done with the child's corpse'. That Sunday Marion Henrysdaughter was summoned to the Dunrossness kirk session and declared that the child was the result of a sexual assault by a married man when she was herding her father's cows in a barn. She also confessed to her father that she had buried the child in the skeo and claimed it had been stillborn. For his part Malcolm Malcolmson was contrite. He acknowledged 'with tears in his eyes' when interrogated before the session that he was the father of the child, but 'was conscious that he had no blame in what had happened and that even his own wife declared that she would have provided for the child as if it had been her own.'

Marion Henrysdaughter's story belongs to the pre-modern moral world of Shetland. She understood the strict norms governing sexual behaviour, and this understanding must have informed her decision not to reveal her pregnancy, even to the father of the child, to give birth in secret, to conceal the child's body and thereafter to claim she had been the victim of rape. This was a world in which women's bodies were observed and policed by family and neighbours, ministers and kirk sessions. Indeed, single women's bodies were public property, especially when they were suspected of being pregnant or having given birth. In 1815 Margaret Fraser's body was not only subject to constant observation and comment by other women – one neighbour exhorted her 'not to conceal the pregnancy if she was really in that state' – but was also subjected to frequent poking and pressing while she complained of nothing more than a swelling in her belly.[60] One of her neighbours, who wished to test the rumour that Margaret was with child, 'felt Margaret's belly and distinctly was aware of the moving of a child within it'. Another who suspected the true cause of Margaret's illness, visited after Margaret had given birth, 'felt her breasts and body and was immediately convinced that she had been recently delivered not only from the empty feeling of her belly and stomach and her body being tied round with a napkin as is customary with women after childbirth but also from the appearance of blood about her person and other convincing circumstances.'[61] Church ministers and elders, on the other hand, regarded the observation and control of women's sexual comportment as a central part of their disciplinary role. Ministers regularly reminded their parishioners from the pulpit of the consequences of sexual misconduct, including the punishment for concealment and child murder.[62] Session elders were often among the first on the scene following the rumour of a dead child, and it was they who set the wheels for a prosecution in motion.

Within this context of shame, guilt and punishment the role of women was compromised. Female knowledge and skill were, in normal circumstances, beneficial to a pregnant woman. The gossip and rumour that surrounded women who denied they were with child were intended to elicit from her an admission of her condition so that she might become part of that element of women's world centred upon motherhood. But a woman who steadfastly denied her condition alienated other women who did not wish to be associated with the arrival of an unwanted child. In the summer of 1853 Mary Twatt gave birth to an illegitimate child in her father's house. For some time rumours had circulated that the father of the child was Mary's brother-in-law, in whose house she had worked as a servant. This allegation helps to explain the intense interest in Mary's condition but also, perhaps, the reactions of her mother and female neighbours upon the birth of the child. Margaret Twatt heard her daughter cry out in the ben end of the house. She went to attend her and turned the blankets down and 'when she saw what had happened she said "I'll have to go and leave thee" and I [Mary] scarcely knowing what I said replied "Go".' The blankets were replaced. Some considerable time later Margaret returned and found the child dead. Asked whether the child was born alive Margaret replied, 'I suppose it was I saw it breathe once, but I gave it no help.' Neither mother nor daughter touched the child until Margaret Twatt wrapped it in cloth and placed it back in the bed, where it was left to lie for a day. Her neighbours Catherine Moffat, Elizabeth Jamieson and Christina Twatt also heard Mary's screams but none entered the house; the latter, who was Mary's aunt, refused saying 'that if they wanted her they would have sent for her'. Barbara Jamieson, another near neighbour, did confront Mary's mother as she was returning from the peat hill saying: 'Maggy there must have been something extraordinary in your house this morning as Mary's cries have alarmed the neighbours. What is the meaning of it?' Barbara had been unable to enter the house as the door had been shut. Margaret Twatt did not reply, whereby Barbara Jamieson remarked, 'friend there can be no secrets from god'.[63] The child was later placed in a box and buried by Mary's father. The attitude of Mary and her mother in denying Mary's pregnancy and the birth isolated Mary from a female culture which, in normal conditions, would have been beneficial.

Fifty years later, attitudes towards the infanticidal mother in Shetland had altered. The moral discourse propagated by the church – particularly as it pertained to female sexuality – had gradually given way to a new discourse which elevated and revered the maternal woman, and which represented women as victims of men's aggression and lust. And it is this shift in attitudes that helps to explain the treatment of our final infanticidal mother, Gina Skaar. Gina was a twenty-three-year-old Norwegian domestic servant found guilty of concealment of pregnancy by the Shetland sheriff court in 1899.[64] The full story of the circumstances resulting in her pregnancy are unknown. However, we do know a great deal about the public reaction to her condition and her actions. Whilst she was in the service of the Pole family in Mossbank her employer was informed by the local doctor that Gina was pregnant. Gina, however, denied this, and Mrs Pole, despite the evidence of her own eyes – 'she was growing bigger and bigger' – was inclined to believe her because 'she had been such a good servant and had always been so trustworthy'. In court Gina was treated with considerable sympathy. Her own defence lawyer made much of her youth, her ignorance of the language and her isolation from friends and family, 'especially females in whom she might have confided and consulted.'[65] Indeed, he urged the sheriff, 'One cannot but sympathise and feel sorry for the poor girl . . . No-one, my Lord, can have any idea as to the amount of suffering, both physical and mental, she has already undergone.' The sheriff accepted, to a degree, the mitigating circumstances. Gina was found guilty of concealment of pregnancy and sentenced to nine months' imprisonment instead of the maximum of two years, but this was not the end of the matter. The outpouring of public sympathy for the girl and the tenor of popular opinion stands in marked contrast to earlier attitudes. Gina, 'a poor Norwegian girl', was seen not as a perpetrator but as a victim of male mistreatment according to one correspondent to the *Shetland Times* who signed himself 'a Father':

> I have often wondered why the other, and generally more guilty party, should get off scot free, while the poor female has to bear all the suffering and terrible disgrace . . . in our laws regarding such cases there is something worse than rotten: there is a cruel, horrid, burning shame. If the blackguard who may have ruined a poor girl cannot be put in as a criminal beside her, his name should be published . . . I do not know who her destroyer is, but I hope her sad case will stick to his guilty soul and lead him to do something for the girl he has ruined.[66]

Another supporter similarly argued that Gina was being made to suffer for 'the mean conduct of the male participant, whom I will not call a man . . . The girl has done wrong, no doubt, but she has suffered for it . . . we do not kill the fatted calf for the female prodigal in such cases; we reserve this entirely for the male.'[67] Henceforth a campaign to release Gina from prison was launched and, following the delivery of a petition to the Scottish Secretary signed by a number of residents of her parish of Mossbank, the sentence was reduced to six months.[68]

Gina Skaar's story is part of the modern moral world, of which Shetland was very much a part by 1900. She was portrayed as a respectable young woman, a domestic servant for a respected merchant's family, and her plight was treated with sympathy because she was deemed to be a victim. The 'modern' discourse on ideal womanhood could accept Gina Skaar, notwithstanding the fact that she had been pregnant with an illegitimate child and had caused the child to die, because she was, in the words of her mistress, a good servant and trustworthy. At her trial her defence effectively employed language that would appeal to the sentiments of those who had acculturated the ideals of nineteenth-century domestic and maternal womanhood. Perhaps Gina Skaar more closely epitomised the ideal of womanhood – weak, submissive, domestic, disempowered – than native Shetland females, who presented a more assertive identity. Marion Henrysdaughter, on the other hand, was condemned by her actions, and her body betrayed her. She was judged by the standards of a different set of values, those which regarded womanhood as sexually dangerous.

Respectability

By 1900 Shetland was immersed in the language of respectability, tinged with evangelical preoccupations with Christian morality, temperance and purity. These had pervaded public life and were being used in all kinds of circumstances to police a range of moral behaviour by men and women. Those who drank to excess, who beat their wives, or who engaged in lewd behaviour liable to be an affront to public decency were castigated by the courts and the press. In this way the discourses on morality and respectability in one's private affairs were circulated and reinforced in the public domain. Typical was the message imparted by Provost Porteous when sitting in judgement on Catherine Mouat in the Lerwick police court in 1908. Catherine, the wife of a cooper, had been found drunk in the High Street one Tuesday at noon. 'It is bad enough to see a man drink', exclaimed Porteous, 'but it is a disgraceful thing to see a young woman like you here on a similar charge. You should give up the drink altogether.' Catherine Mouat, having been let off with a warning, was duly chastised: 'Thank you, sir, I will never taste liquor again.'[69]

Shetland, and more particularly Lerwick, was changing from a rough little place to a more prosperous and socially mixed town containing a sizeable number of middle-class inhabitants imbued with Victorian evangelical sensibilities. As the town expanded it acquired new churches and mission halls, and all the accoutrements of provincial bourgeois respectable sociability: women's and youth organisations, teetotalism, freemasonry and civic ritual. Embodied within this culture were the values of self-control, restraint and decency, and one of the routes by which the discourses on respectability were circulated amongst the wider Shetland population was the Shetland press. From the 1880s prosecutions of domestic and marital violence were regularly reported in the newspapers. Stories of husbands mentally and physically abusing their wives and families were used to impart the message that such behaviour was unacceptable. Magistrates never missed an opportunity to teach a moral lesson, not only to those present in court but also to the broader reading public. Thus, when the labourer Laurence Jamieson came before the police court in 1901 charged with being drunk and incapable in Lerwick's Mounthooly Street, the magistrate Baillie Porteous grasped the opportunity to preach a lesson on the evils of drink and the duties of a good husband. 'It is a terrible thing that a man should drink all his earnings as you do and leave his wife and family to look after themselves . . . I fancy a man like you would have very limited credit. Every penny you spend in drink is taken away from your family, and should be spent for their comfort and maintenance.'[70] When Jamieson protested that his wife had not fulfilled her side of the marriage bargain – 'She hasn't made me meat nor yet washed me clothes for the past six months' – the magistrate was unimpressed by his excuses and absence of genuine regret. Laurence Jamieson had not embraced the language of Christian respectability or the demeanour of the redeemed sinner, unlike his compatriot Robert Anderson, whose 'conversion' from wife-beater to good Christian husband exemplifies the acculturation of evangelical discourses on respectability amongst all social classes and both sexes in Shetland at the end of the nineteenth century.

In December 1886 Betsy Nicholson, wife of Robert Anderson, a fishcurer and crofter residing on the northern tip of the Shetland mainland, made a statement to a local policeman about her predicament:

My name is . . . Betsy Nicolson, 36 years of age and at present residing with my husband Robt. Anderson. I was married to him in 1870, we have 7 of a family, the oldest is 16 years old and the youngest 1 year old. My marriage life has been very unhappy on account of cruel treatment by my husband towards myself and family. He is often in the habit of locking up all the food in the house and threatens to take my life if I should put a finger on it. He bakes his bread and cooks his food for himself, it is my belief that we shall be starved to death if we shall be any longer depending upon my cruel and unnatural husband, there is not long since he said to me that it was of no use to be bothering ourselves about the world when one of us was to be murdered and the other hanged.[71]

Betsy's fear of her husband's violence intensified in the new year of 1887, after an incident in which Robert struck her eldest child Isa and then struck her too, 'a hard blow on the forehead which remained black and painful for several days'.[72] Following this incident Robert was arrested, charged with assault and put in prison to await trial. The witness statements by Betsy and two of her children testified to a long history of violence. Betsy explained that after the couple married in Leith they returned to Shetland with nowhere to live, so they each stayed with their respective parents until Robert found them a house at North Roe. Shortly after the birth of their first child in 1872 Robert began to ill-use her. 'He has gone on getting worse but I have stopped for the sake of my seven children.'[73] Isa, aged fifteen, confirmed her mother's story – 'I have heard my father say that he would put my mother to her grave' – and fourteen-year-old James stated that 'I have heard him threaten to kill my mother several times.'[74] Robert, then, had never been a good husband or father. Not only was he violent but he failed to fulfil the most basic function of the good man, providing for his family. Betsy, on the other hand, presented herself as the ideal wife and mother, a woman who sacrificed herself for sixteen years for the sake of her children. Such narrative constructions of the bad husband and the good wife can be seen repeatedly in the records of the civil courts of Europe throughout the century as the gendered discourses of respectability and morality became embedded at all levels of society. But in this case the use of idealised constructions of gender roles and their antithesis took an added significance when Betsy suddenly withdrew her complaint:

I withdraw the proceedings against my husband, Robert Anderson, as he is come home a new man in the Lord Jesus, and promised to lead a new life, so we have forgiven each other. I could have proved every word of it, yet we all need mercy, and I do not want to persevere in it, if he will be in peace. May I never more need the protection of the law again; but I hope you will see that it is not because I could not prove it, but because he forgives me, I forgive him.[75]

The procurator fiscal and the judge in the case were not entirely convinced of Robert's sudden conversion. Robert had spent five days in prison and had then been allowed home, during which time it was suggested 'he might have used influence.'[76] In the light of current understandings of the psychology of domestic abuse, the modern reader is likely to side with the cynicism of the judge who refused to dispose of the case entirely and instead let it lie on the table, allowing for it to be resurrected if new evidence came to light. But, in the context of evangelical Britain, where conversion of the male unconverted and redemption of the male sinner by a good Christian woman was a constant theme in popular novels, tracts, magazines and obituaries, Robert Anderson's conversion and his wife's willingness to believe in his transformation become understandable. Indeed, as the historian Callum Brown argues, women were invariably the agents of men's redemption. In this case it was Betsy who was empowered to change her husband from a mean and violent heathen to a 'new man', a respectable husband.[77] Betsy Anderson clearly fulfilled the requisite qualities of nineteenth-century female piety. She was most likely a practising Christian and a good wife and mother. Robert may have come to see himself as a sinner, an unworthy husband and father. Certainly his sense of masculine identity was challenged in the private sphere of the home and in the public domain of the court and the media. Conversion was the only route to redemption by his family and society as a whole.

The court case marked a hiatus in the affairs of the Anderson family. Two years after Robert's court appearance Betsy gave birth to her eighth child, whom she named Harriet Beecher Stowe Anderson after the American evangelical abolitionist and author of *Uncle Tom's Cabin*. Betsy would have been familiar with this 'icon of female evangelicalism' from her readings of popular religious magazines and tracts, and her decision to give her daughter this remarkable name – and surely it was Betsy's decision to do so – is not only an indication of her strong identity as a Christian woman but also an affirmation, both to itself and to the community beyond, of her family's commitment to the morals of evangelical Christianity. We know nothing more of the fate of Betsy and Robert, but it appears that the family maintained its evangelical adherence as second- and third-generation Andersons were baptised and married in either Baptist or Congregational churches.[78]

Betsy Anderson's decision to accept her husband's conversion was perhaps not solely informed by her religious faith and the evangelical imperative to forgive her sinful husband. Like any woman in Shetland she was in a fragile economic situation. Unlike some of their neighbours in North Roe the Andersons had little land; Robert is described in the 1881 census as a fisherman's labourer and farmer; Betsy is described as a farmer's wife. With seven children they would have struggled. And Betsy must have known that without a husband her chances of survival would have been seriously harmed. She only needed to read the local newspapers to understand that the authorities could not be relied upon to support the abused wife. A case in point is that of Gilbert and Margaret Williamson, who lived not far from the Andersons at North Roe. In 1883 John Thompson, a neighbour of the Williamsons, wrote to the procurator fiscal Thomas Gifford at the behest of Margaret Williamson.

> I am sorry to inform you that Margaret Anderson or Williamson came here to me today asking me if I would write and let you know that they cannot stop with Gilbert W any longer as he is getting worse and worse every day. Dear Sir Margaret tells me today that she came in from giving the cattle their dinner he was standing over the fire naked with a knife in his hand and when she saw him made for the door he got hold of her and very likely would have put an end to her life if it had not been the New Town folks and the daughter that was working near the door which fled to her relief . . . he is saying that he is going to take away his own life also and we cannot tell how soon the devil may tempt him to put his words into action.[79]

John Thompson had offered Margaret Williamson and her daughter a refuge at his house until the authorities decided to act. But investigations by the medical officer, the local poor inspector and the local policeman all failed to find a reason to intervene. The medical officer considered Gilbert Williamson 'to be of sound mind'.[80] The parish poor inspector refused to take action on the grounds that the man was not a pauper but added that, 'If it is true, as it seems to be, that he is threatening violence for his wife and daughter . . . and that he has actually committed, or tried to commit an assault on his wife – should he not be apprehended on a criminal charge?'[81] Yet when PC Urquhart enquired into the situation, he merely presented a picture of a quarrelsome household which did not justify police intervention.

> In the first place I found that Williamson is not in the habit of disturbing his neighbours, there is none of them afraid of him, they say he is very seldom seen outside, but it is well known that there are

quarrels and almost continual disturbance between Williamson and his wife and daughter . . . but as far as I could learn Williamson has not committed assault which can be proven against him.[82]

The fact that Gilbert Williamson's behaviour was not a disturbance to his neighbours was of some importance, particularly in view of the fact that PC Urquhart witnessed Williamson's appalling manners but felt unable to pursue the case further. 'He is indolent and abusive in his manners, and always uttering profane language. I may mention that when I came to the house he seemed to be unruly, he had the door off the hinges, and he threw a kettle of boiling water on the floor, but he got very quite (sic) as soon as he saw me.'[83]

In the absence of a criminal conviction Margaret Williamson had few choices. If she made herself homeless she was unlikely to receive support from the parochial board. Such was the plight of Williamina Craigie from the island of Whalsay, who alleged that she was so cruelly treated by husband William that she was forced to 'flee for safety' to Lerwick leaving her seven children behind.[84] In 1900, unable to support herself owing to a dislocation of the coccyx as a result of her husband kicking her in the back, Williamina applied for an interim award of aliment against her husband and custody of her children. She also applied for admission to the poor roll in order that she might take action against her husband. But despite evidence of a catalogue of the most severe ill-treatment against her, including mental and physical cruelty by William's daughter from his first marriage, Williamina's case was dismissed by the sheriff.

The moral order that came to dominate at the end of the nineteenth century incorporated a mainstream British rhetoric of respectability, of moral probity, of public decency. Drinking in public, upsetting the neighbours and disturbing the peace were regarded as unacceptable threats to social order. The town elites were importing their ideas about decency and respectability into people's private lives. Betsy Anderson took it upon herself to reform her household. Other women possessing less strength of will or belief in redemption had to rely on the courts to order their private lives by fining or imprisoning their cruel and violent husbands. By 1900 it was increasingly likely that the courts would act on the turn to respectability, reflected in the comments by Sheriff Broun in a case of marital assault on the pier at Bressay in 1910: 'it is not a nice thing to strike a woman in the face.'[85] But female victims of this kind of behaviour possibly suffered not merely from a patriarchal legal system but from the widespread perception in Shetland that women here rarely conformed to the image of the respectable domestic wife.

Conclusions

The ideals of Victorian womanhood, of separate spheres, domesticity and respectability which are so central to all our traditional understandings of women and gender relations appear to have had little relevance for most Shetland women. The majority engaged in economic production, were little concerned with the domestic sphere, had limited opportunities to fulfil the domestic ideal and possessed a strong sense of where their rights lay. They had clear ideas of the rules of sexual liaison, though these became muddied by laddish men and alien lawyers when they got to court. From the 1860s to the 1900s, this culture suffered the attrition of invading discourses disseminated by a new bourgeoisie and visiting fishers, missionaries and tourists. By 1900, women had no choice but to utilise the language of idealised womanhood in order to offset the language and actions they were forced to describe in court. In contrast with the pre-modern style of the kirk session system, which judged a woman by her actions and dealt with her accordingly, the civil and criminal courts allowed for far greater use of rhetorical language and alternative readings of events. Women had to stand up in court and describe, often in some detail, the nature of their experiences in the sexual domain. Women's voices were not oppressed or silenced by discourses of domesticity and respectability, but Shetland women, with their strong sense of self, confidence in themselves and sureness about their identity drawn from their economic role, were willing to use the legal system in order to gain economic recompense for dashed hopes and disappointed expectations. Women found the civil and criminal courts a place where they could speak about their own understandings of appropriate or acceptable sexual behaviour. Far from adopting a weak or passive demeanour in court, many of these women, especially those who claimed financial damages for breach of promise or in the form of aliment for an illegitimate child, used their opportunity to establish their reputation. Indeed, Shetland women were litigious to an extraordinary degree. They sought to use the system and needed no invitation. These women did not have power in the traditional sense but they possessed an identity as workers and aspired to independence. Their sexuality was not the sole or determining element of their identity.

Notes

1 Brettell, *Men who Migrate*; Brettell, 'Male migrants and unwed mothers'.
2 Alexander Trotter (1856) quoted in Flinn, *Travellers in a Bygone Shetland*, p. 80.
3 Brown, *Up-helly-aa*, pp. 63–81.

4 Brown, *Up-helly-aa*, pp. 84–96.

5 Revd G. T. Ridlon, *Shetland News*, 14 Jan. 1888.

6 *Shetland News*, 28 Jan. 1888.

7 John Laing (1822) quoted in Flinn, *Travellers in a Bygone Shetland*, p. 71.

8 A. Edmonston (1809) quoted in Kendall, *With Naught but Kin*, p. 105.

9 SA, SC 12/6/1811/60: Petition and complaint, 21 Oct. 1811.

10 SA, SC 12/6/1811/60: Petition and complaint, 21 Oct. 1811.

11 SA, AD 22/2/40/40: Andres Plokker, indecent assault, 16 June 1905.

12 'J. M. E. Saxby', in H. C. G. Matthew and B. Harrison (eds), *Oxford Dictionary of National Biography* (Oxford, Oxford University Press, 2004).

13 SA, D 1/134: unidentified newspaper cutting, dated 1894.

14 See R. Mitchison and L. Leneman, *Sexuality and Social Control: Scotland 1660–1780* (Oxford, Blackwell, 1989); L. Leneman and R. Mitchison, *Girls in Trouble: Sexuality and Social Control in Rural Scotland 1660–1780* (Edinburgh, Scottish Cultural Press, 1998); L. Leneman and R. Mitchison, *Sin in the City: Sexuality and Social Control in Urban Scotland 1660–1780* (Edinburgh, Scottish Cultural Press, 1998); G. DesBrisay, 'Wet nurses and unwed mothers in seventeenth century Aberdeen', in E. Ewan and M. M. Meikle (eds), *Women in Scotland c.1100–c.1750* (East Linton, Tuckwell Press, 1999), pp. 210–20.

15 See, for example, Leneman and Mitchison, *Girls in Trouble*, pp. 13 and 82–8.

16 See M. Todd, *The Culture of Protestantism in Early Modern Scotland* (New Haven and London, Yale University Press, 2002).

17 Cole, *Women of the Praia*, p. 77.

18 Corbin (1987) quoted in Cole, *Women of the Praia*, p. 78.

19 On this reorientation amongst anthropologists see Moore, *Feminism and Anthropology*, pp. 38–41 and A. Weiner, *Women of Value, Men of Renown: New Perspectives in Trobriand Exchange* (Austin, TX, 1976).

20 Cole, *Women of the Praia*, p. 79.

21 See T. C. Smout, *A Century of the Scottish People 1830–1950* (London, Fontana, 1987), pp. 166–74; A. Blaikie, 'A kind of loving: illegitimacy, grandparents and the rural economy of north east Scotland 1750–1900', *Scottish Economic and Social History* 14 (1994), pp. 41–57.

22 See the collection of studies of 'deviant' Scottish women in Y. G. Brown and R. Ferguson (eds), *Twisted Sisters: Women, Crime and Deviance in Scotland since 1400* (East Linton, Tuckwell Press, 2002). See also E. Ewan, 'Disorderly damsels: women and assault in late medieval Scotland', unpublished paper, 2002, and E. Ewan, 'Alison Rough: a woman's life and death in sixteenth-century Edinburgh', *Women's History Magazine* 45 (2003), pp. 4–13.

23 De Certeau, *The Practice of Everyday Life*.

24 SA, SC 12/6/1894/24: Georgeson v. Walterson, breach of promise to marry. Robina also threatened to sue Walterson for libel if his counsel persisted in the allegation that she had had an abortion, 'thereby implying that she was a woman of low character and had also been guilty of a criminal act'.

25 *Shetland Times*, 9 June 1894.

26 *Shetland Times*, 9 June 1894.

27 SA, SC 12/6/1894/24: Petition for damages (for £100 for breach of promise to marry).

28 SA, SC 12/6/1894/24: Petition for damages (for £100 for breach of promise to marry).

29 SA, SC 12/6/1894/24: Petition for damages (for £100 for breach of promise to marry).

30 *Shetland Times*, 9 June 1894.

31 SA, SC 12/6/1888/12: Petition for damages for breach of promise, 18 Feb. 1888.

32 R. Cowie, *Shetland: Descriptive and Historical* (Edinburgh, John Menzies and Co., 1st edn 1871), p. 102.

33 T. C. Smout, 'Aspects of sexual behaviour in nineteenth century Scotland', in A. A. Maclaren (ed.), *Social Class in Scotland: Past and Present* (Edinburgh, John Donald, 1976), pp. 55–85.

34 SA, SC 12/6/1823/13: Summons for damages for failure to marry, 5 March 1823.

35 SA, SC 12/6/1870/5: Summons of aliment, 20 Jan. 1870.

36 SA, SC 12/6/1870/5: Summons of aliment, 20 Jan. 1870.

37 SA, CH 2/380/3: Walls and Sandness kirk session minutes, 1771–1802, 10 March–27 May 1793.

38 SA 12/6/1888/12: Petition for damages for breach of promise to marry, 18 Feb. 1888.

39 *Shetland News*, 16 June 1888.

40 *Shetland News*, 7 July 1888.

41 SA, AD 22/2/17/23: Rape or assault with intent, 12 Oct. 1880.

42 SA, SC 12/6/1870/4: Summons for breach of promise to marry, 21 Jan. 1870.

43 Census, 1881: Walls.

44 SA, SC 12/6/1880/07: Petition for damages, 9 Feb. 1880.

45 Census, 1881.

46 SA, SC 12/36/4: Last will and testament of Hugh Williamson, 14 March 1858.

47 SA, SC 12/6/1871/60: Summons for damages, 9 Nov. 1871.

48 SA, SC 12/6/1888/12: Petition for damages, 18 Feb. 1888.

49 SA, SC 12/6/1888/12: Petition for damages, 18 Feb. 1888.

50 See A.-M. Kilday, 'Maternal monsters: murdering mothers in south-west Scotland, 1750–1815', in Brown and Ferguson (eds), *Twisted Sisters*, pp. 156–79.

51 Edmonston, *Present State of the Zetland Islands*, p. 63.

52 See D. A. Symonds, *Weep Not for Me: Women, Ballads and Infanticide in Early Modern Scotland* (University Park, PA, Pennsylvania State University Press, 1997), pp. 124–5.

53 SA, SC 12/6/1859/2: Judicial declaration of Jemima Nicolson, 19 Feb. 1859.

54 See, for example, S. Wilson, 'Infanticide, child abandonment and female honour in nineteenth century Corsica', *Comparative Studies in Society and History* 30 (1988), pp. 762–83.

55 227 aliment petitions are recorded in the Shetland sheriff court records between 1800 and 1890.

56 SA, SC 12/6/1868/62: Summons of aliment, 3 Oct. 1868; 1881 census: Shetland.

57 SA, SC 12/6/1794/17: Marion Henrysdaughter (evidence of Malcolm Malcolmson).

58 SA, SC 12/6/1859/4: 15 March 1859.

59 SA, SC 12/6/1794/17: Child murder, 8 Nov. 1794.

60 SA, SC 12/6/1815/44: Margaret Fraser, 27 Sept. 1815 (evidence of Catherine Mouat). See L. Gowing, *Common Bodies: Women, Touch and Power in Seventeenth Century England* (New Haven and London, Yale University Press, 2003).

61 SA, SC 12/6/1815/44: Evidence of Magdalene Moncrieff.

62 See SA, SC 12/6/1783/8: Margaret Omond, child murder, July 1783. William Mitchell, minister of Tingwall parish, stated, 'I have made the enquiry desired relative to the shocking affair of Margaret Omond . . . now in the Presbytery's opinion guilty of child murder by the Act of William and Mary which I have read several times from the pulpit . . .' (12 July 1873).

63 SA, AD 22/2/1/8/2: Mary Twatt, 1853 (precognition of Barbara Jamieson).

64 SA, AD 22/2/34/40: Gina Skaar, concealment of pregnancy, 10 Feb. 1899. See L. Abrams, 'The case of Gina Skaar', *The New Shetlander* 226 (Yule 2003), pp. 24–7.

65 *Shetland News*, 4 March 1899.

66 *Shetland Times*, 18 March 1899.

67 *Shetland News*, 25 March 1899.

68 *Shetland News*, 13 May 1899.

69 *Shetland News*, 15 Feb. 1908.

70 *Shetland Times*, 1 June 1901.

71 SA, AD 22/2/102/1886/101: Letter of Police Constable P. Urquhart to James Kirkland Galloway Esq., procurator fiscal for Zetland, 21 Dec. 1886.

72 SA, AD 22/2/22/58: Precognitions in action by procurator fiscal against Robt. Anderson, 10 Feb. 1887.

73 SA, AD 22/2/22/58: Action against Robt. Anderson, 10 Feb. 1887.

74 SA, AD 22/2/22/58: Action against Robt. Anderson, 10 Feb. 1887.

75 *Shetland Times*, 26 Feb. 1887.

76 *Shetland Times*, 26 Feb. 1887.

77 See C. G. Brown, *The Death of Christian Britain* (London, Routledge, 2001), pp. 88–114; C. G. Brown, 'The unconverted and the conversion: gender relations in the salvation narrative in Britain 1800–1960', in W. J. van Bekkum, J. N. Bremmer and A. Molendijk (eds), *Cultures of Conversion* (Brussels, Peeter, 2005).

78 Information provided by Bruce Benson.

79 SA, AD 22/2/102/1883/58/2: Letter from John Thompson to Thomas Gifford, 12 March 1883.

80 SA, AD 22/2/102/1883/58/2: Wm. Creau, medical officer, 17 March 1883.

81 SA, AD, 22/2/102/1883/58/3: Jas. Bruce inspector to Messrs Duncan & Galloway solicitors, 17 March 1883.

82 SA, AD 22/2/102/1883/58/1: PC Urquhart to procurator fiscal, 2 April 1883.

83 SA, AD 22/2/102/1883/58/1: PC Urquhart to procurator fiscal, 2 April 1883.

84 SA, SC 12/6/1900/03: Petition for admission to poors' roll anent action concerning ill treatment, March 1900; SC 12/6/1900/05: Petition for maintenance of 10s a week and custody of children, 26 March 1900.

85 *Shetland News*, 16 April 1910.

7

Power

Da women den could do laek men. (Shetland Archive, 3/1/124: Katie Inkster)

VISITORS TO SHETLAND in the nineteenth century regarded the women they encountered as subordinate and put-upon. But at the same time they admired their physical and mental strength. Outsiders understood that this society could not be compared with other rural communities in other parts of the British Isles, and they frequently used the iconic crofting and knitting female as a symbolic means of conveying this difference. Implicit in their descriptions of women was an ambiguity about the power women possessed. The wife of a fisherman who carried his sea-chest on her back for miles while he walked beside her or rode on a pony, or the woman who carried her husband to and from his boat to prevent his feet from getting wet, appeared to represent the very worst kind of exploitation at a time when ideas about woman's domestic role pervaded discourses on womanhood elsewhere in Europe and North America. Yet those visitors also recognised and admired women's industry and saw that it was often the women who 'wore the breeches' at home.

Like the new visitors to Shetland, the historians of the early twenty-first century would ordinarily reach the same conclusions. They would do so, at root, because we are equipped with the same myth system of discourse about what constitutes women's subordination and power. This chapter seeks to navigate the issue of 'power' by approaching it in terms which the Shetland woman understood in the nineteenth and early twentieth centuries, and which survive in women's contemporary understanding of their own heritage.

Gender

The pervasiveness of the ideology of domesticity and the desirability of the withdrawal of women from productive work amongst the middle classes of western Europe and North America during the nineteenth century had a powerful impact upon travellers during that era who encountered alternative cultures or modes of living. Whether visiting the lesser-known parts of Europe or the unknown imperial posses-sions, these men and women judged the peoples they encountered according to their own world view. Likewise, modern anthropologists have tended in the past to make glib assumptions about power relations in any given society, based upon often superficial observations. Thus the appearance to outsiders of seemingly downtrodden, passive and submissive women in many parts of Europe led to the depiction of these women as subordinate and oppressed. For instance, images of rural Greek women clothed in dark apparel, 'formless, effaced and self-effacing', symbolised to outsiders an apparent subordination of women in rural Greek society which anthropologists began to question only in the late 1960s.[1] Amongst the Andalusian gypsy community the women were 'deliberately dowdy' in their dress, always wearing an apron which suggested, to the uninitiated, female subordination.[2] The fishwives of the east coast of Scotland were depicted as drudges for carrying baskets of fish for miles to sell to rural households.[3] The 'Lady Correspondent' of the *Dundee Advertiser* drew similar conclusions upon encountering Shetland women in 1898. 'They are never without their burden, never at rest from toil. They look overdriven and weighed down with unremitting labour.'[4] In some societies in western Europe, as well as further afield in so called 'primitive' communities, the restrictive spatial nature of women's lives, their containment within the home and even the taboos governing where they could or could not go led to assumptions of women's second-class status and exclusion from all structures of power.[5] And women themselves may have conspired to create an illusion of a male-dominated society which outsiders easily accepted because it coincided with their preconceived ideas.[6] Thus women who were hidden away were labelled subordinate; women who were undertaking paid work in the public domain were judged to be unfortunate, exploited or dangerous. In Shetland, where it was common to see women working in public view, the latter conclusion was easily drawn. Walter Scott echoed the views of the majority of his contemporaries when he 'deprecated the invincible native habit of making the women burden-bearers'.[7]

The second assumption that has encouraged both outside observers and more recent scholars to represent women as subordinate in peasant societies has been a common understanding about where power resides in such communities. The androcentrism of much early writing within history and anthropology was manifested in a focus on formal structures and hierarchies which could be easily seen and understood within western frameworks of public power. Thus power was seen to rest upon ownership of property, control over major resources and access to the institutions and processes of political decision making. In most societies men have clearly dominated these realms. Systems of property inheritance – whether based on primogeniture or partible inheritance – tend to favour sons, and landownership commonly trans- lates into other forms of power, authority and status in rural cultures.[8] Societies in which women inherit land as a matter of course, or where they own significant wealth, are rare and tend to be noted as exceptions rather than alternative models which may have applicability elsewhere. The tendency to describe such societies – such as Galicia in northern Spain – as matriarchies merely turns the patriarchal model on its head rather than offering a more nuanced understanding of how power is distributed in gendered ways.[9]

Historians have found the notion of separate spheres, the division between the private and the public, a useful means of talking about access to power. Neither sphere is necessarily gendered, but in the nine- teenth century the private sphere became associated more exclusively with the domestic, the home and reproduction and thus became identified with female roles. Conversely, the public sphere of work, commerce, politics and sociability became identified with male roles. The public–private distinction gives rise to two explanatory models. The first model is a society where the distinction between public and private spheres is sharply drawn and where women are primarily associated with the private or domestic sphere. In this model women are more likely to have a low status. The second model is a society where the public–private distinction is blunter, where gender roles are less sharply defined and hence where egalitarian relationships are more likely.[10] In the context of fishing communities both models have been applied. Within those of north-east Scotland and elsewhere around the North Sea, where the men were forced to become mere wage earners on deep-sea trawlers instead of owning their own boats, and where men were absent from home for long periods, it has been argued that the men's experience of exploitation was manifested in their dominance in the home expressed through heavy drinking, selfishness and domestic violence.[11] Elsewhere, such as in Shetland, it is suggested by some scholars that more equal gender relations were the consequence of more flexible understandings of public and private spheres.[12] In this kind of society power is less likely to be exclusively associated with public roles, and public decisions may be made at the level of the household. Where public and private roles are seen as complementary and where neither sphere is exclusively the domain of one sex, it is likely that the domestic sphere, broadly defined, may provide an alternative or competing basis for power.

Since the 1970s, feminist historians and anthropologists have effectively challenged this androcentric way of reading power relations.[13] They have recognised that women's modes of action have often been ignored or misunderstood, that behaviour patterns have been interpreted too literally and that taboos and cultural obligations have been interpreted invariably as restraints and as straightforward signs of subordination.[14] Taking a woman-centred perspective as the starting point, these scholars have radically shifted the language and interpretation of power in rural and peasant societies by looking for power in different places and interpreting its expressions in different ways. The mere fact that women displayed a subordinate, passive or deferent demeanour to ethnologists or to their social and political superiors does not mean that they necessarily occupied a subordinate position in the community hierarchy, or that they lacked authority in either the private or the public sphere. And even though women in many – probably most – peasant societies did not own land or property, and did not directly influence political decision making, it does not follow that they were universally subordinate. This perspective has reconceptualised power, its locus and its nature.

Feminist scholars have thus worked with more complex and diffuse notions of power which take into account a variety of ways in which power may be distributed. Ownership of property and land is not excluded from the analysis but, especially in land-poor societies, or in those where ownership of land and property is concentrated in the hands of the very few, power relations are determined by different factors and may be observed in different places. In peasant societies where 'real' or formal power is believed to be situated outside the community (with the landowners for instance, or the church), informal power is more significant in determining day-to-day relations.[15] There are three ways of thinking about gendered power relations in these societies. The first is focused upon women's role as producers; the second concerns power within the household; and the third perspective broadens the understanding of power to include the power of knowledge.

Property

In Shetland these alternative models are especially helpful because neither the majority of men nor the majority of women owned the land they cultivated or the houses they lived in. Here, property ownership and inheritance patterns had little bearing upon gendered power relations. The land on Shetland was owned by landlords – some resident, others absentee – some of whom leased their estates to merchant-lairds who in turn received rents from tenants. The majority of Shetlanders who lived outside Lerwick were tenants of a farm or croft on which they conducted subsistence agriculture in addition to the living they gained from the sea. In 1861, for example, in the parish of Dunrossness in South Mainland, John Bruce of Sumburgh was one of the major landowners, with 309 tenants, along with William Bruce of Symbister, who had 188 tenants.[16] These parcels of land ranged in size and value but most were small patches of between 0.5 and 8 merks and rarely exceeded £7 in value.[17] The tenancy of a croft, then, did not directly confer power on the named tenant. Indirectly, though, the tenant did assume various responsibilities. One of the conditions of lease on Thomas Cameron's Garth and Annsbrae estate stated that 'the head of the family is responsible for the conduct of all the members of same' and that the tack (or land lease) was to pass to the 'lawful heirs male of the tenant . . . and failing heirs male to the heirs female by the same rules, without division', although the tenant was permitted to name any child the rightful successor.[18] Thus there were rights and responsibilities assigned to a named tenant, and it is possible that he or she may have assumed a degree of power or status from these, although this very much depended on the value of the land. Conversely, the loss of a tenancy through eviction appears to have had a symbolic significance and of course a very real material impact. A crofter who refused to 'submit to this assumed patriarchal Government' (of the landlord or merchant) might face eviction and was perceived to have been 'robbed of his manhood', in the words of the *Shetland News* of 1889.[19] It is a moot point whether a woman who was likewise evicted was similarly perceived to have lost status amongst her peers.

If we assume for a moment that the tenancy of a farm or croft was associated with some status in Shetland society, then the proportion of female tenants at any one time should interest us. There was no prohibition against a woman signing a tenancy agreement, although it seems more likely that wives inherited tenancies in the event of a husband's death. Proportions of female tenants varied substantially in different parts of the islands and at different times. In 1861 only 8 per cent of South Mainland tenancies were held by women, and half of these were widows, which suggests that a goodly proportion of female tenants had inherited from their husbands. Moreover, the average value of the female tenancies – £233 – was significantly lower than the average value of all tenancies – £398.[20] Almost thirty years later in 1889, proportions of female tenants on various estates ranged from a high of 27 per cent on the Bruce estate at Sumburgh in South Mainland to a low of 7 per cent on the neighbouring Bruce of Symbister estate.[21] The assertion by Paul Thompson that in the early twentieth century Shetland women held a compensating power through owning the land they worked – and he suggests that 'nearly a third of the farms were held by women' – is misleading in that it exaggerates the percentage of female croft tenancies across the islands as a whole. Moreover, it would be wrong to suggest that a tenancy, even after the Crofters' Holdings Act of 1886, conferred economic or political power.[22] What it did provide was a means to a living as long as one was physically able to nurture the land.

Before the fixing of rents by the Crofters' Commission in 1889, many tenants in Shetland were tied into fishing contracts. As women did not go to sea, a female tenant of a croft required a man to fish for the landlord in order to pay the rent. A widow who inherited a croft tenancy from her husband would quickly fall into debt if she did not have a son or other male relative to fish. Drowning at sea was a commonplace event, but two fishing disasters – the Gloup disaster of 1881 with the loss of fifty-eight fishermen and the Delting tragedy of 1900 when twenty-two men drowned – highlighted the plight of the families left without a means of support. Following the Gloup disaster thirty-four widows and eighty-five children were left to manage without a male earner. One such was the widow of Alexander Moar, who, along with his eldest son, had drowned that July day. Left with five children to care for, Alexander Moar's widow had only a croft with a few cattle and sheep, one or two ponies and a debt of £2 to James Hoseason, the merchant.[23] Widows commonly found themselves indebted to the merchants in the event of the loss of a husband at sea if his boat and equipment was also lost. Merchants advanced lines and tackle on credit to fishermen but demanded repayment in the event of a tragedy. Following the establishment of the Shetland Fishermen's Widows' Relief Fund in 1881 after the Gloup disaster, widows and other dependants of fishermen did receive small amounts of charitable aid, and this additional income may have helped them to remain on the croft. However, it was not uncommon for landlords or their agents to retain sums paid out by insurance funds to widows of seamen. In Ursula Smith's case, the £24 she was due from the Shipwrecked Mariners' Society following the loss of her husband at sea was appropriated by the landlord to set against her rent and arrears. Ursula Smith received only £1 to use as she wished.[24]

In 1886 the Crofters' Holdings Act granted crofters security of tenure. This was followed by the fixing of fair rents and the writing off of debts by the Crofters' Commission in 1889 and 1892. At the same time the fishing-tenure system disappeared and was followed by the herring boom, which offered much greater rewards to fishermen and boosted the Shetland economy in general. By the end of the century the croft was no longer such an essential means to survival. If there was ever a time when female tenancies increased it was coterminous with the marginality of crofting, reflecting the low status of the occupation and the availability of alternative occupations for men. For women, crofting tenancies conferred little if any status before 1886 because of the insecurity of tenure, the constant indebtedness, the need for a man to fish and the threat of eviction. From 1886 the existence of secure tenancies and fixed rents improved tenants' rights, but on account of the poor quality and value of the land and the increasing opportunities for cash earnings in other sectors, the value of the croft shifted. It remained important at a subsistence level and as a source of additional income in cash and in kind, at least until the Second World War. Thereafter, it has been argued, the croft itself took on more symbolic than economic value. For the whole period, then, it was not women's legal status as tenants that was significant, but their economic contribution to the household.

Production

In land-poor societies and in maritime communities which depend upon an unreliable resource, power and status derive less from property ownership than from one's contribution to productive activity. In a marginal or subsistence economy, the work of all members of the community or household is essential to that group's well-being. Households depend upon a multiplicity of seasonal production activities – both subsistence production on the croft and commodity production for cash or barter. The ideological division between male wage earners or breadwinners and female homemakers has much less material relevance in this context (except as a discursive power mediated through institutions like the church, the legal system and so on). Men and women depend on one another but, at the same time, the economic independence of each gender, and the division between male-dominated occupations and those carried out predominantly by women, give females economic authority and thus a degree of personal autonomy. This is exaggerated in fishing communities by the physical absence of men for short or long periods of time.

Anthropologists have described a number of 'matricentric regions' in Europe: mainly maritime or mixed fishing and farming regions like Galicia, Malta, parts of northern Portugal and some regions of Scandinavia, where women's labour is valued and where they have achieved a degree of autonomy.[25] In areas like this which contain diverse economic activities, often on land and at sea supplemented by craft production, women and men engage in a variety of production tasks. In northern Portugal, for instance, men were primarily occupied with fishing. Women, though, harvested and sold seaweed, fished with hand lines, worked in onshore fishery activities including the sale of fish, kept gardens for vegetables, farmed hens and rabbits and worked as day labourers on the land.[26] In Swedish coastal communities women ran family farms as well as contributing to the fishery.[27] On the east coast of Scotland women made essential contributions to the fishing economy in their role as net makers and menders, as line baiters and as fish gutters, packers and sellers. In addition they knitted gansies (woollen sweaters) and looked after the house and children.[28] In all these cases women's economic activity brought them in contact with the market and all the issues of economic and cultural production we saw in earlier chapters.

The existence of what have been described as 'matriarchal' societies, notably in Galicia but also in parts of Scandinavia, in Iceland and even in north-east Scotland, suggests that there are precedents for the translation of women's economic participation and autonomous decision making into greater respect and even social and economic power. Galicia represents the most extreme example of a society wherein women, at least until the 1960s, dominated economic and social relations. In this northern Spanish farming and fishing region, the matrilinial family system, whereby the mother is head of the family and property is normally inherited through the female line, endows women with status and authority. Women manage family farms, they make all the decisions regarding the running of the farm, they carry out the financial transactions and they control resources including land and equipment. In fishing communities they control harbour activities, they own boats and they sell the fish, keeping the money.[29] Within Europe Galicia does seem exceptional for the usurpation of patriarchal authority by women. More often it is the case that women's participation in production does not lead to greater power or authority for women in society. They are just as likely to experience exploitation. Management of the household economy and holding the purse strings does not necessarily translate into status or even respect, and it is rare that women are able to convert their earnings into recognised symbols of power such as property. In Newfoundland outport communities, for example, where women contributed economically in any way possible, they were not 'rewarded' by access to property or to the political privileges available to men.[30]

Galicia and Newfoundland sit at either end of a spectrum which attempts to equate women's economic activity with traditional notions of power. However, if we expand our concept of power to include control over resources and we cease analysing women solely in relation to men and male-centred notions of authority and status, then the experience of women in Shetland may be better understood. In a community such as Shetland, where fishing played such a central role in economic life, women's role in the exploitation of the sea was not as great as one might expect. Unlike her counterparts in Portugal, northern Spain, Norway and Sweden, the Shetland woman was rarely found working as part of a crew at sea (although the women were fine rowers and were not averse to inshore line fishing when necessary).[31] Neither did Shetland women have any control over the sale of fish, in contrast with women in maritime communities elsewhere in the United Kingdom such as those in Cornwall, Northumberland and Scotland's east coast. The processing and sale of fish were so controlled by the merchants that women's only form of participation after the catch was as waged labour at the herring stations. Thus we must look at women's control of resources in other realms away from the fishing.

The income, in cash or in kind, brought into the household by women was essential for year-round survival, as was their ability to manage the household resources. Women engaged in both subsistence and commodity production as well as hiring themselves as waged labour on farms. Everything on the croft was treated as an asset: the land, however poor, could produce food in the form of vegetables and meal or fodder for animals. Most crofts kept a small number of livestock – one or two cows, a few sheep, hens and possibly a pony or two. It was women's job to make the most of these meagre resources. Anything not consumed in the household was sold or exchanged.

As independent entrepreneurs and tradeswomen, they took economic decisions, often finding other women with whom to co-operate. Mary Hutchison from Lerwick described to the Truck Commissioners in 1872 how she made a living as a small businesswoman, as a knitter but also as an agent for an Edinburgh wholesaler. She explained how she took orders from Edinburgh and engaged a number of Shetland women to knit for her. Mary Hutchison supplied the wool and paid her knitters in cash. She also traded in credit notes given her by knitters who needed cash.[32] As Chapter 5 illustrated, women's role in production was a significant factor in the formation of a female culture, and in some degree this culture translated into power. In these circumstances it is not surprising that Shetland women have always had a strong identity as workers. In the past their self-image was determined by the work they did rather than their marital or social status. Women's work identity was in part formed by their autonomy as producers, both on the croft and in commodity production. Census returns from Shetland are testament to the importance of work to women's sense of self. Enumerators identified women as workers in discrete occupations rather than as dependants, which must have reflected the will of the women themselves to be so defined as much as the reality observed by the officials. In the 1851 census just 4 per cent of women over the age of fifteen in South Mainland were not given an occupational identity. The majority of adult women – 55 per cent – were explicitly identified as employed in South Mainland, and the rest were defined by a relationship to the head of household as 'wife' or 'daughter'. In the 1881 census for the whole of Shetland, only 16 per cent of women aged over fifteen years were given no occupation. Only 4 per cent of female heads of household were so defined. These figures are significant because in 1881 enumerators were instructed to classify as 'unoccupied' women assisting in family enterprises without pay, a category into which many Shetland women would have fallen if the instruction was taken literally. Moreover, one can assume that those identified as 'crofter's wife' or 'fisherman's wife' were actively employed. The determination of women to be identified as workers is highlighted by individual occupational definitions such as that assigned to seventy-two-year-old Mary Moar living at Kellister, North Yell – 'taking care of children'. Mary was living with her daughter and son-in-law, a fisherman and farmer, and their two young boys. And in the 1901 census, widow Margaret Johnson from Quarff was aptly described as a 'crofteress'.[33]

Personal testimonies recorded since the 1970s affirm the centrality of work to the identity of Shetland women. This suggests that census returns were a true reflection of a distinct female consciousness rooted in the material and cultural realities of life on the islands. Historians have remarked upon the misleading nature of the census as an indicator of the extent and nature of women's work elsewhere in Britain in the nineteenth century, on account of the tendency of enumerators to under-record the work undertaken by women in the light of domestic ideology. Indeed, it has been argued that because the census was organised and produced by men, both the diversity and the quantity of women's employment were misrepresented and underestimated, with many occupied women being defined as 'dependants'.[34] In Shetland, on the other hand, enumerators were recording what they were told in the light of their own understanding of the role of women in the economy of the islands. Thus a woman who engaged in hosiery production in the home was likely to be recorded as a 'knitter' in Shetland. Elsewhere this important economic activity might have been ignored on account of it being regarded as a domestic undertaking and not a legitimate or formal employment category. 'Dependant' was clearly not a status with which Shetland women felt comfortable. In 1881 only three adult women in the whole of Shetland were so defined and one of these was an 'imbecile'.

The census is one of the most anonymous of sources, but even in the barest of entries we can uncover something of the ways in which Shetland women interpreted their experiences and represented them-selves to others. Life stories, on the other hand, are rich, multi-layered portrayals of women's subjectivities. Women who narrate their lives have the opportunity to present themselves to others as they would wish to be presented. As Sally Cole remarks in her study of Portuguese women, life stories 'present women as social actors constructing their lives in ways that empower them and employing strategies to achieve goals that they define within their particular historical and social contexts.'[35] In the Mediterranean, women's personal testimonies have challenged the construction of themselves in the anthropological literature as trapped within the honour-and-shame code. In Shetland women's narratives do counter outsiders' conceptions of the downtrodden and exploited female, but they do so by engaging with and utilising an idealised discourse of the Shetland woman which stresses her strength, her inde-pendence and her equality.[36] Consequently, work features at the heart of oral and written testimonies.

For seven years, between 1968 and 1974, Mary Manson from Westsandwick on the island of Yell kept a diary.[37] Every day, without fail, she recorded the weather conditions and the activities undertaken on the croft. The seasonal round of crofting tasks dominates the entries. Subjective feelings and personal experiences feature rarely, despite the fact that the author was well known throughout Shetland as a storyteller. Mary Manson's story of a journey to fetch a cure from a wise-woman has already been analysed in Chapter 2. She was born in

1897 into a crofting family. She married a seaman and crofter and lived in Yell all her life, rarely leaving Shetland. Her daily routine was dominated by croft work, starting in April with the sowing and drilling and finishing in November with the killing of pigs to supply the family with meat for the winter. Her diary entries tell us that she identified herself as a worker, both on the croft and in the house. Mary was an active participant in all the major crofting activities, from gathering the sheep in the spring to raising the peats and hoeing turnips through the summer months and cutting the hay and gathering the potatoes at the end of the crofting year. In addition she did all the housework and prepared meals for the family and neighbours. In a typical entry for 1 and 2 May 1969 she writes:

> 1 May: Beautiful morning but came away torrential showers in the afternoon, dried up later SE [south-east]. Dad [Mary's husband] and Hughie shifting the sheep to the hill park. Dad up with a bag of hay for the sheep. Robert Keith ploughed up the ground and also ploughed up Jeanie Smith's . . . Too wet to do any sowing of corn today. Hughie started to cart out the Noosterhouse byre.
> 2 May: Dad and Mum [Mary Manson] sowing the corn. Harrowed it all with a tractor. In for tea after harrowing. Sausages and scrambled eggs. Mum and Dad spread the artificial manure on the corn and the tatties after teatime.[38]

Mary Manson's diary gives a privileged position to croft work. She decided on the balance between family events, personal experience and emotion, events in the wider world and day-to-day economic activities. The last of these almost always predominated. One of the few exceptions was the entry for 14 May 1968: there she wrote in red ink on what was undoubtedly a red-letter day, when electricity arrived on Yell: 'Electric lights switched on today. Mum and Dad celebrating with a bottle of white wife [a Shetland beer]. Mum and Dad carting out the last of the manure.'

The discourse within Shetland which constructs women as workers has strongly influenced the content of female personal narratives recorded since the 1970s. In a place where men were often absent or at least have no prominent place in women's discourses of work, women are keen to speak about the work carried out by their mothers. When asked by an interviewer to say more about her father, Katie Inkster replied: 'He sailed da sea – he wis at sea a lot and he wis on da navy. An he lived ta come through it. It wis an aaful worry for my mother – she's five peerie bairns and sho worked da croft. But we got it aa plooed you see, so I hed ta start, and no wonder I wis da youngest een aroond Weisdale dat could milk a coo . . . Just hed ta learn ta do it you see.'[39] This respondent falls immediately into the dominant narrative of men away at sea and women left at home to run the croft. Once she has dismissed her father Katie Inkster can return to the more familiar and self-affirming story of hard-working women. Even when she admits that some men did not go to sea she returns swiftly to the dominant narrative of crofting women: 'I'll tell you whar some o dem worked, on da coonty roads, because dey hed big crofts and their wives couldna manage. They couldna leave da bairns in even ta go oot ta da milking . . . But it wis a job, you ken, you could manage if you were maybe keepin one cow, but you couldna manage wi a lot.'[40]

Women's pride in their identity as workers can also be seen in the detailed descriptions of work skills. Historians of women's work have argued for some time that the identification of women with the domestic sphere in dominant discourses did not necessarily mean that women's own responses to work were defined by their domestic responsibilities. Oral histories in particular have allowed women to express their identities with greater reference to work experiences relative to home and family.[41] In Shetland there has never been any reluctance amongst women to celebrate their working identity as productive workers and as household managers, but in recent years the dramatic economic and social changes in Shetland – the shift to sheep farming, the decline of the fishing industry and the impact of the oil industry – have legitimated women's pride in skills now lost. Even herring gutting, which elsewhere in Britain was regarded as a rough occupation comparable to factory work for its exploitative conditions and the transient nature of the workers, has been reclaimed and represented as a noble form of women's work of which women are now proud.[42] The inclusion of women's work at the herring stations into public representations of the fishing industry, such as at the Scottish Fisheries Museum at Anstruther, has contributed to the recognition and rehabilitation of women's work in fishing communities and legitimates women's recollections of the knowledge and skills they acquired as gutters. Agnes Tulloch started work gutting herring in Lerwick at the age of seventeen before the First World War. Interviewed in 1983, she recalled her work in immense detail:

> this matjah herring [fat herring] we got to take out that fatty gut. Weel some would take it out perfectly, you had to gut up the gills first and then a second dab would get out this fatty gut . . . you came

ashore wi' dem and the cooper was there to take a note of it, and they were put in this boxes for wis tae gut, but just salt on them to rouge them, just as much you ken, you couldna have tae have herring in a box without, wi' the one sticking tae the idder, so we roused them, pretty weel roused, and then we packed that empty, what you would call an empty herring, intae barrels, and on the herring you would just have put as much salt . . . as you would put on an egg.[43]

Through their personal testimonies it is easy to detect women's pride in their work roles. Like the women from Cole's Portuguese maritime community, women in Shetland have a sense of 'having a life'.[44] Their strong sense of autonomous self is expressed in oral and written texts as women weave their autobiographies into Shetland's history. Their identification as workers gives them a status and a stake in the representation of the past.

Domesticity

In western feminist historiography the association of women with the private or domestic sphere has often been interpreted as a constraining ideology. The domestic was often equated with reproduction and non-productive economic functions in a gender hierarchy that assigned status to productive work and civic responsibility. However, this interpretation of separate spheres has been subjected to critiques from feminist anthropologists and historians who have reclaimed the domestic sphere. Anthropologists have forcefully argued that assumptions of universal female subordination are unhelpful and that each society must be scrutinised on its own terms. Historians, instead of interpreting the domestic realm, broadly conceived, as a universal form of female imprisonment, have identified it as a significant site of female power and a foundation for the extension of this power beyond the private sphere. Power is always social, and therefore the private or domestic sphere can form as legitimate a forum for the exercise of power as any other.[45] Thus historians of the urban bourgeoisie have argued that women made the domestic sphere their own, fashioned an environment that suited their needs and used it to extend their maternalism into the civic and political arena.[46] Studies of the urban working classes have identified women's networks organised around domestic tasks such as doing the laundry and shopping which allow women a space in which to articulate their concerns and their interests.[47] As Melanie Tebbutt points out, 'the burden of domestic survival which fell on women's shoulders left no scope for weakness or vulnerability', and women's political consciousness was likely to be grounded in pragmatic day-to-day experiences.[48] Similarly, studies of rural and peasant societies challenge the view that women were universally subordinate and show how outward appearances conceal a more subtle reality.[49] For instance, Friedl's examination of Greek village women demonstrates how, although men possess the prestige in the village – it is men who gather in public, who hold the prestigious religious and political positions and who are accorded deference from women – it is women who wield considerable power based on their economic value as dowry and their decision making within the household.[50] And Martine Segalen argues that in France women became 'social beings' and achieved social status through their work in the household.[51] In most peasant societies the household is the primary economic and social unit. Men's work activities tend to take place away from the domestic sphere but they contribute to it. Women's economic role, on the other hand, is more often spatially centred on the domestic sphere, and because decisions taken here are of primary importance, the fact that political positions outside the household are dominated by men may be of little significance.[52] In his study of kinship relations in a southern German village David Sabean comes to just this conclusion. During the nineteenth century women 'negotiated a central place in the productive structures of the village and in the consumption decisions of their households. If formal offices remained in the hands of men . . . women came to find a parallel field for political and social activity in caring for kin, negotiating networks, brokering alliances, and maintaining the viability of agriculture and flax production.'[53]

How do these theoretical perspectives apply in Shetland? Women's numerical preponderance and their dominance of household structures meant that many households 'tended to be woman-centred whether men were absent or present.'[54] Just as in Portugal, men in Shetland were marginalised in the context of domestic production. Men had little say. Household resources were in the control, in the main, of women. By their sheer absence, men were less influential than in the management of most European households. But the historian of the nineteenth century encounters obstacles to demonstrating this. For the twentieth century the scholar can use oral history techniques to discern the details of intimate decisions and who took them, and anthropologists and ethnologists may observe and record the day-to-day detail of household relations. It is more difficult to uncover the texture of everyday relationships in the more distant past. Who in the household decided to sell a cow? How were decisions made about where a couple would live, and who would take in the elderly parent? Official sources provide only tantalising glimpses of people's everyday conundrums.

For all that, it seems both plausible and likely that Shetland homes were overwhelmingly female-governed. We know from Chapter 4 that it was women who linked the Shetland household to the trading networks and market place. It seems inconceivable that this exchange function of women could have rested on anything other than predominantly female decision making. It is women's role in marketing the household that compels us to the conclusion that they managed it too. In a society in which resources were limited, women needed a wide network of kin, neighbours and acquaintances and a variety of strategies to maximise their likelihood of survival. These strategies and networks could effectively bolster the domestic authority of the females at the expense of absent males.[55] In accepting the intrinsic value of women's labour – both the production of hosiery and work on the land as well as wage earning – we must also accept that despite the dominance of men in formal positions of power (in the church, in law, in government and as landowners and merchants), at the level of the household and the local community women possessed a degree of authority and even confidence in their own decision making. And arguably, if a woman had a sense of security within her own domestic sphere she was likely to establish supportive relations with other women.[56]

Knowledge

Knowledge is gendered, and access to it and its dissemination are also gendered. Knowledge is a social construction just as much as gender is. But structuralist scholars place emphasis on the content of knowledge as the source of power, and where information is circulated primarily by word of mouth, that power comes from accessing, circulating or withholding information. Knowledge is an instrumental mechanism for community stability. Historians of early modern societies and anthropologists working in pre-literate communities and in remote rural societies have placed most emphasis on the value of recognising the importance of gossip or oral modes of information exchange as a means of understanding how communities regulate themselves.[57] 'Gossip is a hallmark of membership' of a demarcated group, argues Gluckman, and 'the values of the group are clearly asserted in gossip and scandal.'[58] But this structuralist approach to gossip takes knowledge as a fixed body of attitudes and information and sees it as a means of affirming group values and maintaining group equilibrium. Women's historians approach the nature of this knowledge as fluid. They have used the study of gossip to interrogate women's lives, accepting that 'the study of gossip is the study of women's concerns and values, a key to the female subculture.'[59] Additionally they have examined the language of insult, defamation and slander, or 'gossip elevated into the public arena', in order to analyse understandings of gender difference in pre-modern society.[60] Women are more often associated with informal, verbal modes of communication and information exchange than men. This is largely on account of their exclusion from the formal and literary modes of communication, and a recognition that women's social networks are based on conversation, but it is also based on beliefs about women's unruly tongues, their fondness for gossip, for the passing on of rumour, information or 'tittle-tattle' about others. This makes women's knowledge different. Multiple knowledges exist in every society, and women's is a very powerful one. Moreover, as historians have suggested, the nature of knowledge changes dramatically with period.

Historians have pointed to a qualitative difference in nature between pre-modern and modern mentalités, especially in regard to gender relations. In Europe from around the sixteenth century to the mid-eighteenth century, a person's character and reputation were delineated by verbal descriptors that had a power to confer, not merely to convey, the qualities they suggested. Words like 'witch' and 'whore' had a literalness to the early modern world that gave them a potency they were to lose when, after around 1750, they became used as pejoratives of a mere verbal abuse. Calling someone a 'witch' in sixteenth- or seventeenth-century Scotland was something that could, if left unchecked, lead to that person being accused of witchcraft, being tried and being executed. 'Whore' similarly could lead to so-called evidence of 'repute' which could result in damaging ecclesiastical censure. In the late eighteenth and nineteenth centuries, such language came to be used metaphorically, not literally. This was a change in the gendered nature of knowledge (of, in this case, women).

What immediately strikes the historian of Shetland is that this pre-modern mentalité survived considerably longer. Well into the nineteenth century the characteristic female reaction to defamation of the early modern world was still evident in court cases. Elsewhere in Scotland, slander cases had changed to a late modern form.

Most historians of women rather take for granted that early modern defamation ceased in the eighteenth century. Certainly such cases stopped reaching the courts because legal systems had by then discarded the empirically informed notion of a link between word and reality. Well into the nineteenth century people in Shetland valued the information they possessed about others, and they understood the potency of the words they uttered in public. Shetlanders were noted for a predilection for 'inquisitiveness'. Critics warned of the danger whereby 'this same trait too often degenerates into a passion for gossip, hunting out private history, and finally into the most reckless slander . . . which begets and fosters habits of evil speaking and suspicion.'[61] Slander and defamation cases were heard in the sheriff court intermittently during the first half of the nineteenth century, suggesting that here, unlike elsewhere in the British Isles, what we now regard as a pre-modern mindset, whereby character and reputation were measured by the spoken word, was still in existence.[62] Insults like 'whore' and 'witch' were heavy with meaning and were used deliberately. Both the person who uttered the insult and the intended recipient would have been aware of the significance of such words, although the significance of 'witch' in particular was lessening by the middle of the century.[63] Thus, in 1849, when James Peterson 'in the fields of Gott, in presence of several people, most wickedly and maliciously [called] the [Elizabeth Nicolson] "a damned eternal bitch and a common whore"', he was sued for damages by his victim on the grounds that his words were 'calculated utterly to ruin the claimant's character'.[64] And similarly, in 1841, when Christina Stanley was described as a 'lying bitch, and also a thief and a common whore', she retaliated by calling her assailant a 'tongue thief and robber in his heart', words which, according to the sheriff, 'seemingly intended to convey the idea that she felt as if he was stealing or robbing her reputation'.[65] But this popular world view was clearly in conflict with a more 'modern' ideology held by the legal system which was less likely to give credence to the impact of the spoken word, especially if the power of the supernatural had been invoked. In 1803, the case of a Lerwick boatman who was being sued by a merchant for asserting that the merchant's wife was a 'witch, and that she had witched him by setting five corbies [crows] on him at different times who were like to tear him to pieces and that he knew her to be one of them' was given short shrift by the sheriff substitute, who found that 'all prosecutions for imputing witchcraft to another person is discharged in as much as it is held to be an absurd and incredible imputation by which no person can be injured in point of fame.'[66] 'Incredible' was the epithet used by Sheriff Rampini more than seventy years later in another imputation of witchcraft. When one woman from Mid Yell called another a witch and accused her of 'having taken away the "profit" from their cow's milk', there was no doubt that the parties well understood the power of the words used and their implication, as the verbal confrontation soon degenerated into a physical one.[67] Yet Sheriff Rampini was not convinced, stating that

> He was surprised to see a party of respectable looking people making asses of themselves ... it was incredible that such gross superstition [should] still persist among our islanders, and yet these people seemed quite in earnest in their belief that one of themselves had the power of preventing the milk in their churns to yield butter. It seems a satire on our boasted civilisation and 'abundant means of Grace'.[68]

Reputation for women in Shetland was a valued commodity throughout the century. It was key to their economic activity and their chances in the marriage market, and thus words spoken in public possessed considerable weight and significance, despite the dismissive attitude of the legal authorities. This linkage of reputation to economic market status and to marriageability was a characteristic of the early modern world. It was vital, clearly, in a society like Shetland where women's survival was dependent on their autonomous economic functions. In an economy dominated by women, the slur of language sustained a potency that could threaten livelihood.

In the case of communities where the sexes experience separation of roles (and more especially perhaps where significant members of one sex are absent for long periods), it is argued that oral forms of communication can operate to create and cement a discrete cultural community based on a 'common set of signifying practices' which may include rituals, beliefs, behaviours and understandings expressed via coded messages.[69] Again, it is women who are more likely to form themselves into such a community on account of their exclusion or marginalisation from the world of men. The separate characters of men's and women's spheres encourage women to form what has been termed an 'interpretive community'.[70] Within this framework the two forms of communication – gossip and coded language – are joined by a third, the supernatural and the corporeal. Women's knowledge of the female body and of cures and healing processes allied to the supernatural has been identified in many pre-modern societies as a source of female authority and of female solidarity, at a time when medical understandings of the female body in particular were still in their infancy. All three forms of female knowledge have been explored by historians in the context of Mediterranean societies where, such is the imbalance of power between the sexes, in part bolstered by the honour–shame value system, women have found ways of sharing information and preserving knowledge in the face of a dominant culture that dismisses their needs and desires.[71]

In other words, gossip has been interpreted as an effective means by which women may achieve a degree of autonomy in patriarchal societies.

Shetland is a different case. Women predominated on the islands, and their active role in the Shetland economy meant a lively verbal female information exchange system. Women hustled and bustled around the streets and lanes of Lerwick and to and fro between the town and the countryside. Their work necessitated that they be constantly in the public domain, in the fields, travelling to and from the peat hill, backwards and forwards to and from the store to sell hosiery, in and out of neighbours' houses to exchange credit notes for foodstuffs and so on. And there was ample opportunity for gossip to be shared at the regular spinning and knitting parties attended by the women of a neighbourhood. As they engaged in these activities they passed on useful information: who was prepared to exchange some milk for tea; which merchant was giving a good price for hosiery; where there was wool to be purchased; where work was to be had; and they would have passed on news about ships and men lost, the circumstances of widows and their children, suspected illegitimate births, marriages and promises broken. In the hurly-burly of economic exchange and competition for scarce resources, heated words led to defamation of character in early modern style, and thus to court, where sheriffs educated in Enlightenment Scottish universities despaired.

Gossip, then, can help us to draw maps of female interaction and social space in private and in public.[72] Of course this kind of gossip or 'idle talk' was a staple of all communities, but in a face-to-face community like Shetland, information gained and exchanged was a form of currency which could confer value or authority on the woman who imparted the knowledge, it could cement relationships and it could bolster or harm reputations. Moreover, gossip can also be used to define community morals. It has what scholars used to call a 'social control' function, whereby certain behaviours may be tolerated or suppressed and whereby certain individuals may be isolated or subjected to ridicule.[73] Anthropologists have tended to interpret gossip as a functional activity which serves to regulate behaviour and release tensions, thus maintaining social stability. If all members of a community know that they are being observed they are obliged to remain vigilant for fear of being the subject of gossip. According to Parman's work in a Scottish crofting community, 'the watchful neighbour, the gossiping tongue . . . is an important element in social control. Even the thought that someone might think you were doing something keeps behaviour circumspect.'[74]

And Shetland culture had, and still has, many overt and prominent forms of community regulation. The best-known is that which occurs in the winter fire-festival and its antecedent forms dating from around 1805, in which masked guisers heap ridicule on offending community spoilsports and transgressors, through verbal and property attacks and through written and dramatic 'jokes'. From the 1890s, Lerwick inhabitants used Up-helly-aa, and more specifically the Bill – a satirical placard containing jokes, defamatory comments and scathing attacks on local dignitaries and members of the festival committee, posted in public on the Market Cross – to settle scores, to defuse tensions and to unsettle hierarchies, as a form of charivari.[75] The Bill was essentially just a ritualised form of gossip, designed to siphon off criticisms and to prick pretensions, and ultimately to maintain community unity. However, the festival was controlled by men and the Bill became a public text, written down and posted in a public place, and nowadays published in the local newspaper and the Up-helly-aa programme. Women's gossip, however, remained oral and thereby unfixed, constantly open to re-interpretation and shifts of meaning. This flexible and mutable means of communication could operate strategically in women's interests.

However, women's control over the dissemination of information and their maintenance of a privileged set of knowledges was double-edged. Women did not have a monopoly on gossip and they could not always control the ways in which their knowledge was used. While gossip and coded language could be used to facilitate women's networks, it could also be directed against women who did not conform to cultural norms. And in some instances women consciously used their monopoly on female knowledge to marginalise other women. In nineteenth-century Shetland the combination of a strong female community and a patriarchal legal and moral system meant that women did wield power via their strong networks of information exchange. At the same time, though, in the absence of any systematic or island-wide policing system or a medical service, women's knowledge, particularly in regard to other women, was useful to the church and to the civil authorities.

Certain domains of knowledge and experience were controlled by women. Pregnancy and childbirth, and indeed all aspects of a woman's body and natural functions, were considered to be in the female realm, at least until the 1890s. This included the provision of cures and healing for women's complaints. All women, and especially mothers, were deemed to have access to this kind of knowledge but midwives, howdies (untrained midwives) and wise-women had privileged powers. Before the end of the century doctors were rare in rural Shetland and would have attended births very seldom. Most women relied upon their mothers, female relatives and howdies during pregnancy and childbirth and upon wise-women for cures for unknown ailments. Married women most likely welcomed the interest shown in their bodies by other women. Pregnancy and childbirth were surrounded by ritual and social custom designed to support the mother and child. In order to be emotionally prepared for the birth it was necessary that a mother be emotionally and socially 'open' so that she would be able to call on assistance if needed.[76] A married woman would submit to public interest in her condition because she knew it was to her benefit. Secrecy and silence were interpreted as potentially dangerous for the life of the child and the social position of the mother. Some believed, for instance, that childbirth was a time when a mother was particularly vulnerable to enchantment by fairies or that new-born babies were at risk of being stolen away by fairies.[77] This is one area, then, where women's power was largely unchallenged until the advent after the First World War of a trained midwifery and medical service.

Within the woman's world of knowledge, so-called wise-women were still accorded respect up until the end of the nineteenth century. Every parish had a howdie-woman; 'they couldn't do without them'.[78] These women 'mainly delivered, I don't think they ever fetched them for anything other than somebody in an absolute jam at child-birth . . . they were fetched if there were difficulties and they learned from there.'[79] One Whalsay midwife was described as 'a capable woman, who was full of old lore, not as a student but as part of her inherit-ance.'[80] Wise-women, on the other hand, were thought to possess more wide-ranging powers. Wise-women, witches and old wives inhabited a liminal space. They were thought to possess powers to cure the sick and the enchanted and, conversely, they could use their powers to harm: 'These were the women, if they had a spote against someone, they went and put alum in their wells where they drew water . . . yes, you see, that would destroy the milk.'[81] And, as we have already seen in the case of accusations of bewitchment, beliefs about the magical powers of some women were not uncommonly remarked upon as late as the 1880s.[82] Merran Winwick (1820–1895) is probably the most well-known wise-woman in Shetland, featuring in many oral narratives and stories about the islands. Her mother was a midwife on Unst, and Merran inherited her mother's knowledge and skills. 'Weel, dey wir a woman at wis born here in Yell', narrated Bruce Henderson, interviewed in 1974. 'An sho seemed at sho knew everything in da world dis wife. Sho wis a woman at attended ladies whin it wis at dey wir haein babies an sho knew greatly aboot medicine an da most o da people, some frae Yell gud till her.'[83] Merran Winwick also features in Mary Manson's story of the journey taken by her mother to fetch a cure for a sick cousin from a wife, discussed in Chapter 2, 'because everybody said that she never gave them any sort of medicine but what didna cure them.'[84] The combination of knowledge, skill and magic or superstition ensured that these women were treated with respect in a community which was ill-served by conventional medicine.

Knowledge of women's matters was not, however, restricted to howdies and wise-women. In Shetland, as in many rural societies, a woman's body was closely observed or policed by others in the community and especially by other women. Here, people spoke of rumours of women being with child, of reports being 'prevalent in the neighbourhood', of a woman's pregnancy being 'the talk of the place'. Those who heard the rumours tried to verify the information; 'In consequence of the talk of the place', said Catherine Johnson in 1885 in respect of rumours that Mary Williamson was pregnant, 'I then looked at her . . . She was dressed in a white muslin dress with a tight fitting body . . . I was then of the opinion that she is eight months with child. It became the talk of the district [Westsandwick, Yell] that she gave birth to a child.'[85] In strict Protestant communities just as in Catholic ones, where pre-marital sex, illegitimacy and adultery were condemned, it was the female body that signalled non-conformity. In this context gossip and the exchange of information and knowledge about a woman's body could be supportive or it could be used to condemn a woman. In circumstances where a woman was pregnant with an illegitimate child the dynamics of female information exchange or gossip subtly altered. Most of our understanding about what women knew and understood about pregnancy and childbirth is derived from the records of infanticide cases.[86] When a woman suspected of having killed her new-born infant was prosecuted, the authorities gathered a great deal of evidence from her family and neighbours concerning public knowledge or rumour of her condition. In these rare cases we can observe the ways in which women's authority in the domain of pregnancy and childbirth could be beneficial both to the accused and to the legal and religious authorities.

It is important to remember that women's bodies were regarded as unstable; physical processes and signs were ambiguous.[87] It was not until the very end of the nineteenth century that medical diagnoses pronounced by medical doctors were given greater weight than the observations and interpretations of women themselves. Indeed, doctors throughout the century appear to have concurred with the uncertainty of diagnosis and the range of interpretations of symptoms adopted by their patients. The symptoms normally associated with a pregnancy today – cessation of menstruation, a swelling belly, enlarged breasts, swollen legs, sickness, tiredness and even food cravings – were all open to a number of interpretations. Dropsy, a cyst or boil, a 'swelling' of the stomach – all of these were commonly cited as explanations for a woman assuming the appearance of a woman with child. Elizabeth Williamson, the sister of Christina Williamson who was investigated for concealment of pregnancy in 1857, was, when questioned, ambivalent about her sister's state of health. Although she was aware of rumours that Christina was pregnant, she declared that she never spoke to her sister on the subject. 'I had frequent opportunities of seeing her both dressed and undressed but I cannot say I observed any change in her figure or appearance . . . she maybe was rather fuller than she ought to have been. I think she was but I do not know what was the matter with her.'[88] In 1859 Jemima Nicolson was suspected of having concealed her pregnancy. Rumours of her being with child circulated amongst her neighbours on the island of Unst, but no-one would admit to being certain of her condition. Her sister-in-law Charlotte, a woman who herself was pregnant and who lived in the same house as Jemima, had her suspicions but even she could not be certain.

> I fancied from Jemima's appearance that she was in a similar state with myself. Her face seemed occasionally flushed . . . but I never communicated my suspicions to anyone . . . It was a mere passing suspicion . . . Sometimes I fancied she looked stouter than usual and at other times I thought I had been mistaken. I sometimes spoke to her sister Jane about her and we did think at times that there might be truth in the rumour, but we never could come to any decided opinion . . . Jemima has ever since I came to the house appeared strong and healthy and wrought well and actively.[89]

From the accused woman's perspective, the privileging of a premodern, unscientific understanding of the female body with all its uncertainties and ambiguities could be empowering.

Appearance was not the only indicator of a woman's state. Different interpretations were ascribed to physical changes in the body which, according to the context in which these symptoms were understood, could mean either pregnancy or something else such as a growth, a swelling, a temporary blockage or even weight gain. A woman's age and experience, her reputation and the vehemence of her denial of pregnancy all determined the way in which her physical symptoms were understood by community members. Lillias Peterson was shocked when she was told that Margaret Fraser had given birth. She had been told her neighbour was sick with a stomach complaint 'and the suppression of her monthly courses', but she 'never supposed that the girl was pregnant both in consequence of her professions and of her being apparently extremely religious'.[90] Gina Skaar's mistress was inclined to believe her servant's denial of pregnancy despite the evidence before her own eyes that Gina was 'growing bigger and bigger' because 'she had been such a good servant and had always been so trustworthy'.[91]

Gossip about a woman's condition created a community of women who would be on hand to support a pregnant woman through her pregnancy and delivery. Conversely, a woman who denied her condition shut herself off from the community of women who normally would have facilitated her transformation into a mother. Female knowledge and authority in this domain were potentially enabling, and women who took advantage of them would be welcomed into the community of mothers, even if the child was illegitimate. Women who were suspected of concealing their pregnancy or of murdering their infant forfeited their right to this support. In such cases those individuals who were privileged with greater knowledge of women's bodies possessed powers outside the female community. Until the 1850s women who had already borne children, and midwives, possessed a degree of power in the criminal system otherwise dominated by legal and religious men. Prosecutors, sheriffs and church elders used women's knowledge and insight in an attempt to gain evidence and understanding of a female world of pregnancy and childbirth. It was only later that medical doctors came to usurp the knowledge and power of women in the community. However, the evidence given by these women frequently exposed the fragility of the case constructed by the suspect. Their privileged knowledge of the female body gave them authority amongst men like kirk session elders, who were often among the first on the scene following the rumour of a dead child. But whereas during the eighteenth century elders would have requested to see a woman's breasts and may well have carried out the examination themselves, in the nineteenth century they required women to assist them in their interrogatory duties.

Margaret Walterson was reported to have been delivered of an illegitimate child one morning in May 1855. Gilbert Williamson, the local schoolmaster and an elder of the Church of Scotland, wasted no time in visiting her, accompanied by another elder and two women, one of whom was an occasional midwife. Margaret Walterson was still in bed when they arrived. 'She was not aware of me and the other Elder being in the room as we thought it better to allow the women to interrogate her as if by themselves for fear of agitating her if she knew that we were present. Ann Harrison put the questions to her, some of which suggested by me.'[92] However, elders also used midwives for more than verbal interrogations. It was commonly believed that the only sure sign that a woman had given birth was that her breasts contained milk. Elspeth White, a midwife in Lerwick in 1830, was called to examine Janet Leisk, just eighteen years old, who had reportedly been delivered of a child a few days previously. News spread quickly around the town. Janet Leisk's neighbour upon hearing the rumour mentioned it to Janet's grandfather, who spoke to Janet's mother, who in turn went to see the elder of the parish, and he sent Elspeth White to Janet's home. The midwife requested that Janet show her breasts:

> she objected at first to show her breasts but at last consented at her mother's request and came forward . . . trembling and crying; that on seeing the breasts [Elspeth White] remarked that she did not like their appearance, meaning their appearance indicated that the said Janet Leisk had recently brought forth a child, upon which her mother remarked that she had been wearing tight stays during the summer which had bruised her breasts. Declares that she [Elspeth White] then tried if there was any milk in them and obtained a small quantity by sucking.[93]

Midwives occupied a privileged place in the investigation process, but the evidence of other female witnesses – women who were themselves mothers – also assumed importance precisely because childbirth was a female domain. 'Having had a family myself', remarked Andrina Sinclair in the case of Agnes Hawick in 1854, 'I was satisfied both from what she told me of her state and from her appearance that she had been delivered.'[94] And in 1885, Mary Jane Smith, mother of seven, was an authoritative witness on the appearance of Mary Williamson from Yell, whom she met at a wedding: 'I had not taken any notice of her before this although it was the talk of the place that she was with child. She was in my house that night. She was dressed in a black dress. She then had the appearance of a woman close to confinement. In looks she was pale and weak looking and full in the body. She was full from the breast down as full as she could be.'[95]

The female community continued to watch out for its own as a means of protecting women from the censure of the church and from the harm they might do to themselves and the unborn child. Gossip about a woman's body had a protective function. And knowledge of all matters associated with women's bodies was a form of cultural power in a society where doctors were sparse. However, if an infanticide was suspected, women's knowledge became a threat rather than a support within a culture of suspicion and control of women's sexuality. It is dangerous to assume that women always supported one another or that female solidarity could overcome institutionalised male power.

Here then was an isolated island archipelago which, well into the nineteenth century, provides us with rich documentary evidence of an early modern gendered knowledge of womanhood. Victorian Shetland allows a unique window in to a highly documented modern society in which a woman's pre-modern world thrived, despite the best offices of the state legal apparatus and modern evangelical religion.

Conclusions

Access to political and economic power in Shetland was dominated by men in their public roles as merchants, landlords and church elders and, to a lesser extent, as crofting tenants and fishermen. Shetland women did not, in the main, occupy formal positions holding legitimate authority and had little direct influence over institutions of power. On the other hand, they engaged in a series of economic and cultural relationships which gave them a degree of power which was different from the kind of power possessed by men.[96] This is not to say that women were equal to men. In these islands, where women were demographically dominant and where their productive activity was central to the viability of the household, women constructed a series of relationships centred upon women's knowledge and women's networks. Using models borrowed from feminist social anthropology it has been possible to show that the domestic space is just as much a centre of power as the public space. That power can be expressed and experienced through skill and knowledge and control of cultural resources as much as through property ownership and political influence. Shetland women's productive and reproductive roles were enmeshed in a female world which in turn created and reinforced women's sturdy sense of identity as workers and as key members of the community. By the end of the nineteenth century some of women's power in these realms was diminishing. The abandonment of fishing-tenure, the gradual decline of truck, the fixing of croft rents and the rise of the herring industry and employment opportunities in the service industries meant that the barter economy gradually gave way to a cash economy and that women no longer needed to entangle themselves in complicated exchange relationships. Economic relationships became more direct; trust and reputation were less important. Additionally, the introduction of a medical service for the islands, the decline of the moral power of the church and the expansion of civil policing all contributed to a reduction in women's knowledge power base. Nevertheless, the legacy of woman-centredness in the nineteenth century was, and still is, evident in women's narratives celebrating the heroines of the past, who stand as memorials for a time when women were respected and were at the heart of economic and cultural life.

Notes

1 J. Dubisch (ed.), *Gender and Power in Rural Greece* (Princeton, Princeton University Press, 1986), p. ix.

2 B. Quintana and L. Floyd, *!Que Gitano* (New York, 1972) quoted in Delamont, *Appetites and Identities*, pp. 182–3.

3 Nadel-Klein, *Fishing for Heritage*, p. 60.

4 SA, D 1/135: *Dundee Advertiser*, 9 Sept. 1898.

5 For example, see J. K. Campbell, *Honour, Family and Patronage* (Oxford, Clarendon Press, 1964) on the Sarakatsani people of northern Greece. For general discussions of this issue see Delamont, *Appetites and Identities*, pp. 180–91, and S. C. Rogers, 'Female forms of power and the myth of male dominance: a model of female/male interaction in peasant society', *American Ethnologist* 2:4 (1975), pp. 727–56.

6 See Rogers, 'Female forms of power', particularly the discussion of deference customs, and S. G. Berkowitz, 'Familism, kinship and sex roles', *Anthropological Quarterly* 57:2 (1984), pp. 83–92.

7 SA, D 1/135: *The Scotsman*, 2 Sept. 1903.

8 See S. Shortall, *Women and Farming: Property and Power* (Basingstoke, Macmillan, 1999) for a discussion of this in the context of the family farm in Ireland.

9 See M.-L. Rey-Henningsen, 'Galicia, state of women', *Spare Rib* 70 (1980), pp. 27–9 and Rey-Henningsen, *The World of the Ploughwoman*, where she states, 'Not only does the woman dominate social relations in community life; in economic, work and family matters too, the man is completely subordinate to his wife and/or mother-in-law' (p. 98).

10 See M. Z. Rosaldo, 'Woman, culture and society: a theoretical overview', in M. Z. Rosaldo and L. Lamphere (eds), *Woman, Culture and Society* (Stanford, CA, Stanford University Press, 1974), pp. 17–42, here pp. 36–7. See also Dubisch (ed.), *Gender and Power*, pp. 12–13.

11 Thompson, 'Women in the fishing', pp. 21–3.

12 Thompson et al., *Living the Fishing*, esp. chapters 10, 14 and 15.

13 This challenge has been particularly effective in Mediterranean studies, where it was often assumed that the subordination of women was a cultural norm. See Cole, *Women of the Praia*, p. 40.

14 There are too many examples of this literature to list but see, for example, Weiner, *Women of Value, Men of Renown*; M. Strathern, *Women in Between: Female Roles in a Male World: Mount Hagen, New Guinea* (Lanham, MD, and London, Rowmen and Littlefield, 1995); Dubisch (ed.), *Gender and Power*.

15 Rogers, 'Female forms of power', p. 737.

16 SA, CO 8/1/7/10: Valuation roll, Dunrossness, Sandwick and Cunningsburgh, 1861.

17 A mark or merk of land was so called because its purchase price was one merk (or mark), equivalent to 13s $^1/_3$d: sterling.

18 Napier Commission, Appendix LI: Articles, regulations and conditions of lease.

19 *Shetland News*, 31 Aug. 1889.

20 SA, CO 8/1/7/10: Valuation roll, Dunrossness, Sandwick and Cunningsburgh, 1861.

21 *Shetland News*, 9 Nov. 1889, 'Decisions by Crofters Commissioners in Shetland Cases'.

22 Thompson, 'Women in the fishing', p. 20.

23 SA, D 1/357/6: Papers of Shetland Fishermen's Widows' Relief Fund, 1881.

24 *Shetland News*, 26 Oct. 1889.

25 Brettell, *Men who Migrate*; Cole, *Women of the Praia*; Rey-Henningsen, *The World of the Ploughwoman*; Byron, 'The maritime household in northern Europe'; Boissevain, 'Towards a social anthropology of the Mediterranean'.

26 Cole, *Women of the Praia*, pp. 73–6.

27 Thompson et al., *Living the Fishing*, pp. 174–5.

28 Nadel-Klein, *Fishing for Heritage*, pp. 51–91.

29 Rey-Henningsen, *The World of the Ploughwoman*, pp. 115–27.

30 G. George, *The Rock where we Stand: An Ethnography of Women's Activism in Newfoundland* (Toronto, University of Toronto Press, 2000), pp. 27–30. See also M. Porter, '"She was skipper of the shore crew": notes on the development of the sexual division of labour in Newfoundland', *Labour* 15 (1985), pp. 105–23.

31 Thompson et al., *Living the Fishing*, pp. 174–5.

32 Truck 1872, lines 1,561–607.

33 Census, 1881 and 1901.

34 E. Higgs, 'Women, occupations and work in nineteenth century censuses', *History Workshop Journal* 23 (1987), pp. 59–80.

35 Cole, *Women of the Praia*, p. 40.

36 See Jack, 'Shetland women and crofting'.

37 Mary Manson's diary, 1969 (unpublished), courtesy of Mrs Netta Inkster.

38 Mary Manson's diary.

39 SA, 3/1/124/1–2: Katie Inkster.

40 SA, 3/1/124/1–2: Katie Inkster.

41 See E. Gordon, 'Women, work and collective action: Dundee jute workers, 1870–1906', *Journal of Social History* 21 (1987), pp. 27–48; D. Gittins, *Fair Sex: Family Size and Structure 1900–39* (London, Hutchinson, 1982); J. D. Stephenson and C. G. Brown, 'The view from the workplace: women's memories of work in Stirling c.1910–c.1950', in E. Gordon and E. Breitenbach (eds), *The World is Ill Divided: Women's Work in Scotland in the Nineteenth and Early Twentieth Centuries* (Edinburgh, Edinburgh University Press, 1990), pp. 7–28; S. Reynolds, 'Women in the printing and paper trades in Edwardian Scotland', in Gordon and Breitenbach (eds), *The World is Ill Divided*, pp. 49–69.

42 See Nadel-Klein, *Fishing for Heritage*, pp. 68–79.

43 SA, 3/1/103: Agnes Tulloch.

44 Cole, *Women of the Praia*, p. 40.

45 J. Dubisch, 'Introduction', in Dubisch (ed.), *Gender and Power*, pp. 3–41, here p. 19.

46 See, for example, L. Davidoff and C. Hall, *Family Fortunes: Men and Women of the English Middle Class, 1780–1850* (London, Routledge, 1987); E. Gordon and G. Nair, *Public Lives: Women, Family and Society in Victorian Britain* (New Haven and London, Yale University Press, 2003); B. Smith, *Ladies of the Leisure Class: The Bourgeoisie of Northern France in the Nineteenth Century* (Princeton, NJ, Princeton University Press, 1981).

47 See Ross, 'Survival networks'; T. Kaplan, Female consciousness and collective action: the case of Barcelona, 1910–18', *Signs* 7 (1982), pp. 545–66.

48 M. Tebbutt, *Women's Talk: A Social History of 'Gossip' in Working-Class Neighbourhoods, 1880–1960* (Aldershot, Scolar Press, 1995), p. 11.

49 For a survey of some of this literature see Rogers, 'Female forms of power'.

50 E. Friedl, 'The position of women: appearance and reality', in Dubisch (ed.), *Gender and Power*, pp. 42–52.

51 M. Segalen, *Historical Anthropology of the Family* (Cambridge, Cambridge University Press, 1986), p. 205. See also M. Segalen, *Love and Power in the Peasant Family: Rural France in the Nineteenth Century* (Oxford, Blackwell, 1983).

52 Rogers, 'Female forms of power', p. 746.

53 D. W. Sabean, *Kinship in Neckarhausen 1700–1870* (Cambridge, Cambridge University Press, 1998), p. 490.

54 Cole, *Women of the Praia*, p. 63.

55 For a discussion of these strategies in a completely different context see C. B. Stack, 'Sex roles and survival strategies in an urban black community', in M. Z. Rosaldo and L. Lamphere (eds), *Woman, Culture and Society* (Stanford, CA, Stanford University Press, 1974), pp. 113–28.

56 Rogers, 'Female forms of power', p. 746.

57 For a summary of some of this literature see Delamont, *Appetites and Identities*, pp. 177–80. For an illuminating case study see S. Hindle, 'The shaming of Margaret Knowsley: gossip, gender, and the experience of authority in early modern England', *Continuity and Change* 9 (1994), pp. 391–419.

58 M. Gluckman, 'Gossip and scandal', *Current Anthropology* 4 (1963), pp. 307–16, here p. 313. For a critique of the structuralist position see R. Paine, 'What is gossip about? An alternative hypothesis', *Man*, new series, 2 (1967), pp. 278–85.

59 D. Jones, 'Gossip – notes on women's oral culture', in D. Cameron (ed.), *The Feminist Critique of Language* (London, Routledge, 1990), pp. 242–9. For an application of this principle see Tebbutt, *Women's Talk*.

60 L. Gowing, *Domestic Dangers: Women, Words, and Sex in Early Modern London* (Oxford, Oxford University Press, 1996).

61 Eliza Edmondston (1856) quoted in Kendall, *With Naught but Kin*, pp. 43–4.

62 See L. Leneman, 'Defamation in Scotland, 1750–1800', *Continuity and Change* 15 (2000), pp. 209–34.

63 On the role of gossip in witchcraft accusations see W. Bleek, 'Witchcraft, gossip and death: a social drama', *Man*, new series, 11 (1976), pp. 526–41.

64 SA, SC 12/6/1849/83: Summons for defamation, 20 April 1849.

65 SA, SC 12/6/1841/111: Summons of defamation, 22 June 1841.

66 SA, SC 12/6/1803/30: Petition for defamation, 2 Aug. 1803.

67 *Shetland Times*, 20 Sept. 1879.

68 *Shetland Times*, 20 Sept. 1879.

69 J. N. Radner and S. S. Lanser, 'Strategies of coding in women's cultures', in J. N. Radner (ed.), *Feminist Messages: Coding in Women's Folk Culture* (Urbana and Chicago, University of Illinois Press, 1993), pp. 1–29, here p. 2.

70 Radner and Lanser, 'Strategies of coding', p. 2.

71 See Kennedy, 'Women's friendships on Crete'.

72 See Hindle, 'The shaming of Margaret Knowsley', p. 393.

73 For a discussion of gossip and community unity see Gluckman, 'Gossip and scandal'. On ridicule see A. Gustavsson, 'Folklore in community conflicts: gossip in a fishing community', *Scandinavian Yearbook of Folklore* 35 (1979), pp. 49–85.

74 S. Parman, *Scottish Crofters* (Fort Worth, Holt, Rinehart and Winston, 1990), pp. 102–3.

75 Brown, *Up-helly-aa*, p. 143.

76 See A. Rowlands, ' "In great secrecy": the crime of infanticide in Rothenburg ob der Tauber, 1501–1618', *German History* 15 (1997), pp. 101–21, here pp. 106–7. On the rituals surrounding women who had just given birth see S. Wilson, *The Magical Universe: Everyday Ritual and Magic in Pre-Modern Europe* (London, Hambledon, 2000), pp. 171–95.

77 'Women at the time of child-bearing were especially liable to be taken by *hillfolk*, and hence the midwife was generally an expert in the art of preserving her charge from the *trows*' (J. Spence, *Shetland Folk-Lore* (Lerwick, Johnson and Greig, 1899, reprinted 1973), p. 165). See also Henderson and Cowan, *Scottish Fairy Belief*, pp. 74–6.

78 Interview with Mary Ellen Odie.

79 Interview with Mary Ellen Odie.

80 SA, John Stewart of Whalsay (uncatalogued manuscript).

81 SA, 3/1/264: Robina Bruce.

82 See Marwick, *The Folklore of Orkney and Shetland*, pp. 47–57 for numerous examples.

83 SA, 3/1/290: Bruce Henderson.

84 SA, 3/1/77/2: Mary Manson.

85 SA, AD 22/2/20/29: Precognition – concealment of pregnancy, 25 April 1885.

86 For a fuller discussion of infanticide see L. Abrams, 'From demon to victim: the infanticidal mother in Shetland, 1699–1899', in Brown and Ferguson (eds), *Twisted Sisters*, pp. 180–203.

87 See U. Rublack, *The Crimes of Women in Early Modern Germany* (Oxford, Oxford University Press, 1999), pp. 172–4. On women's interpretations of the body see B. Duden, *The Woman Beneath the Skin: A Doctor's Patients in Eighteenth Century Germany* (Cambridge, MA, Harvard University Press, 1991).

88 SA, AD 22/2/3/39: Christina Williamson, concealment of pregnancy, 7 May 1857.

89 SA, AD 22/2/4/24: Jemima Nicolson, concealment of pregnancy, 21 Feb. 1859.

90 SA, SC 12/6/1815/44: Margaret Fraser, child murder, 27 Sept. 1815.

91 SA, AD 22/2/24/40: Gina Skaar, 10 July 1899.
92 SA, AD 22/2/2/8: Margaret Mitchell or Walterson, child murder, 23 May 1855.
93 SA, SC 12/6/1830/111: Janet Leisk, child murder, 8 Oct. 1830.
94 SA, AD 22/2/1/55: Agnes Hawick, 25 May 1854.
95 SA, AD 22/2/20/29: Mary Williamson, 24 April 1885.
96 This analysis is influenced by Weiner, *Women of Value, Men of Renown*.

8

Reflections

The past as personal

THIS STUDY has been a work of historical anthropology. It has been impossible to separate the past from the present because the past is constantly reified and reconstituted in the present. The combination of approaches – historical and anthropological – has proved essential in Shetland, where the past is not somewhere or something forgotten but a vibrant, living place which is constantly evoked in order to make sense of the present.[1] And women have a prominent place in both time-scapes.

The past is personal in the stories narrated by Shetland women. The Shetland landscape is populated by individuals whose experiences have come to signify and embody the myth of Shetland womanhood. This use of personal experience to talk about a generalised culture in the past is a valuable tool in the hands of the historian who wishes to reconcile the grand narrative with the particular and the personal. Oral historians have long struggled with the tension between the personal – the individual life experience as narrated by a respondent – and the general culture or the broad normative trends within which the personal is constructed. Historians today are less concerned with corroboration of personal testimonies and more interested in how 'the individuality of each life story . . . becomes instead a vital document of the construction of consciousness, emphasising both the variety of experience in any social group, and also how each individual story draws on a common culture.'[2] This study has attempted to take on board the conflation of the self and culture that is exhibited in personal narratives and to use it to analyse narratives created in the past and now accessible only via written archival sources.

The result of this process is a history of Shetland women which is embedded in women's own understandings and interpretations of their present and past lives. It is what might be described as a woman-centred analysis of a place or a culture which self-consciously represents itself as woman-centred. Today Shetland is not a woman-centred place in the same sense, if in any. Women are in a slight minority in the population, and their work roles are not dissimilar to those undertaken by the majority of women elsewhere in Europe. In 1999 the sectors employing the highest proportion of women were the service sector and the public services. Croft work has been relegated to a part-time activity for a minority of women. Yet crofting and the 'way of life' it connotes still carry cultural weight in public and personal representations of the past.

It is possible that this study, like previous academic and popular studies of Shetland history, may contribute to the continuation and reinforcement of the myth it purports to investigate, essentially becoming part of the broader discourse on the Shetland past. But discursive constructions of the past do not exist beyond the point at which they cease to be relevant. The myth of a woman-centred, egalitarian Shetland was most pertinent and achieved its greatest public assent in the 1970s and 1980s, following the challenges posed by the oil industry. Shetland is currently experiencing economic uncertainty as both the oil and the fishing industries contract. However, in comparison with other areas of Scotland where a way of life has been threatened or totally wiped out, and where local expressions of identity and difference have been used to stimulate a sense of worth within the community and tourism from without, Shetland is less well placed to use its collective identity in this way on account of its geographical location.

Anthropologists and ethnographers have become increasingly explicit about the place and role of the individual scholar in the field.[3] Historians, on the other hand, are unused to placing themselves in the analytical frame, at least consciously. However, Shetland is a place where one cannot remain anonymous for long. The archive is a hub of activity where, if one stays for long enough, one will encounter, in person or by reputation, a cross-section of Shetland society, all of whom are knowledgeable about Shetland history and have stories to tell. But it is the increasing use of oral history methodology and the application of post-modernist techniques of analysis that has moved the historian closer to the position of the anthropologist. Oral history work involves recognising the play of inter-subjectivity between the interviewer and the respondent, and thus acknowledging that the subjective position of the researcher will help shape the narrative that is constructed by the interviewee. At the same time, the respondent will create for himself or herself an appropriate mode of performance for the interview.[4] In my oral history interviews and in the many more informal conversations I had with Shetland women and men during my research trips, my identity – as a woman, an academic historian, and English – must be acknowledged as one influence on the contents and forms of narratives told to me.

The story of women in the Shetland past resembles a fairy-tale. It contains heroines and 'witches', tragedy and triumph over adversity, magic and happy endings, and yet the story is embedded in the materiality of Shetland society. The heroines are crofters, the witches are wise-women. Of course the fairy-tale is an ever-shifting narrative, constantly adapted to suit the circumstances of the teller and her audience. In this way the tale can remain relevant and can continue to fulfil its objectives. As the historian Marina Warner explains:

> Fairy tales exchange knowledge between an older voice of experience and a younger audience, they present pictures of perils and possibilities that lie ahead, they use terror to set limits on choice and offer consolation to the wronged, they draw social outlines around boys and girls, fathers and mothers, the rich and the poor, the rulers and the ruled, they point out the evildoers and garland the virtuous, they stand up to adversity with dreams of vengeance, power and vindication.[5]

The stories narrated by women in Shetland continue to be relevant in what is today a modern society struggling to cope with the complexities of the global economy. In most respects women's experience in twenty-first-century Shetland mirrors that of women elsewhere in modern western societies, but in Shetland the past continues to serve as a referent of identity. At a time when Shetland is searching for home-made survival solutions, women's narratives are used to engage in a political dialogue about Shetland identity and social change.

Disturbing narratives

Shetland is a prize for the scholar. It disturbs our concepts of progress, our accepted notions of gender structures, our sense of when the past stopped and our understanding of when women's liberation occurred and what it achieved. The history of women in modern western Europe has at its core a story of uneven progression, from a time when women were subordinate on the grounds of their sex to the present, where gender equality is more than just an aspiration. Shetland subverts this narrative. It subverts it because here is a place where women's culture still in the early years of the twenty-first century resonates (if faintly now) with a notion of a past – of female relatives of one, two, three or more generations ago – who were in control, numerically in charge, running not just household economies, but farms and trading networks, all operating in a culture of their own making and distinction. This is recalled in Shetland culture as a meta-narrative of women's power vested in knowledge, economic activity and household survival. Women so outnumbered men that a qualitatively different culture nurtured the continuance of a pre-modern world through the nineteenth century and into – just – the twentieth century. Women's narratives about each other and the material reality of their lives had a potency that surprised and alarmed the off-island-educated elites who brought 'enlightened' visions of women's virtues and their 'proper' roles and functions. This is not to say that women were 'liberated' at an early date in Shetland – just that the patriarchal system was so incredibly limited by the shortage of men as to leave a vacuum filled by a women's culture of control. This did *not* make women more free, better-off, more prosperous or more in control than their sisters elsewhere, or their granddaughters later on. It does not mean that things were better for women. Rather, it means merely that it was *a woman's world* that operated with very distinctive female rules, stories and understandings, and which became in the twentieth century the basis for a meta-narrative of a past in which the classic story of female subordination (with which European culture is familiar) did not apply.

This meta-narrative spoke of this woman's world as in existence as late as the first half of the twentieth century. But the story is fading now. The women I was privileged to interview for this book, and those interviewed in the 1970s and 1980s whose testimony I was fortunately able to access, still keep this story alive. What they show us, I believe, is that the feminist narrative of progress is not the only way to envisage women's destinies in the western world. They point to a way of constructing women's history that does not envisage women engaging in an organised struggle for equality through the nineteenth and twentieth centuries. They point to a way of looking at women's history as based on a different myth – that of women's past as having included a woman's world. It may not have been perfect; it may have been harsher indeed than for many women elsewhere. It did not detract from patriarchy, indeed. But though the suffering of women was just as bad in 'objective' economic, bodily and medical senses, patriarchy was shuffled off to the corners of a society in which men were just plain absent for most of the time.

The past never stops. The oral testimonies consulted for this book show that the world most historians imagine and categorise as 'early modern' was still alive in Shetland in the nineteenth century, with strong residues lingering through much of the twentieth century. From mother to daughter, there remained a strong memory of a world of empowered women. The testimony of Mary Manson, speaking in 1982, is quite astonishing to a western, well-educated woman such as myself.[6] Its story, construction, manner of delivery, allusions and presumptions about power and knowledge are like something out of a forgotten or imagined fairy-tale of centuries ago, something retrieved by the medieval scholar, not the late twentieth-century oral historian. Mary spoke for a whole world of Shetland women in which the very notion of female subord-ination is conceived very differently from that in most of the rest of Britain and Europe in the late modern period. In Shetland culture, it is not something that women have emerged from at some point in the 1960s and 1970s. Rather, it is something enduring and unrelenting, located in wise-women and female epic voyages, in the woman at the tended croft, the woman with a kishie on her back and knitting in her hands, bringing peats from moor to stack. The world in which she lived was the product of the unforgiving landscape, weather and economy, of men's absence and premature death at sea, of a landlord class that operated a perverse and cruel form of tenancy and of a merchant class that held women knitters in thrall to low-paid piece work. The woman's world operated within and despite these structures. Mary Manson's narrative, Shetland women's narrative, stands aside from that conven-tional story we write, re-tell and revise in our history books. It may not be *totally* divorced from it, but Shetland women construct their past as largely un-deflected by the new forms of female empowerment thrown up by modern feminism. There was an older women's empowerment which neither Shetland sheriffs nor even the local novelist and woman's champion Jessie Saxby could wholly understand.

The woman's world was constructed on the interaction of myth and materiality. The one did not exist without the other. The woman's world was bounded (or structured) by demographic and economic realities, by a landscape and agrarian system of some distinctive harshness and marginality in European terms and by the necessities of survival within those limits. But society is never merely material; it is also cultural. Knowledge and power were constructed by women and largely operated by them, and made for an entirely different way of perceiving their destiny from that we historians have ascribed to western womanhood.

The woman's world exposed by Shetland women reveals to the feminist scholar a different way of viewing the world and women's place within it. The question arises – was Shetland unique, or does it reveal a conception of the world and women's position in it that lies hidden within other European or western societies in the nineteenth and twentieth centuries? The women's stories that combine in this book suggest that there may be a different narrative of women in the past. This book has shown that women live in worlds of myth and of materiality, but these two worlds are interdependent; one cannot exist without the other.

Notes

1 See M. Silverman and P. H. Gulliver (eds), *Approaching the Past: Historical Anthropology through Irish Case Studies* (New York, Columbia University Press, 1992).
2 Samuel and Thompson (eds), *The Myths We Live By*, p. 2.
3 See, for example, J. Okely and H. Callaway (eds), *Anthropology and Autobiography* (London, Routledge, 1992).
4 See Summerfield, *Reconstructing Women's Wartime Lives*, pp. 20–3.
5 Warner, *From the Beast to the Blonde*, p. 21.
6 SA, 3/1/77/2: Mary Manson.

Bibliography

Primary sources

UNPUBLISHED DOCUMENTARY SOURCES
(ALL LOCATED AT SHETLAND ARCHIVE,
LERWICK (SA), EXCEPT WHERE INDICATED)

AD 22/2: Procurator fiscal precognitions, 1850–1926.

AD 22/2/102: Police letter book.

CH 2/1072/3: Lerwick kirk session minutes, 1780–1842.

CH 2/286/2: Northmavine kirk session minutes, 1765–1834.

CH 2/380/3: Walls and Sandness kirk session minutes, 1771–1802.

CO 6/5/14: Record of applications for parochial relief, parish of Dunrossness, 1892–1906.

CO 6/5/30: Minutes of Dunrossness, Sandwick and Cunningsburgh parochial board, 1845–71.

CO 6/5/36/14/1: List of widows in south Cunningsburgh.

CO 6/6/7: Record of applications for parochial relief, parish of Fetlar 1882–1945.

CO 6/7/23: General register of poor belonging to the parish of Lerwick, 1865–72.

CO 6/7/32: Record of applications for parochial relief, parish of Lerwick, 1857–69.

CO 8/1/7/10: Valuation roll, parish of Dunrossness, 1861–62.

D 1/83: Journal of Sarah Squire, Quaker, kept during a religious visit to Shetland, Orkney and the north of Scotland, 1835. With typed transcriptions by Marjorie Dell.

D 1/134–5: Scrapbooks compiled by James Shand, late nineteenth century to early twentieth century.

D 1/228: Records of J. Mitchell, fishcurer, 1882.

D 1/228/11: Ledger with accounts of 'women's work', etc., 1880–82.

D 1/357/3–6: Shetland Fishermen's Widows' Relief Fund, 1881–1936.

D 1/378/1–2: Journal kept by John Lewis, Methodist missionary in Shetland, 31 May 1823–1 April 1824, 30 April 1824–9 November 1825.

D 24: Nicolson Estate papers.

D 27/10/13: Notebooks with extensive notes by John Stewart anent Shetland folk-lore and ethnology, 1950–1970s.

SC 12/6: Sheriff court processes, 1692–1900.

SC 12/36: Wills and inventories.

1/8/1: Lerwick Prison criminal register, 1837–78.

2/216/9: Factories and workshops: annual report for 1905 (material on Lerwick and Baltasound gutting stations).

ORAL HISTORY INTERVIEWS
(TAPES AND TRANSCRIPTS IN SA)

3/1/20: Ida Manson.
3/1/37/1: Nina Charleson.
3/1/55/2: Henry Hunter.
3/1/77/2: Mary Manson.
3/1/99: Barbara Williamson.
3/1/103: Agnes Tulloch.
3/1/112: Margaret Shearer.
3/1/123/1: John Gear.
3/1/124/1–2: Katie Inkster.
3/1/130/1: Ruby Ewenson.
3/1/154: Agnes Halcrow.
3/1/162/2: Agnes Leask.
3/1/178: Harriet Robertson.
3/1/179: Jessie Sinclair.
3/1/237: Nan Paton.
3/1/264: Robina Bruce.
3/1/290: Bruce Henderson.
3/2/10/1: Jeannie Hardie.
3/2/19/2: Joan Williamson.
3/2/102: Mrs K. Laurenson.
3/2/103/2: Magnus and Helen Anderson.
3/2/109/2: Katherine Bairnson.
3/75/1: Ella Law.

ORAL HISTORY INTERVIEWS CONDUCTED BY THE
AUTHOR (TAPES AND TRANSCRIPTS IN POSSESSION
OF THE AUTHOR AND DEPOSITED WITH SA)

Netta Inkster, interviewed 9 April 2001 and 19 March 2002.
Agnes Leask, interviewed 20 March 2002.
Mary Ellen Odie, interviewed 4 April 2001.

DIARY

Mary Manson's diary, 1969 (unpublished), in possession of Mrs Netta
Inkster.

Published primary sources

British Parliamentary Papers, C (1st series) 555 I: *Commission to Inquire into
the Truck System, Second Report (Shetland), 1872.*
British Parliamentary Papers, 1 C (1st series) 3980 I–IV: *Royal Commission
of Inquiry into the Condition of Crofters and Cottars in the Highlands and Islands
of Scotland* (Napier Commission), *1884.*

Registrar General for Scotland Annual Report, 1881 (Edinburgh, HMSO, 1881).
Royal Commission on Housing in Scotland, Shetland evidence (1913).
Census of Scotland, 1851, 1861, 1871, 1881, 1901, 1911, 1921 (Edinburgh, HMSO).

Film / video

The Rugged Island: A Shetland Lyric, directed by Jenny Brown (1934), Scottish Film and Television Archive, Glasgow.
The Work They Say is Mine, directed by Rosie Gibson (made for Channel 4 television, 1986).

Newspapers and magazines

Daily Record.
The Herald.
Irish News.
The New Shetlander.
Northern Ensign.
The Scotsman.
The Shetland News.
The Shetland Times.
Tocher.

Published secondary sources

Abrahams, R. D., 'A performance-centred approach to gossip', *Man*, new series, 5:2 (1970), pp. 290–301.

Abrams, L., '"The best men in Shetland": women, gender and place in peripheral communities', in P. Payton (ed.), *Cornish Studies: Eight* (Exeter, University of Exeter Press, 2000), pp. 97–114.

Abrams, L., 'From demon to victim: the infanticidal mother in Shetland, 1699–1899', in Y. G. Brown and R. Ferguson (eds), *Twisted Sisters: Women, Crime and Deviance in Scotland since 1400* (East Linton, Tuckwell Press, 2002), pp. 180–203.

Abrams, L., *The Making of Modern Woman: Europe 1789–1918* (London, Longman, 2002).

Abrams, L., 'The case of Gina Skaar', *The New Shetlander* 226 (Yule 2003), pp. 24–7.

Anderson, M., 'Why was Scottish nuptiality so depressed for so long?', in I. Devos and L. Kennedy (eds), *Marriage and Rural Economy: Western Europe since 1400* (Brepols, Turnhout, 1999), pp. 49–84.

Anthony, R., *Herds and Hinds: Farm Labour in Lowland Scotland, 1900–1939* (East Linton, Tuckwell Press, 1997).

Ardener, E., '"Remote areas": some theoretical considerations', in A. Jackson (ed.), *Anthropology at Home* (London, Tavistock, 1987), pp. 38–54.

Arwill-Nordbladh, E., 'The Swedish image of Viking age women: stereotype, generalisation, and beyond', in R. Samson (ed.), *Social Approaches to Viking Studies* (Glasgow, Cruithne Press, 1991), pp. 53–64.

Barnard, A., *History and Theory in Anthropology* (Cambridge, Cambridge University Press, 2000).

Barnard, F., *Picturesque Life in Shetland* (Edinburgh, George Waterston & Sons, 1890).

Barthes, R., *Mythologies* (London, Vintage, 1993).

Bauman, R. (ed.), *Folklore, Cultural Performances, and Popular Entertainments* (Oxford, Oxford University Press, 1992).

Bauman, R., 'Performance', in Bauman (ed.), *Folklore*, pp. 41–9.

Bennett, J., 'History that stands still: women's work in the European past', *Feminist Studies* 14 (1988), pp. 269–83.

Berkowitz, S. G., 'Familism, kinship and sex roles', *Anthropological Quarterly* 57:2 (1984), pp. 83–92.

Black, G. F., *County Folklore*, vol. III: *Orkney and Shetland Islands* (orig. 1903; reprint Felinfach, Llanerch Publishers, 1994).

Blaikie, A., *Illegitimacy, Sex and Society: Northeast Scotland 1750–1900* (Oxford, Oxford University Press, 1993).

Blaikie, A., 'A kind of loving: illegitimacy, grandparents and the rural economy of north east Scotland 1750–1900', *Scottish Economic and Social History* 14 (1994), pp. 41–57.

Bleek, W., 'Witchcraft, gossip and death: a social drama', *Man*, new series, II (1976), pp. 526–41.

Blind, K., 'Shetland folklore and the old faith of the Scandinavians and Teutons', *Saga-Book of the Viking Club* 1 (1896), pp. 163–81.

Boissevain, J., 'Towards a social anthropology of the Mediterranean', *Current Anthropology* 20 (1979), pp. 81–93.

Bourke, J., *Husbandry to Housewifery: Women, Economic Change and Housework in Ireland 1890–1914* (Oxford, Clarendon Press, 1993).

Brettell, C., 'Male migrants and unwed mothers: illegitimacy in a northwestern Portuguese town', *Anthropology* 9 (1985), pp. 87–110.

Brettell, C., *Men who Migrate, Women who Wait: Population and History in a Portuguese Parish* (Princeton, NJ, Princeton University Press, 1986).

Brock, J. M., *The Mobile Scot: A Study of Emigration and Migration 1861–1911* (Edinburgh, John Donald, 1999).

Brown, C. G., *Up-helly-aa: Custom, Culture and Community in Shetland* (Manchester, Manchester University Press, 1998).

Brown, C. G., *The Death of Christian Britain* (London, Routledge, 2001).

Brown, C. G., 'The unconverted and the conversion: gender relations in the salvation narrative in Britain 1800–1960', in W. J. van Bekkum, J. N. Bremmer and A. Molendijk (eds), *Conversion in Modern Times* (Leuven, Peeters, 2005).

Brown, Y. G. and R. Ferguson (eds), *Twisted Sisters: Women, Crime and Deviance in Scotland since 1400* (East Linton, Tuckwell Press, 2002).

Byron, R., *Sea Change: A Shetland Society, 1970–79* (St John's, Newfoundland, Institute of Social and Economic Research, 1986).

Byron, R., 'The maritime household in northern Europe', *Comparative Studies in Society and History* 36 (1994), pp. 271–91.

Byron, R. and D. Chalmers, 'The fisherwomen of Fife: history, identity and social change', *Ethnologia Europaea* 23 (1993), pp. 97–110.

Byron, R. and G. McFarlane, *Social Change in Dunrossness*, report for Shetland Islands Council, 1979.

Campbell, J. K., *Honour, Family and Patronage* (Oxford, Clarendon Press, 1964).

Canning, K., *Languages of Labor and Gender: Female Factory Work in Germany, 1850–1914* (Ithaca, NY, Cornell University Press, 1996).

Carter, A. (ed.), *The Virago Book of Fairy Tales* (London, Virago, 1990).

de Certeau, M., *The Practice of Everyday Life* (Berkeley, University of California Press, 1984).

Chanfrault-Duchet, M.-F., 'Narrative structures, social models and symbolic representation in the life story', in S. B. Gluck and D. Patai (eds), *Women's Words* (London, Routledge, 1991), pp. 77–92.

Cohen, A. P. (ed.), *Belonging: Identity and Social Organisation in British Rural Cultures* (Manchester, Manchester University Press, 1982).

Cohen, A. P., 'Belonging: the experience of culture', in Cohen (ed.), *Belonging*, pp. 1–17.

Cohen, A. P., *The Symbolic Construction of Community* (London, Tavistock, 1985).

Cohen, A. P., *Whalsay: Symbol, Segment and Boundary in a Shetland Island Community* (Manchester, Manchester University Press, 1987).

Cohen, A. P. (ed.), *Signifying Identities: Anthroplogical Perspectives on Boundaries and Contested Values* (London, Routledge, 2000).

Cole, S., 'The sexual division of labour and social change in a Portuguese fishery', in J. Nadel-Klein and D. L. Davis (eds), *To Work and To Weep*, pp. 169–89.

Cole, S., *Women of the Praia: Work and Lives in a Portuguese Coastal Community* (Princeton, NJ, Princeton University Press, 1991).

Cosslett, T., C. Lury and P. Summerfield (eds), *Feminism and Autobiography: Texts, Theories, Methods* (London, Routledge, 2000).

Coull, J. R., 'The boom in the herring fishery in the Shetland Islands, 1880–1914', *Northern Scotland* 8 (1988), pp. 25–37.

Cowie, R., *Shetland: Descriptive and Historical* (Edinburgh, John Menzies and Co., 1st edn 1871).

Cruikshank, J., *Life Lived Like a Story: Life Stories of Three Yukon Native Elders* (Vancouver, University of British Columbia Press, 1990).

Cruikshank, J., 'Myth as a framework for life stories: Athapaskan women making sense of social change in northern Canada', in R. Samuel and P. Thompson (eds), *The Myths we Live By* (London, Routledge, 1990), pp. 174–83.

Cruikshank, J., 'Claiming legitimacy: prophecy narratives from northern Aboriginal women', *American Indian Quarterly* 18:2 (1994), pp. 147–67.

Davidoff, L. and C. Hall, *Family Fortunes: Men and Women of the English Middle Class, 1780–1850* (London, Routledge, 1987).

Davis, D. L. and J. Nadel-Klein, 'Terra cognita? A review of the literature', in Nadel-Klein and Davis (eds), *To Work and To Weep*, pp. 19–50.

Davis, N. Z., *Women on the Margins: Three Seventeenth Century Lives* (London, Harvard University Press, 1995).

Davis, N. Z., *The Gift in Sixteenth Century France* (Oxford, Oxford University Press, 2000).

Dégh, L., *Narratives in Society: A Performer-Centred Study of Narration* (Bloomington, IN, Indiana University Press, 1995).

Delamont, S., *Appetites and Identities: An Introduction to the Social Anthropology of Western Europe* (London, Routledge, 1995).

DesBrisay, G., 'Wet nurses and unwed mothers in seventeenth century Aberdeen', in E. Ewan and M. M. Meikle (eds), *Women in Scotland c.1100–c.1750* (East Linton, Tuckwell Press, 1999), pp. 210–20.

Devine, T. M., 'Women workers, 1850–1914', in T. M. Devine (ed.), *Farm Servants and Labour in Lowland Scotland 1770–1914* (Edinburgh, John Donald, 1984), pp. 98–123.

Dommasnes, L. H., 'Women, kinship and the basis of power', in R. Samson (ed.), *Social Approaches to Viking Studies* (Glasgow, Cruithne Press, 1991), pp. 65–73.

Dubisch, J. (ed.), *Gender and Power in Rural Greece* (Princeton, NJ, Princeton University Press, 1986).

Dubisch, J., 'Introduction', in Dubisch (ed.), *Gender and Power*, pp. 3–41.

Duden, B., *The Woman Beneath the Skin: A Doctor's Patients in Eighteenth Century Germany* (Cambridge, MA, Harvard University Press, 1991).

Edmonston, A., *A View of the Present State of the Zetland Islands*, 2 vols (Edinburgh, James Ballantyne & Co., 1809).

Edmonston, B. and J. M. E. Saxby, *The Home of a Naturalist* (London, Nesbit, 1888).

Elphinstone, M., *The Sea Road* (Edinburgh, Canongate, 2000).

Ennew, J., *The Western Isles Today* (Cambridge, Cambridge University Press, 1980).

Ewan, E., 'Alison Rough: a woman's life and death in sixteenth-century Edinburgh', *Women's History Magazine* 45 (2003), pp. 4–13.

Ewan, E., S. Innes, S. Reynolds and R. Pipes (eds), *Biographical Dictionary of Scottish Women* (Edinburgh, Edinburgh University Press, forthcoming 2006).

E. Ewan and M. M. Meikle (eds), *Women in Scotland c.1100–c.1750* (East Linton, Tuckwell Press, 1999).

Fenton, A., *The Northern Isles: Orkney and Shetland* (East Linton, Tuckwell Press, 1997).

Flinn, D., *Travellers in a Bygone Shetland: An Anthology* (Edinburgh, Scottish Academic Press, 1989).

Flinn, M. (ed.), *Scottish Population History from the 17th Century to the 1930s* (Cambridge, Cambridge University Press, 1977).

Forster, G. M., 'Peasant society and the image of limited good', *American Anthropologist*, new series, 67:2 (1965), pp. 293–315.

Fox, R., *The Tory Islanders: A People of the Celtic Fringe* (Cambridge, Cambridge University Press, 1978).

Fraser, F., *The Christian Watt Papers* (Edinburgh, Paul Harris, 1983).

Frater, A. C., 'Women of the Gàidhealtachd and their songs to 1750', in Ewan and Meikle (eds), *Women in Scotland*, pp. 67–79.

Friedl, E., 'The position of women: appearance and reality', in J. Dubisch (ed.), *Gender and Power*, pp. 42–52.

Fryer, L. G., *Knitting by the Fireside and on the Hillside: A History of the Shetland Hand Knitting Industry c.1600–1950* (Lerwick, Shetland Times Ltd, 1995).

Geertz, C., 'Deep play: notes on the Balinese cockfight', in C. Geertz (ed.), *Myth, Symbol and Culture* (New York, Norton, 1971), pp. 1–37.

George, G., *The Rock where we Stand: An Ethnography of Women's Activism in Newfoundland* (Toronto, University of Toronto Press, 2000).

Gifford, T., *An Historical Description of the Zetland Islands* (London, Nicholson, 1786).

Gilroy, A., 'Introduction', in Gilroy (ed.), *Romantic Geographies*, pp. 1–15.

Gilroy, A., (ed.), *Romantic Geographies: Discourses of Travel 1775–1844* (Manchester, Manchester University Press, 2000).

Gittins, D., *Fair Sex: Family Size and Structure 1900–39* (London, Hutchinson, 1982).

Gluckman, M., 'Gossip and scandal', *Current Anthropology* 4 (1963), pp. 307–16.

Goffmann, E., *The Presentation of Self in Everyday Life* (London, Penguin, 1990).

Gordon, E., 'Women, work and collective action: Dundee jute workers, 1870–1906', *Journal of Social History* 21 (1987), pp. 27–48.

Gordon, E., *Women and the Labour Movement in Scotland 1850–1914* (Oxford, Oxford University Press, 1991).

Gordon, E. and G. Nair, *Public Lives: Women, Family and Society in Victorian Britain* (New Haven and London, Yale University Press, 2003).

Gowing, L., *Domestic Dangers: Women, Words, and Sex in Early Modern London* (Oxford, Oxford University Press, 1996).

Gowing, L., *Common Bodies: Women, Touch and Power in Seventeenth Century England* (New Haven and London, Yale University Press, 2003).

Graham, J. J. and L. I. Graham (eds), *A Shetland Anthology: Poetry from Earliest Times to the Present Day* (Lerwick, Shetland Publishing Company, 1998).

Graham, M. F., 'Women and the church courts in Reformation-era Scotland', in Ewan and Meikle (eds), *Women in Scotland*, pp. 187–98.

Grant, R., *The Lone Voyage of Betty Mouat* (Aberdeen, Impulse Books, 1973).

Gray, J., 'Open spaces and dwelling places: being at home on hill farms in the Scottish Borders', in S. M. Low and D. Lawrence-Zúñiga (eds), *The Anthropology of Space and Place: Locating Culture* (Oxford, Blackwell, 2003), pp. 224–44.

Gustavsson, A., 'Folklore in community conflicts: gossip in a fishing community', *Scandinavian Yearbook of Folklore* 35 (1979), pp. 49–85.

Guttentag, M. and P. F. Secord, *Too Many Women? The Sex Ratio Question* (London, Sage, 1983).

Heenan, B., 'Living arrangements among elderly Shetlanders in the parishes of Lerwick, Yell and Unst between 1851 and 1891', in A. H. Dawson, H. R. Jones, A. Small and J. A. Soulsby (eds), *Scottish Geographical Studies* (Dundee and St Andrews Universities, 1993), pp. 218–28.

Henderson, L. and Cowan, E. J., *Scottish Fairy Belief* (East Linton, Tuckwell Press, 2001).

Hibbert, S., *A Description of the Shetland Islands* (Edinburgh, Constable, 1822).

Higgs, E., 'Women, occupations and work in nineteenth century censuses', *History Workshop Journal* 23 (1987), pp. 59–80.

Hill, B., *Women Alone: Spinsters in England 1660–1850* (New Haven and London, Yale University Press, 2001).

Hindle, S., 'The shaming of Margaret Knowsley: gossip, gender, and the experience of authority in early modern England', *Continuity and Change* 9 (1994), pp. 391–419.

Honeyman, K., *Women, Gender and Industrialisation in England, 1700–1870* (Basingstoke, Macmillan, 2000).

van Houts, E., *Memory and Gender in Medieval Europe 900–1200* (London, Macmillan, 1999).

Hufton, O., 'Women without men: widows and spinsters in Britain and France in the eighteenth century', *Journal of Family History* 9 (1984), pp. 355–76.

Hunter, J., *The Making of a Crofting Community* (Edinburgh, John Donald, 1976).

Jackson, A. (ed.), *Anthropology at Home* (London, Tavistock, 1987).

Jamieson, C., 'The women of Shetland', *The New Shetlander* 177 (Hairst 1991), pp. 31–3.

Jesch, J., *Women in the Viking Age* (Woodbridge, Boydell Press, 1991).

Johnson, M., 'Domestic work in rural Iceland: an historical overview', in N. Long (ed.), *Family and Work in Rural Societies: Perspectives on Non-Wage Labour* (London, Tavistock, 1984), pp. 160–74.

Johnson, R. L., *A Shetland Country Merchant: A Biography of James Williamson of Mid Yell: 1800–1872* (Scalloway, Shetland Publishing Company, 1979).

Johnston, G., 'Widow Laurenson of Da Wilmin', *The New Shetlander* 221 (Hairst 2002), pp. 55–8.

Johnston, G., 'An inspector calls: poor relief in Cunningsburgh before and after the First World War', *The New Shetlander* 227 (Voar 2004), pp. 16–22.

Jones, D., 'Gossip – notes on women's oral culture', in D. Cameron (ed.), *The Feminist Critique of Language* (London, Routledge, 1990), pp. 242–9.

Kaplan, T., 'Female consciousness and collective action: the case of Barcelona, 1910–18', *Signs* 7 (1982), pp. 545–66.

Kendall, N., *With Naught but Kin behind them: The Shetland of its Early Emigrants* (Melbourne, Brown Prior Anderson, 1998).

Kennedy, R., 'Women's friendships on Crete: a psychological perspective', in Dubisch (ed.), *Gender and Power in Rural Greece*, pp. 121–38.

Kilday, A.-M., 'Maternal monsters: murdering mothers in south-west Scotland, 1750–1815', in Brown and Ferguson (eds), *Twisted Sisters*, pp. 156–79.

Laslett, P. and R. Wall (eds), *Household and Family in Past Time* (Cambridge, Cambridge University Press, 1978).

Leneman, L. 'Defamation in Scotland, 1750–1800', *Continuity and Change* 15 (2000), pp. 209–34.

Leneman, L. and R. Mitchison, *Girls in Trouble: Sexuality and Social Control in Rural Scotland 1660–1780* (Edinburgh, Scottish Cultural Press, 1998).

Leneman, L. and R. Mitchison, *Sin in the City: Sexuality and Social Control in Urban Scotland 1660–1780* (Edinburgh, Scottish Cultural Press, 1998).

Livingstone, W. P., *Shetland and the Shetlanders* (London, Thomas Nelson & Sons, 1947).

Macdonald, D., *Tales and Traditions of the Lews* (Edinburgh, Birlinn, 2000).

Macdonald, S., *Reimagining Culture: Histories, Identities and the Gaelic Renaissance* (Oxford, Berg, 1997).

McFarlane, G., 'Shetlanders and incomers: change, conflict and emphasis in social perspectives', in L. Holy and M. Stuchlik (eds), *The Structure of Folk Models* (London, Academic Press, 1981), pp. 119–36.

McGrath, C., B. Neis and M. Porter (eds), *Their Lives and Times: Women in Newfoundland and Labrador* (St John's, Killick Press, 1995).

McLintock, A., *Imperial Leather: Race, Gender and Sexuality in the Colonial Contest* (New York, Routledge, 1995).

Manson, T. M. Y., *Drifting Alone to Norway* (Shetland, Nelson Smith Printing Services, 1996).

Marwick, E., *The Folklore of Orkney and Shetland* (Edinburgh, Birlinn, 2000).

Massey, D., *Space, Place and Gender* (Cambridge, Cambridge University Press, 1994).

Matthew, H. C. G. and B. Harrison (eds), *Oxford Dictionary of National Biography* (Oxford, Oxford University Press, 2004).

Mewett, P. G., 'Associational categories and the social location of relationships in a Lewis crofting community', in Cohen (ed.), *Belonging*, pp. 101–30.

Mewett, P. G., 'Exiles, nicknames, social identities and the production of local consciousness in a Lewis crofting community', in Cohen (ed.), *Belonging*, pp. 222–46.

Mills, S., 'Written on the landscape: Mary Wollstonecraft's *Letters Written During a Short Residence in Sweden, Norway and Denmark*', in A. Gilroy (ed.), *Romantic Geographies: Discourses of Travel 1775–1844* (Manchester, Manchester University Press, 2000), pp. 19–34.

Mitchell, I., *Ahint da Deeks* (Lerwick, Shetland Amenity Trust, 1987).

Mitchell, I., A. Johnson and I. Coghill, *Living Memory: A Photographic and Oral History of Lerwick, Gulberwick and Sound* (Lerwick, Shetland Amenity Trust, 1986).

Mitchison, R. and L. Leneman, *Sexuality and Social Control: Scotland 1660–1780* (Oxford, Blackwell, 1989).

Moffatt, W., *Shetland: The Isles of Nightless Summer* (London, Heath Cranton Ltd, 1934).

Moore, H. L., *Feminism and Anthropology* (London, Polity, 1988).

Moreton, C., *Hungry for Home: Leaving the Blaskets: A Journey from the Edge of Ireland* (London, Viking, 2000).

Moring, B., 'Household and family in Finnish coastal societies 1635–1895', *Journal of Family History* 18 (1993), pp. 395–414.

Moring, B., 'Marriage and social change in south-western Finland, 1700–1870', *Continuity and Change* 11 (1996), pp. 91–113.

Morrison, I. A., 'The Auld Rock: the physical environment as an element in the interplay of continuity and change in Shetland's history', in Waugh (ed.), *Shetland's Northern Links*, pp. 84–9.

Morrow, P., 'On shaky ground: folklore, collaboration and problematic outcomes', in Morrow and Schneider (eds), *When Our Words Return*, pp. 27–51.

Morrow, P. and W. Schneider (eds), *When Our Words Return: Writing, Hearing, and Remembering Oral Traditions of Alaska and the Yukon* (Logan, UT, Utah State University Press, 1995).

Nadel-Klein, J., 'A fisher laddie needs a fisher lassie: endogamy and work in a Scottish fishing village', in Nadel-Klein and Davis (eds), *To Work and To Weep*, pp. 190–210.

Nadel-Klein, J., *Fishing for Heritage: Modernity and Loss along the Scottish Coast* (Oxford, Berg, 2003).

Nadel-Klein, J. and D. L. Davis (eds), *To Work and To Weep: Women in Fishing Economies* (St John's, Memorial University of Newfoundland, 1988).

Nelson, J. L., 'Gender, memory and social power', *Gender & History* 12:3 (2000), pp. 722–34.

The New Statistical Account for Scotland, vol. XV (Edinburgh and London, William Blackwood & Sons, 1845).

Okely, J. and H. Callaway (eds), *Anthropology and Autobiography* (London, Routledge, 1992).

Paine, R., 'What is gossip about? An alternative hypothesis', *Man*, new series, 2 (1967), pp. 278–85.

Parman, S., *Scottish Crofters* (Fort Worth, Holt, Rinehart and Winston, 1990).

Personal Narratives Group, 'Forms that transform', in Personal Narratives Group (ed.), *Interpreting Women's Lives: Feminist Theory and Personal Narratives* (Bloomington, IN, Indiana University Press, 1989).

Porter, M., '"She was skipper of the shore crew": notes on the development of the sexual division of labour in Newfoundland', *Labour* 15 (1985), pp. 105–23.

Pugh, S., *Kirstie's Witnesses* (Lerwick, Shetland Times Ltd, 1988).

Purkiss, D., *Troublesome Things: A History of Fairies and Fairy Stories* (London, Penguin, 2000).

Radner, J. N. and S. S. Lanser, 'Strategies of coding in women's cultures', in J. N. Radner (ed.), *Feminist Messages: Coding in Women's Folk Culture* (Urbana and Chicago, University of Illinois Press, 1993), pp. 1–29.

Rey-Henningsen, M.-L., 'Galicia, state of women', *Spare Rib* 70 (1980), pp. 27–9.

Rey-Henningsen, M.-L., *The World of the Ploughwoman: Folklore and Reality in Matriarchal Northwest Spain* (Helsinki, Academia Scientiarum Fennica, 1994).

Reynolds, S., 'Women in the printing and paper trades in Edwardian Scotland', in E. Gordon and E. Breitenbach (eds), *The World is Ill Divided: Women's Work in Scotland in the Nineteenth and Early Twentieth Centuries* (Edinburgh, Edinburgh University Press, 1990), pp. 49–69.

Roberts, E., *A Woman's Place: An Oral History of Working-Class Women 1890–1940* (Oxford, Blackwell, 1984).

Robertson, M. S., *Sons and Daughters of Shetland 1800–1900* (Lerwick, Shetland Publishing Company, 1991).

Rogers, S. C., 'Female forms of power and the myth of male dominance: a model of female/male interaction in peasant society', *American Ethnologist* 2:4 (1975), pp. 727–56.

Rosaldo, M. Z., 'Woman, culture and society: a theoretical overview', in M. Z. Rosaldo and L. Lamphere (eds), *Woman, Culture and Society* (Stanford, CA, Stanford University Press, 1974), pp. 17–42.

Rose, S., *Limited Livelihoods: Gender and Class in Nineteenth Century England* (London, Routledge, 1992).

Ross, E., 'Fierce questions and taunts: married life in working-class London, 1870–1914', *Feminist Studies* 8 (1982), pp. 575–602.

Ross, E., 'Survival networks: women's neighbourhood sharing in London before World War One', *History Workshop* 15 (1983), pp. 4–27.

Rowlands, A., ' "In great secrecy": the crime of infanticide in Rothenburg ob der Tauber, 1501–1618', *German History* 15 (1997), pp. 101–21.

Rublack, U., *The Crimes of Women in Early Modern Germany* (Oxford, Oxford University Press, 1999).

Sabean, D. W., *Kinship in Neckarhausen 1700–1870* (Cambridge, Cambridge University Press, 1998).

Samuel, R., *Theatres of Memory*, vol. I: *Past and Present in Contemporary Culture* (London, Verso, 1994).

Samuel, R. and P. Thompson (eds), *The Myths We Live By* (London, Routledge, 1990).

Saxby, J. M. E., *Daala-Mist: Or, Stories of Shetland* (Edinburgh, Andrew Elliot, 1876).

Saxby, J. M. E., *Heim-Laund and Heim-Folk* (Edinburgh, R. and R. Clark, 1892).

Saxby, J. M. E., *A Camsterie Nacket: Being the Story of a Contrary Laddie Ill to Guide* (Edinburgh and London, Oliphant Anderson and Ferrier, 1894).

Saxby, J. M. E., *Shetland Traditional Lore* (Edinburgh, Grant & Murray, 1932).

Sayer, K., *Women of the Fields: Representations of Rural Women in the Nine-teenth Century* (Manchester, Manchester University Press, 1996).

Segalen, M., *Love and Power in the Peasant Family: Rural France in the Nine-teenth Century* (Oxford, Blackwell, 1983).

Segalen, M., *Historical Anthropology of the Family* (Cambridge, Cambridge University Press, 1986).

Sharpe, P., 'Dealing with love: the ambiguous independence of the single woman in early modern England', *Gender & History* 11 (1999), pp. 209–32.

Shortall, S., *Women and Farming: Property and Power* (Basingstoke, Macmillan, 1999).

Silverman, M. and P. H. Gulliver (eds), *Approaching the Past: Historical Anthropology through Irish Case Studies* (New York, Columbia University Press, 1992).

Simonton, D., *A History of European Women's Work, 1700 to the Present* (London, Routledge, 1998).

Skaptadóttir, U. D., 'Housework and wage work: gender in Icelandic fishing communities', in G. Pálsson and P. Durrenberger (eds), *Images of Contemporary Iceland: Everyday Lives and Global Contexts* (Iowa City, IA, University of Iowa Press, 1996), pp. 87–105.

Smith, B., *Ladies of the Leisure Class: The Bourgeoisie of Northern France in the Nineteenth Century* (Princeton, NJ, Princeton University Press, 1981).

Smith, B., 'Kirstie Caddel's Christmas: "national prosperity" and mid-Victorian Shetland', in J. J. Graham and J. Tait (eds), *Shetland Folk Book*, vol. VIII (Lerwick, 1988), pp. 1–13.

Smith, B., 'The development of the spoken and written Shetland dialect: a historian's view', in D. J. Waugh (ed.), *Shetland's Northern Links: Language and History* (Edinburgh, Scottish Society for Northern Studies, 1996), pp. 30–43.

Smith, B., *Toons and Tenants: Settlement and Society in Shetland, 1299–1899* (Lerwick, Shetland Times Ltd, 2000).

Smith, H. D., *Shetland Life and Trade 1550–1914* (Edinburgh, John Donald, 1984).

Smith, M. E., 'Comments on the heuristic utility of maritime anthropology', *The Maritime Anthropologist* 1 (1977), pp. 2–8.

Smout, T. C., 'Aspects of sexual behaviour in nineteenth century Scotland', in A. A. Maclaren (ed.), *Social Class in Scotland: Past and Present* (Edinburgh, John Donald, 1976), pp. 55–85.

Smout, T. C., *A History of the Scottish People 1560–1830* (Glasgow, Fontana, 1979).

Smout, T. C., *A Century of the Scottish People 1830–1950* (London, Fontana, 1987).

Spence, J., *Shetland Folk-Lore* (Lerwick, Johnson and Greig, 1899, reprinted 1973).

Spence, J. C., *Inga's Story: Growing Up in Shetland a Century Ago* (Lerwick, Shetland Publishing Company, 1988).

Squires, J., 'Re-visiting "internal colonialism" – the case of Shetland', *Shetland Economic Review* (Lerwick, Shetland Islands Council, 1993), pp. 1,264–9.

Stack, C. B., 'Sex roles and survival strategies in an urban black community', in M. Z. Rosaldo and L. Lamphere (eds), *Woman, Culture and Society* (Stanford, CA, Stanford University Press, 1974), pp. 113–28.

Standen, E., *A Paper on the Shetland Islands* (orig. 1845; Lingfield, Mill Print, 2000).

Stanley, L., *The Auto/biographical I: The Theory and Practice of Feminist Auto/biography* (Manchester, Manchester University Press, 1992).

Stanley, L., 'From self made women to women's made selves? Audit selves, simulation and surveillance in the rise of public woman', in T. Cosslett, C. Lury and P. Summerfield (eds), *Feminism and Autobiography* (London, Routledge, 2000), pp. 40–60.

Stephenson, J. D. and C. G. Brown, 'The view from the workplace: women's memories of work in Stirling c.1910–c.1950', in E. Gordon and E. Breitenbach (eds), *The World is Ill Divided: Women's Work in Scotland in the Nineteenth and Early Twentieth Centuries* (Edinburgh, Edinburgh University Press, 1990), pp. 7–28.

Stiùbhart, D. U., 'Women and gender in the early modern western Gàidhealtachd', in Ewan and Meikle (eds), *Women in Scotland*, pp. 233–49.

Strathern, A. and P. J. Stewart, *Minorities and Memories: Survivals and Extinctions in Scotland and Western Europe* (Durham, NC, Carolina Academic Press, 2001).

Strathern, M., *Women in Between: Female Roles in a Male World: Mount Hagen, New Guinea* (Lanham, MD, and London, Rowmen and Littlefield, 1995).

Strathern, M., *The Gender of the Gift: Problems with Women and Problems with Society in Melanesia* (Berkeley and London, University of California Press, 1988).

Summerfield, P., *Reconstructing Women's Wartime Lives: Discourse and Subjectivity in Oral Histories of the Second World War* (Manchester, Manchester University Press, 1988).

Symonds, D. A., *Weep Not for Me: Women, Ballads, and Infanticide in Early Modern Scotland* (University Park, PA, Pennsylvania State University Press, 1997).

Tebbutt, M., *Women's Talk: A Social History of 'Gossip' in Working-Class Neighbourhoods, 1880–1960* (Aldershot, Scolar Press, 1995).

Telford, S., *'In a World a Wir Ane': A Shetland Herring Girl's Story* (Lerwick, Shetland Times Ltd, 1998).

Thomson, A., 'Anzac memories: putting popular memory theory into practice in Australia', *Oral History Journal* 18 (1990), pp. 25–31.

Thompson, P., 'Women in the fishing: the roots of power between the sexes', *Comparative Studies in Society and History* 27 (1985), pp. 3–32.

Thompson, P., T. Wailey and T. Lummis, *Living the Fishing* (London, Routledge and Kegan Paul, 1983).

Thorvaldsen, G., 'Coastal women and their work roles', in H. Sandvik, K. Telste and G. Thorvaldsen (eds), *Pathways of the Past* (Oslo, Novus, 2002), pp. 139–51.

L. Tilly and J. W. Scott, *Women, Work and Family* (London, Routledge, 1987).

Todd, M., *The Culture of Protestantism in Early Modern Scotland* (New Haven and London, Yale University Press, 2002).

Tosh, J., *A Man's Place: Masculinity and the Middle Class Home in Victorian England* (New Haven and London, Yale University Press, 1999).

Verdon, N., *Rural Women Workers in Nineteenth-Century England: Gender, Work and Wages* (Woodbridge, Boydell Press, 2002).

Wachowich, N., *Saqiyuq: Stories from the Lives of Three Inuit Women* (Montreal and Kingston, McGill Queen's University Press, 1999).

Warner, M., *From the Beast to the Blonde: On Fairy Tales and their Tellers* (London, Vintage, 1995).

Waugh, D. J. (ed.), *Shetland's Northern Links: Language and History* (Edinburgh, Scottish Society for Northern Studies, 1996).

Weiner, A. B., *Women of Value, Men of Renown: New Perspectives in Trobriand Exchange* (Austin, TX, University of Texas Press, 1976).

Wilson, S., 'Infanticide, child abandonment and female honour in nineteenth century Corsica', *Comparative Studies in Society and History* 30 (1988), pp. 762–83.

Wilson, S., *The Magical Universe: Everyday Ritual and Magic in Pre-Modern Europe* (London, Hambledon, 2000).

Yuval-Davis, N., *Gender and Nation* (London, Sage, 1997).

Unpublished secondary sources

Ewen, E., 'Disorderly damsels: women and assault in late medieval Scotland', unpublished paper, 2002.

Hagmark, H., 'Maritime and seafarers' wives in the Åland isles in the 20th century', unpublished paper, 2001.

Jack, C. A. H., 'Shetland women and crofting from the 1930s to the present day: recreating their pasts', unpublished paper, London, 2001.

Jack, C. A. H., 'Women and crofting in Shetland from the 1930s to the present day', PhD thesis, University of the Highlands and Islands Millennium Institute, 2003.

Renwanz, M. E., 'From crofters to Shetlanders: the social history of a Shetland Island community's self image, 1872–1978, PhD thesis, Stanford University, 1981.

Steele, W. R., 'Local authority involvement in housing and health in Shetland c.1900–1950', MPhil thesis, University of Strathclyde, 1992.

Wachowich, N., 'Getting along: life histories as adaptation to changing social climates in the Arctic', unpublished paper, 2002.

Internet sites

Scottish census results 2001 online, www.scrol.gov.uk: Table KS09c, Economic activity – females (consulted 25 March 2004).

Scottish census results online, www.scrol.gov.uk: Table KS11, Industry of employment – females (consulted 25 March 2004).

www.shetland-museum.org.uk/collections/culture/frank_barnard.htm (consulted 2 March 2004).

www.shetland-museum.org.uk/collections/culture/may_moars_medal.htm (consulted 14 Nov. 2002).

Index